Practice*Planners*®

Homework Planners feature dozens of behaviorally based, ready-to-use assignments that are designed for use between sessions, as well as a disk or CD-ROM (Microsoft Word) containing all of the assignments—allowing you to customize them to suit your unique client needs.

Progress Notes Planners contain complete prewritten progress notes for each presenting problem in the companion Treatment Planners.

Client Education Handout Planners contain elegantly designed handouts that can be printed out from the enclosed CD-ROM and provide information on a wide range of psychological and emotional disorders and life skills issues. Use as patient literature, handouts at presentations, and aids for promoting your mental health practice.

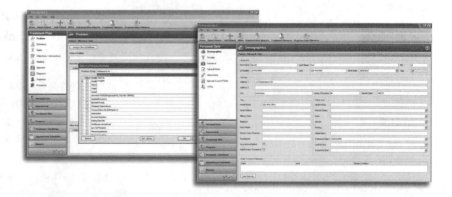

The Adolescent Psychotherapy Treatment Planner, Fourth Edition

Practice*Planners*® Series

Treatment Planners

The Complete Adult Psychotherapy Treatment Planner, Fourth Edition
The Child Psychotherapy Treatment Planner, Fourth Edition
The Adolescent Psychotherapy Treatment Planner, Fourth Edition
The Addiction Treatment Planner, Third Edition
The Continuum of Care Treatment Planner
The Couples Psychotherapy Treatment Planner
The Employee Assistance Treatment Planner
The Pastoral Counseling Treatment Planner
The Older Adult Psychotherapy Treatment Planner
The Behavioral Medicine Treatment Planner
The Group Therapy Treatment Planner, Second Edition
The Gay and Lesbian Psychotherapy Treatment Planner
The Family Therapy Treatment Planner
The Severe and Persistent Mental Illness Treatment Planner
The Mental Retardation and Developmental Disability Treatment Planner
The Social Work and Human Services Treatment Planner
The Crisis Counseling and Traumatic Events Treatment Planner
The Personality Disorders Treatment Planner
The Rehabilitation Psychology Treatment Planner
The Special Education Treatment Planner
The Juvenile Justice and Residential Care Treatment Planner
The School Counseling and School Social Work Treatment Planner
The Sexual Abuse Victim and Sexual Offender Treatment Planner
The Probation and Parole Treatment Planner
The Psychopharmacology Treatment Planner
The Speech-Language Pathology Treatment Planner
The Suicide and Homicide Risk Assessment & Prevention Treatment Planner
The College Student Counseling Treatment Planner
The Parenting Skills Treatment Planner
The Early Childhood Education Intervention Treatment Planner
The Co-Occurring Disorders Treatment Planner

Progress Notes Planners

The Child Psychotherapy Progress Notes Planner, Third Edition
The Adolescent Psychotherapy Progress Notes Planner, Third Edition
The Adult Psychotherapy Progress Notes Planner, Third Edition
The Addiction Progress Notes Planner, Second Edition
The Severe and Persistent Mental Illness Progress Notes Planner
The Couples Psychotherapy Progress Notes Planner
The Family Therapy Progress Notes Planner

Homework Planners

Brief Therapy Homework Planner
Brief Couples Therapy Homework Planner
Brief Employee Assistance Homework Planner
Brief Family Therapy Homework Planner
Grief Counseling Homework Planner
Group Therapy Homework Planner
Divorce Counseling Homework Planner
School Counseling and School Social Work Homework Planner
Child Therapy Activity and Homework Planner
Addiction Treatment Homework Planner, Third Edition
Adolescent Psychotherapy Homework Planner II
Adolescent Psychotherapy Homework Planner, Second Edition
Adult Psychotherapy Homework Planner, Second Edition
Child Psychotherapy Homework Planner, Second Edition
Parenting Skills Homework Planner

Client Education Handout Planners

Adult Client Education Handout Planner
Child and Adolescent Client Education Handout Planner
Couples and Family Client Education Handout Planner

Complete Planners

The Complete Depression Treatment and Homework Planner
The Complete Anxiety Treatment and Homework Planner

Practice*Planners*®

Arthur E. Jongsma, Jr., Series Editor

The Adolescent Psychotherapy Treatment Planner, Fourth Edition

Arthur E. Jongsma, Jr.

L. Mark Peterson

William P. McInnis

Timothy J. Bruce, Contributing Editor

WILEY

JOHN WILEY & SONS, INC.

To our wives:
Judy, Cherry, Lynn, and Lori.
We reach our long-term goals only due to your
faithful interventions of love and encouragement.

CONTENTS

▽ indicates that selected Objective/Interventions are consistent with those found in evidence-based treatments.

PRACTICE*PLANNERS*® SERIES PREFACE

Accountability is an important dimension of the practice of psychotherapy. Treatment programs, public agencies, clinics, and practitioners must justify and document their treatment plans to outside review entities in order to be reimbursed for services. The books and software in the Practice*Planners*® series are designed to help practitioners fulfill these documentation requirements efficiently and professionally.

The Practice*Planners*® series includes a wide array of treatment planning books including not only the original *Complete Adult Psychotherapy Treatment Planner, Child Psychotherapy Treatment Planner,* and *Adolescent Psychotherapy Treatment Planner,* all now in their fourth editions, but also *Treatment Planners* targeted to a wide range of specialty areas of practice, including:

- Addictions
- Behavioral medicine
- College students
- Co-occurring disorders
- Couples therapy
- Crisis counseling
- Early childhood education
- Employee assistance
- Family therapy
- Gays and lesbians
- Group therapy
- Juvenile justice and residential care
- Mental retardation and developmental disability
- Neuropsychology
- Older adults
- Parenting skills
- Pastoral counseling
- Personality disorders
- Probation and parole
- Psychopharmacology

- School counseling
- Severe and persistent mental illness
- Sexual abuse victims and offenders
- Special education
- Suicide and homicide risk assessment

In addition, there are three branches of companion books that can be used in conjunction with the *Treatment Planners,* or on their own:

- ***Progress Notes Planners*** provide a menu of progress statements that elaborate on the client's symptom presentation and the provider's therapeutic intervention. Each *Progress Notes Planner* statement is directly integrated with the behavioral definitions and therapeutic interventions from its companion *Treatment Planner*.
- ***Homework Planners*** include homework assignments designed around each presenting problem (such as anxiety, depression, chemical dependence, anger management, eating disorders, or panic disorder) that is the focus of a chapter in its corresponding *Treatment Planner*.
- ***Client Education Handout Planners*** provide brochures and handouts to help educate and inform clients on presenting problems and mental health issues, as well as life skills techniques. The handouts are included on CD-ROMs for easy printing from your computer and are ideal for use in waiting rooms, at presentations, as newsletters, or as information for clients struggling with mental illness issues. The topics covered by these handouts correspond to the presenting problems in the *Treatment Planners*.

The series also includes:

- **Thera*Scribe*®**, the #1 selling treatment planning and clinical record-keeping software system for mental health professionals. Thera*Scribe*® allows the user to import the data from any of the *Treatment Planner, Progress Notes Planner,* or *Homework Planner* books into the software's expandable database to simply point and click to create a detailed, organized, individualized, and customized treatment plan along with optional integrated progress notes and homework assignments.

Adjunctive books, such as *The Psychotherapy Documentation Primer* and *The Clinical Documentation Sourcebook* contain forms and resources to aid the clinician in mental health practice management.

The goal of our series is to provide practitioners with the resources they need in order to provide high-quality care in the era of accountability. To put it simply: we seek to help you spend more time on patients, and less time on paperwork.

ARTHUR E. JONGSMA, JR.
Grand Rapids, Michigan

ACKNOWLEDGMENTS

I have learned that it is better to acknowledge your weaknesses and to seek out those who complement you with their strengths. I was fortunate enough to have found the right person who brings his expertise in Evidence-Based Treatment to this project. He has contributed wisely and thoughtfully to greatly improve our *Adolescent Psychotherapy Treatment Planner* through his well-informed edits and additions to our content, to bring it in line with the latest psychotherapy research. He has been thoroughly professional in his approach while being a joy to work with, due to his wonderful sense of humor. I have said to many people since beginning this revision, "This guy really knows the literature!" For a person like me, who has spent his career in the psychotherapy trenches, it is a pleasure to get back in touch with my science-based roots by working with a Boulder Model clinician-scientist. I take my hat off to you, Dr. Tim Bruce. You have taken our product to a new level of contribution to the clinicians who are looking for Evidence-Based Treatment guidance. Your students are fortunate to have you for a mentor and we are fortunate to have you for a Contributing Editor. Thank you!

I also want to acknowledge the steady and perceptive work of my manuscript manager, Sue Rhoda. She stays on top of a thousand details while bringing the disjointed pieces of this work to a well organized finished product. Thank you, Sue.

A.E.J.

I want to acknowledge how honored I am to have had this chance to work with Art Jongsma, his colleague Sue Rhoda, and the staff at John Wiley and Sons on these, their well-known and highly regarded, treatment planners. These planners are widely recognized as works of enormous value to practicing clinicians as well as great educational tools for students of our profession. I didn't know Art when he asked me if I would join him on these editions, and the task he had in mind, to help empirically inform objectives and interventions, was daunting. I knew it would be a challenge to retain the rich breadth of options that Art has offered in past editions while simultaneously trying to identify and describe the fundamental features of identified empirically supported treatments. Although I have trained in empirically supported treatment approaches, contributed to this literature, and used them throughout my professional career, I recognize that our product will be open to criticism. I can say that we have done our best to offer a resource to our colleagues and their clients that is practical, flexible, and appreciates the complexities of any of the treatment approaches it conveys. And in the process of working with Art and Sue toward these goals, I have found them not only to be consummate professionals, but also thoughtful, conscientious, and kind persons. It has been a great pleasure working with you, Art and Sue, and a privilege to call you my friends.

T.J.B.

The Adolescent Psychotherapy Treatment Planner, Fourth Edition

INTRODUCTION

ABOUT PRACTICE*PLANNERS*® TREATMENT PLANNERS

Pressure from third-party payors, accrediting agencies, and other outside parties has increased the need for clinicians to quickly produce effective, high-quality treatment plans. *Treatment Planners* provide all the elements necessary to quickly and easily develop formal treatment plans that satisfy the needs of most third-party payors and state and federal review agencies.

Each *Treatment Planner:*

- Saves you hours of time-consuming paperwork.
- Offers the freedom to develop customized treatment plans.
- Includes over 1,000 clear statements describing the behavioral manifestations of each relational problem, and includes long-term goals, short-term objectives, and clinically tested treatment options.
- Has an easy-to-use reference format that helps locate treatment plan components by behavioral problem or DSM-IV™ diagnosis.

As with the rest of the books in the Practice*Planners*® series, our aim is to clarify, simplify, and accelerate the treatment planning process, so you spend less time on paperwork, and more time with your clients.

HOW TO USE THIS TREATMENT PLANNER

Use this *Treatment Planner* to write treatment plans according to the following progression of six steps:

1. **Problem Selection.** Although the client may discuss a variety of issues during the assessment, the clinician must determine the most significant problems on which to focus the treatment process. Usually a primary problem will surface, and secondary problems may also be evident. Some other problems may have to be set aside as not urgent enough to require treat-

ment at this time. An effective treatment plan can only deal with a few selected problems or treatment will lose its direction. Choose the problem within this *Planner* which most accurately represents your client's presenting issues.

2. **Problem Definition.** Each client presents with unique nuances as to how a problem behaviorally reveals itself in his or her life. Therefore, each problem that is selected for treatment focus requires a specific definition about how it is evidenced in the particular client. The symptom pattern should be associated with diagnostic criteria and codes such as those found in the *DSM-IV* or the International Classification of Diseases. This *Planner* offers such behaviorally specific definition statements to choose from or to serve as a model for your own personally crafted statements.

3. **Goal Development.** The next step in developing your treatment plan is to set broad goals for the resolution of the target problem. These statements need not be crafted in measurable terms but can be global, long-term goals that indicate a desired positive outcome to the treatment procedures. This *Planner* provides several possible goal statements for each problem, but one statement is all that is required in a treatment plan.

4. **Objective Construction.** In contrast to long-term goals, objectives must be stated in behaviorally measurable language so that it is clear to review agencies, health maintenance organizations, and managed care organizations when the client has achieved the established objectives. The objectives presented in this *Planner* are designed to meet this demand for accountability. Numerous alternatives are presented to allow construction of a variety of treatment plan possibilities for the same presenting problem.

5. **Intervention Creation.** Interventions are the actions of the clinician designed to help the client complete the objectives. There should be at least one intervention for every objective. If the client does not accomplish the objective after the initial intervention, new interventions should be added to the plan. Interventions should be selected on the basis of the client's needs and strengths and the treatment provider's full therapeutic repertoire. This *Planner* contains interventions from a broad range of therapeutic approaches, and we encourage the provider to write other interventions reflecting his or her own training and experience.

Some suggested interventions listed in the *Planner* refer to specific books that can be assigned to the client for adjunctive bibliotherapy. Appendix B contains a full bibliographic reference list of these materials, including these two popular choices: *Read Two Books and Let's Talk Next Week: Using Bibliotherapy in Clinical Practice* (2000) by Maidman Joshua and DiMenna and *Rent Two Films and Let's Talk in the Morning: Using Popular Movies in Psychotherapy, Second Edition* (2001) by Hesley and Hesley (both books are published by Wiley). For further information about self-help books, mental health professionals may wish to consult *The Au-*

thoritative Guide to Self-Help Resources in Mental Health, Revised Edition (2003) by Norcross et al. (available from The Guilford Press, New York).

6. **Diagnosis Determination.** The determination of an appropriate diagnosis is based on an evaluation of the client's complete clinical presentation. The clinician must compare the behavioral, cognitive, emotional, and interpersonal symptoms that the client presents with the criteria for diagnosis of a mental illness condition as described in *DSM-IV.* Despite arguments made against diagnosing clients in this manner, diagnosis is a reality that exists in the world of mental health care, and it is a necessity for third-party reimbursement. It is the clinician's thorough knowledge of *DSM-IV* criteria and a complete understanding of the client assessment data that contribute to the most reliable, valid diagnosis.

Congratulations! After completing these six steps, you should have a comprehensive and individualized treatment plan ready for immediate implementation and presentation to the client. A sample treatment plan for Oppositional Defiant is provided at the end of this introduction.

INCORPORATING EVIDENCE-BASED TREATMENT INTO THE *TREATMENT PLANNER*

Evidence-based treatment (that is, treatment which is scientifically shown in research trials to be efficacious) is rapidly becoming of critical importance to the mental health community as insurance companies are beginning to offer preferential pay to organizations using it. In fact, the APA Division 12 (Society of Clinical Psychology) lists of empirically supported treatments have been referenced by a number of local, state and federal funding agencies, which are beginning to restrict reimbursement to these treatments, as are some managed-care and insurance companies.

In this fourth edition of *The Adolescent Psychotherapy Treatment Planner* we have made an effort to empirically inform some chapters by highlighting Short-Term Objectives (STOs) and Therapeutic Interventions (TIs) that are consistent with therapies that have demonstrated efficacy through empirical study. Watch for this icon as an indication that an Objective/Intervention is consistent with those found in evidence-based treatments.

References to their empirical support have been included in the reference section as Appendix B. Reviews of efforts to identify evidence-based therapies (EBT), including the effort's benefits and limitations, can be found in Bruce and Sanderson (2005), Chambless and colleagues (1996, 1998), and Chambless and Ollendick (2001). References have also been included to therapist- and client-oriented treatment manuals and books that describe the step-by-step use of noted EBTs or treatments consistent with their objectives and interventions. Of course, recognizing that there are STOs and TIs that practicing clinicians have found useful but that have not yet received empirical scrutiny, we have included those that reflect common practice among experienced clinicians. The goal is to provide a range of treatment plan options, some studied empirically, others reflecting common clinical practice, so the user can construct what they believe to be the best plan for their particular client.

In many instances, EBTs are short-term, problem-oriented treatments that focus on improving current problems/symptoms related to a client's current distress and disability. Accordingly, STOs and TIs of that type have been placed earlier in the sequence of STO and TI options. In addition, some STOs and TIs reflect core components of the EBT approach that are always delivered (e.g., exposure to feared objects and situations for a phobic disorder; behavioral activation for depression). Others reflect adjuncts to treatment that are commonly used to address problems that may not always be a feature of the clinical picture (e.g., assertive communication skills training for the social anxious or depressed client whose difficulty with assertion appears contributory to the primary anxiety or depressive disorder). Most of the STOs and TIs associated with the EBTs are described at a level of detail that permits flexibility and adaptability in their specific application. As with previous editions of this *Treatment Planner,* each chapter also includes the option to add STOs and TIs that are not listed.

Criteria for Inclusion of Evidence-Based Therapies

Not every treatment that has undergone empirical study for a mental health problem is included in this edition. In general, we have included EBTs the empirical support for which has either been well established or demonstrated at more than a preliminary level as defined by those authors who have undertaken the task of identifying EBTs, such as Chambless and colleagues (1996, 1998) and Nathan and Gorman (1998, 2002). At minimum, this requires demonstration of efficacy through a clinical trial or large clinical replication series that have features reflective of good experimental design (e.g., random assignment, blind assignments, reliable and valid measurement, clear inclusion and exclusion criteria, state-of-the-art diagnostic methods, and adequate sample size). Well established EBTs typically have more than one of these types of studies demonstrating their efficacy as well as other desirable features, such as demonstration of efficacy by independent research groups and specification of client characteristics for which the treatment was effective. Because treatment literatures for various problems develop at different paces, treatment STOs and TIs that have been included may have the most empirical support for their problem area, but less than that found in more heavily studied areas. For example, Cognitive Behavior Therapy (CBT) has the highest level of empirical support of tested psychotherapies for Childhood Obsessive Compulsive Disorder (OCD), but that level of evidence is lower than that supporting, for example, exposure-based therapy for phobic fear and avoidance. The latter has simply been studied more extensively. Nonetheless, within the psychotherapy outcome literature for OCD, CBT clearly has the highest level of evidence supporting its efficacy and usefulness. Accordingly, STOs and TIs consistent with CBT have been included in this edition. Lastly, just as some of the STOs and TIs included in this edition reflect common clinical practices of experienced clinicians, those associated with EBTs reflect what is commonly practiced by clinicians that use EBTs.

Summary of Required and Preferred EBT Inclusion Criteria

Required
- Demonstration of efficacy through at least one randomized controlled trial with good experimental design, or
- Demonstration of efficacy through a large, well-designed clinical replication series.

Preferred
- Efficacy has been shown by more than one study.
- Efficacy has been demonstrated by independent research groups.
- Client characteristics for which the treatment was effective were specified.
- A clear description of the treatment was available.

There does remain considerable debate regarding evidence-based treatment amongst mental health professionals who are not always in agreement regarding the best treatments or how to weigh the factors that contribute to good outcomes. Some practitioners are skeptical about the wisdom of changing their practice on the basis of research evidence, and their reluctance is fuelled by the methodological problems of psychotherapy research. Our goal in this book is to provide a range of treatment plan options, some studied empirically, others reflecting common clinical practice, so the user can construct what they believe to be the best plan for their particular client. As indicated earlier, recognizing that there are interventions which practicing clinicians have found useful but that have not yet received empirical scrutiny, we have included those that reflect common practice among experienced clinicians.

A FINAL NOTE ON TAILORING THE TREATMENT PLAN TO THE CLIENT

One important aspect of effective treatment planning is that each plan should be tailored to the individual client's problems and needs. Treatment plans should not be mass-produced, even if clients have similar problems. The individual's strengths and weaknesses, unique stressors, social network, family circumstances, and symptom patterns must be considered in developing a treatment strategy. Drawing upon our own years of clinical experience, we have put together a variety of treatment choices. These statements can be combined in thousands of permutations to develop detailed treatment plans. Relying on their own good judgment, clinicians can easily select the statements that are appropriate for the individuals whom they are treating. In addition, we encourage readers to add their own definitions, goals, objectives, and interventions to the existing samples. As with all of the books in the *Treatment Planners* series, it is our hope that this book will help promote effective, creative treatment planning—a process that will ultimately benefit the client, clinician, and mental health community.

SAMPLE TREATMENT PLAN

OPPOSITIONAL DEFIANT

Definitions: Displays a pattern of negativistic, hostile, and defiant behavior toward most adults.

Often defies or refuses to comply with reasonable requests and rules.

Consistently is angry and resentful.

Often is spiteful or vindictive.

Goals: Replace hostile, defiant behaviors toward adults with respect and cooperation.

Reach a level of reduced tension, increased satisfaction, and improved communication with family and/or other authority figures.

Parents learn and implement good child behavioral management skills.

OBJECTIVES

1. Identify situations, thoughts, and feelings that trigger angry feelings, problem behaviors, and the targets of those actions.

2. Learn and implement calming strategies as part of a new way to manage reactions to frustration and defiance.

3. Identify, challenge, and replace self-talk that leads to anger and misbehavior with self-talk that

INTERVENTIONS

1. Actively build the level of trust with the client through consistent eye contact, active listening, unconditional positive regard, and warm acceptance to help increase his/her disclosure of thoughts and feelings.

2. Thoroughly assess the various stimuli (e.g., situations, people, thoughts) that have triggered the client's anger and the thoughts, feelings, and actions that have characterized his/her anger responses.

1. Teach the client calming techniques (e.g., muscle relaxation, paced breathing, calming imagery) as part of a tailored strategy for responding appropriately to angry feelings and the urge to defy when they occur.

1. Explore the client's self-talk that mediates his/her angry feelings and actions (e.g., demanding expectations

facilitates a more constructive reaction.

reflected in should, must, or have to statements); identify and challenge biases, assisting him/her in generating appraisals and self-talk that corrects for the biases and facilitates a more flexible and temperate response to frustration.

4. Learn and implement thought-stopping to manage intrusive unwanted thoughts that trigger anger and acting out.

1. Assign the client to implement a "thought-stopping" technique on a daily basis to manage intrusive unwanted thoughts that trigger anger and acting out between sessions (or assign "Making Use of the Thought-Stopping Technique" in the *Adult Psychotherapy Homework Planner,* 2nd ed. by Jongsma); review implementation; reinforce success, providing corrective feedback toward improvement.

5. Verbalize feelings of frustration, disagreement, and anger in a controlled, assertive way.

1. Use instruction, modeling, and/or role-playing to teach the client assertive communication; if indicated, refer him/her to an assertiveness training class/group for further instruction.

6. Parents learn and implement Parent Management Training skills to recognize and manage problem behavior of the client.

1. Teach the parents how to specifically define and identify problem behaviors, identify their own reactions to the behavior, determine whether the reaction encourages or discourages the behavior, and generate alternatives to the problem behavior.

2. Teach the parents how to implement key parenting practices consistently, including establishing realistic age-appropriate rules for acceptable and unacceptable behavior, prompting of positive behavior in the environment, use of positive reinforcement to encourage behavior (e.g., praise), use of calm clear direct instruction, time out, and other loss-of-privilege practices

for problem behavior (or assign "Switching from Defense to Offense" in the *Adolescent Therapy Homework Planner,* 2nd ed. by Jongsma, Peterson, and McInnis).

3. Assign the parents home exercises in which they implement and record results of implementation exercises (or assign "Clear Rules, Positive Reinforcement, Appropriate Consequences" in the *Adolescent Therapy Homework Planner,* 2nd ed. by Jongsma, Peterson, and McInnis); review in session, providing corrective feedback toward improved, appropriate, and consistent use of skills.

7. Decrease the frequency and intensity of hostile, negativistic, and defiant interactions with parents/adults.

1. Track the frequency and intensity of negative, hostile feelings and defiant behaviors and problem-solve solutions (or assign "Stop Yelling" or "Filing a Complaint" in the *Adolescent Therapy Homework Planner,* 2nd ed. by Jongsma, Peterson, and McInnis); implement plan toward decreasing frequency and intensity.

8. Identify what is wanted from parents and other adults.

1. Assist the client in becoming able to recognize feelings and wants, their connection to behavior, and how to express them in constructive, respectful ways.

2. Assist the client in reframing complaints into requests for positive change (or assign the exercise "Filing a Complaint" or "If I Could Run My Family" from the *Adolescent Therapy Homework Planner,* 2nd ed. by Jongsma, Peterson, and McInnis).

DIAGNOSIS

313.81   Oppositional Defiant Disorder

ACADEMIC UNDERACHIEVEMENT

BEHAVIORAL DEFINITIONS

1. History of academic performance that is below the expected level, given the client's measured intelligence or performance on standardized achievement tests.
2. Repeated failure to complete homework assignments on time.
3. Poor organization or study skills.
4. Frequent tendency to postpone doing homework assignments in favor of engaging in recreational and leisure activities.
5. Positive family history of members having academic problems, failures, or disinterest.
6. Feelings of depression, insecurity, and low self-esteem that interfere with learning and academic progress.
7. Recurrent pattern of engaging in acting out, disruptive, and negative attention-seeking behaviors when encountering frustration in learning.
8. Heightened anxiety that interferes with performance during tests.
9. Parents place excessive or unrealistic pressure on the client to such a degree that it negatively affects the client's academic performance.
10. Decline in academic performance that occurs in response to environmental stress (e.g., parents' divorce, death of loved one, relocation, move).

—. _____
   _____

—. _____
   _____

—. _____
   _____

LONG-TERM GOALS

1. Attain and maintain a level of academic performance that is commensurate with intellectual ability.
2. Complete school and homework assignments on a regular and consistent basis.
3. Achieve and maintain a healthy balance between accomplishing academic goals and meeting social and emotional needs.
4. Stabilize mood and build self-esteem sufficiently to cope effectively with the frustration associated with academic pursuits.
5. Eliminate pattern of engaging in acting out, disruptive, or negative attention-seeking behaviors when confronted with frustration in learning.
6. Significantly reduce the level of anxiety related to taking tests.
7. Parents establish realistic expectations of the client's learning abilities.
8. Parents implement effective intervention strategies at home to help the client achieve academic goals.
9. Remove emotional impediments or resolve family conflicts and environmental stressors to allow for improved academic performance.

—. _____

_____

—. _____

_____

—. _____

_____

SHORT-TERM OBJECTIVES

1. Complete a psychoeducational evaluation. (1)

2. Complete psychological testing. (2)

THERAPEUTIC INTERVENTIONS

1. Arrange for psychoeducational testing to evaluate the presence of a learning disability and to determine whether the client is eligible to receive special education services; provide feedback to the client, his/her family, and school officials regarding the psychoeducational evaluation.

2. Arrange for psychological testing to assess whether it is possible Attention-Deficit/Hyperactivity

Disorder (ADHD) or emotional factors are interfering with the client's academic performance; provide feedback to the client, his/her family, and school officials regarding the psychological evaluation.

3. Parents and client provide psychosocial history information. (3)

3. Gather psychosocial history information that includes key developmental milestones and a family history of educational achievements and failures.

4. Cooperate with a hearing, vision, or medical examination. (4)

4. Refer the client for a hearing, vision, or medical examination to rule out possible hearing, visual, or health problems that are interfering with school performance.

5. Comply with the recommendations made by the multidisciplinary evaluation team at school regarding educational interventions. (5)

5. Attend an individualized educational planning committee (IEPC) meeting with the parents, teachers, and school officials to determine the client's eligibility for special education services, design educational interventions, and establish education goals.

6. Parents and teachers implement educational strategies that maximize the client's learning strengths and compensate for learning weaknesses. (6, 7)

6. Based on the IEPC goals and recommendations, move the client to an appropriate classroom setting to maximize his/her learning.

7. Consult with the client, parents, and school officials about designing effective learning programs or intervention strategies that build on the client's strengths and compensate for his/her weaknesses.

7. Participate in outside tutoring to increase knowledge and skills in the area of academic weakness. (8, 9, 10)

8. Recommend that the parents seek privately contracted tutoring for the client after school to boost his/her skills in the area of his/her academic weakness (i.e., reading, mathematics, written expression).

9. Refer the client to a private learning center for extra tutoring in the areas of academic weakness and assistance in improving study and test-taking skills.

10. Help the client to identify specific academic goals and steps needed to accomplish goals.

8. Implement effective study skills that increase the frequency of completion of school assignments and improve academic performance. (11, 12)

11. Teach the client more effective study skills (e.g., remove distractions, study in quiet places, develop outlines, highlight important details, schedule breaks).

12. Consult with teachers and parents about using a peer tutor to assist the client in his/her area of academic weakness and help improve study skills.

9. Implement effective test-taking strategies that decrease anxiety and improve test performance. (13, 14)

13. Teach the client more effective test-taking strategies (e.g., study in small segments over an extended period of time, review material regularly, read directions twice, recheck work).

14. Train the client in the use of guided imagery or relaxation techniques to reduce anxiety before or during the taking of tests.

10. Parents maintain regular communication (i.e., daily to weekly) with teachers. (15)

15. Encourage the parents to maintain regular (daily or weekly) communication with teachers to help the client remain organized and keep up with school assignments.

11. Use self-monitoring checklists, planners, or calendars to remain organized and help complete school assignments. (16, 17, 18)

16. Encourage the client to use self-monitoring checklists to increase completion of school assignments and improve academic performance.

17. Direct the client to use planners or calendars to record school or homework assignments and plan ahead for long-term projects.

18. Utilize the "Break It Down into Small Steps" program in the *Adolescent Psychotherapy Homework Planner,* 2nd ed. (Jongsma, Peterson, and McInnis) to help the client complete projects or long-term assignments on time.

12. Establish a regular routine that allows time to engage in leisure or recreational activities, spend quality time with the family, and complete homework assignments. (19)

19. Assist the client and his/her parents in developing a routine daily schedule at home that allows him/her to achieve a healthy balance of completing school/homework assignments, engaging in leisure activities, and spending quality time with family and peers.

13. Parents and teachers increase praise and positive reinforcement toward the client for improved school performance. (20, 21, 22)

20. Encourage the parents and teachers to give frequent praise and positive reinforcement for the client's effort and accomplishment on academic tasks.

21. Assign the parents to observe and record responsible behaviors by the client between therapy sessions that pertain to schoolwork. Reinforce responsible behaviors to encourage the client to continue to engage in those behaviors in the future.

22. Help the client identify what rewards would increase his/her motivation to improve academic performance and then make these reinforcers contingent on academic success.

14. Identify and remove all emotional or family conflicts that may be a hindrance to learning. (23, 24)

23. Conduct family sessions to identify any family or marital conflicts that may be inhibiting the client's academic performance; assist the family in resolving conflicts.

24. Conduct individual therapy sessions to help the client work

through and resolve painful emotions, core conflicts, or stressors that impede academic performance.

15. Parents increase time spent involved with the client's homework. (25, 26, 27)

25. Encourage the parents to demonstrate and/or maintain regular interest and involvement in the client's homework (i.e., attend school functions, review planners or calendars to see if the client is staying caught up with schoolwork).

26. Design and implement a reward system and/or contingency contract to help the parents reinforce the client's responsible behaviors, completion of school assignments, and academic success.

27. Assign the parents to observe and record responsible behaviors by the client between therapy sessions that pertain to schoolwork; urge them to reinforce responsible behaviors to encourage the client to continue to engage in those behaviors in the future.

16. Parents decrease the frequency and intensity of arguments with the client over issues related to school performance and homework. (28, 29)

28. Conduct family therapy sessions to assess whether the parents have developed unrealistic expectations or are placing excessive pressure on the client to perform; confront and challenge the parents about placing excessive pressure on the client.

29. Encourage the parents to set firm, consistent limits and utilize natural, logical consequences for the client's noncompliance or refusal to do homework; instruct the parents to avoid unhealthy power struggles or lengthy arguments over the client's homework each night.

17. Parents verbally recognize that their pattern of over-protectiveness interferes with the client's academic growth and assumption of responsibility. (30, 31)

30. Assess the parent-child relationship to help determine whether the parents' overprotectiveness and/or overindulgence of the client contributes to his/her academic underachievement; assist the parents in developing realistic expectations of the client's learning potential.

31. Encourage the parents not to protect the client from the natural consequences of poor academic performance (e.g., loss of credits, detention, delayed graduation, inability to take driver training, higher cost of car insurance) and allow him/her to learn from mistakes or failures.

18. Increase the frequency of on-task behaviors at school, completing school assignments without expressing the desire to give up. (32)

32. Consult with school officials about ways to improve the client's on-task behaviors (e.g., sit the client toward the front of the class or near positive peer role models, call on the client often, provide frequent feedback, break larger assignments into a series of small steps).

19. Increase the frequency of positive statements about school experiences and about confidence in the ability to succeed academically. (33, 34, 35)

33. Reinforce the client's successful school experiences and positive statements about school and confront the client's self-disparaging remarks and expressed desire to give up on school assignments.

34. Consult with the teachers to assign the client a task at school (e.g., giving announcements over the intercom, tutoring another student in his/her area of interest or strength) to demonstrate confidence in his/her ability to act responsibly.

20. Decrease the frequency and severity of acting out behaviors when encountering frustration with school assignments. (36)

21. Identify and verbalize how specific responsible actions lead to improvements in academic performance. (37, 38, 39)

22. Develop a list of resource people within the school setting who can be turned to for support, assistance, or instruction for learning problems. (40)

35. Assign the client the task of making one positive statement daily to himself/herself about school and his/her ability and recording it in a journal or writing it on a sticky note and posting it in the bedroom or kitchen.

36. Teach the client positive coping strategies (e.g., deep breathing and relaxation skills, positive self-talk, "stop, listen, think, and act") to inhibit the impulse to act out or engage in negative attention-seeking behaviors when he/she encounters frustration with schoolwork.

37. Explore for periods of time when the client completed schoolwork regularly and achieved academic success; identify and encourage him/her to use similar strategies to improve his/her current academic functioning.

38. Examine coping strategies that the client has used to solve other problems. Encourage him/her to use similar coping strategies to overcome his/her problems associated with learning.

39. Give the client a homework assignment of identifying three to five role models and listing reasons he/she admires each role model. Explore in the next session the factors that contributed to each role model's success; encourage the client to take similar positive steps to achieve academic success.

40. Identify a list of individuals within the school to whom the client can turn for support, assistance, or instruction when he/she encounters difficulty or frustration with learning.

___. _____   ___. _____

      _____   _____

___. _____   ___. _____

      _____   _____

___. _____   ___. _____

      _____   _____

DIAGNOSTIC SUGGESTIONS

Axis I:	315.00	Reading Disorder
	315.1	Mathematics Disorder
	315.2	Disorder of Written Expression
	V62.3	Academic Problem
	314.01	Attention-Deficit/Hyperactivity Disorder, Combined Type
	314.00	Attention-Deficit/Hyperactivity Disorder, Predominantly Inattentive Type
	300.4	Dysthymic Disorder
	313.81	Oppositional Defiant Disorder
	312.9	Disruptive Behavior Disorder NOS
	_____	_____
	_____	_____
Axis II:	317	Mild Mental Retardation
	V62.89	Borderline Intellectual Functioning
	799.9	Diagnosis Deferred
	V71.09	No Diagnosis
	_____	_____
	_____	_____

ADOPTION

BEHAVIORAL DEFINITIONS

1. Questions are arising regarding family of origin or biological parents.
2. Confusion regarding identity linked to adoption.
3. Statements that reflect a feeling of not being a part of the family (e.g., "I don't fit here," "I'm different").
4. Asking to make a search to get additional information about or make contact with biological parents.
5. Marked shift in interests, dress, and peer group, all of which are contrary to the adoptive family's standards.
6. Exhibiting excessive clingy and helpless behavior that is inappropriate for developmental level.
7. Extreme testing of all limits (e.g., lying, breaking rules, academic under-achievement, truancy, stealing, drug and alcohol experimentation/use, verbal abuse of parents and other authority, promiscuity).
8. Adoptive parents express anxiety and fearfulness because the child wants to meet his/her biological parents.
9. The adoption of an older special-needs child.
10. Parents express frustration with the adopted child's development and level of achievement.

—. _____
   _____
—. _____
   _____
—. _____
   _____

LONG-TERM GOALS

1. Termination of self-defeating, acting out behaviors and acceptance of self as loved and lovable within an adopted family.
2. The weaving of an acceptable self-identify that includes self, biological parents, and adoptive parents.
3. Resolution of the loss of a potential relationship with the biological parents.
4. Completion of the search process that results in reconnection with the biological parent(s).
5. Successful working through of all unresolved issues connected with being adopted.
6. Resolution of the question, "Who am I?"

—. _____

_____

—. _____

_____

—. _____

_____

SHORT-TERM OBJECTIVES	THERAPEUTIC INTERVENTIONS
1. Develop a trusting relationship with the therapist in which feelings and thoughts can be openly communicated. (1)	1. Actively build the level of trust with the client in individual and family sessions through consistent eye contact, active listening, and unconditional acceptance to increase his/her ability to express thoughts and feelings regarding his/her adoption.
2. Family members commit to attending and actively participating in family sessions that address issues related to adoption. (2, 3)	2. Solicit a commitment from all family members to regularly attend and participate in family therapy sessions.
	3. Create a genogram in a family session, listing all family members and what is known about each. Ask the child and the parents what they know or have been told about the biological parents and their families.

3. Verbally identify all the losses related to being adopted. (4)

4. Express feelings of grief connected to the losses associated with being adopted. (5, 6)

5. Report decreased feelings of guilt, shame, abandonment, and rejection. (7, 8, 9, 10)

6. Attend an adoption support group. (11)

4. Ask the client to identify losses connected to being adopted and to process them with the therapist.

5. Assist, guide, and support the client in working through the process of grieving each identified loss associated with being adopted.

6. Assign the client to read *Common Threads of Teenage Grief* (Tyson) and to process the key concepts he/she gains from the reading with the therapist.

7. Help the client identify and verbally express feelings connected to issues of rejection or abandonment.

8. Assign the client to read *Why Didn't She Keep Me?* (Burlingham-Brown) to help him/her resolve feelings of rejection, abandonment, and guilt/shame.

9. Ask the client to read *How It Feels to Be Adopted* (Krementz) and list the key items from each vignette that he/she identifies with. Process completed list.

10. Assist the client in identifying irrational thoughts and beliefs (e.g., "I must have been bad for Mom to have released me for adoption," "I must have been a burden") that contribute to his/her feelings of shame and guilt. Then assist him/her in replacing the irrational thoughts and beliefs with healthy, rational ones.

11. Refer the client and/or parents to an adoption support group.

7. Identify positive aspects of self. (12, 13)

12. Explore with the client what aspects of himself/herself he/she would like to change and develop an action plan to achieve those goals (or assign the exercise "Three Ways to Change Yourself" in the *Adolescent Psychotherapy Homework Planner,* 2nd ed. by Jongsma, Peterson, and McInnis).

13. Assign a self-esteem-building exercise from *SEALS & PLUS* (Korb-Khalsa, Azok, and Leutenberg) to help the client develop self-knowledge, acceptance, and confidence.

8. Verbalize a decrease in confusion regarding self-identity. (14, 15)

14. Provide education to the client about his/her "true and false self or artificial and forbidden self" (see *Journey of the Adopted Self* by Lifton) to give him/her direction and permission to pursue exploring who he/she is.

15. Assign the client the task of creating a list that responds to the question, "Who am I?" Ask him/her to add daily to the list and to share the list with the therapist each week for processing.

9. Parents verbalize an understanding of the dynamics of the struggle with adoption status by adolescents who are searching for identity developmentally. (16, 17)

16. Encourage the parents to read material to increase their knowledge and understanding of the adopted child in adolescence (e.g., *The Whole Life Adoption Book* by Schooler, *Making Sense of Adoption* by Melina).

17. Teach the parents about the developmental task of adolescence that is focused on searching for an independent identity and how this is complicated for an adopted adolescent.

10. Parents report reduced level of fear of the client's interest in and search for information and possible contact with biological parents. (18)

11. Parents verbalize support for the client's search for biological parents. (19)

12. Parents verbalize refusal to support a search for the biological parents and insist it be postponed until the client is 18 or older. (20)

13. Verbalize an acceptance of the need to delay the search for the biological parents until age 18. (20, 21)

18. Conduct a session with the adoptive parents in which their fears and concerns are discussed regarding the client searching for and possibly meeting the biological parents. Confirm the parents' rights and empower them to support, curtail, or postpone the client's search.

19. Hold a family session in which the client's desire to search for his/her biological parents is the issue. If the parents give support to the search, ask them to state verbally their encouragement in going forward. Then elicit from the client a commitment to keep his/her parents informed about the search at a mutually agreed-upon level.

20. Hold a family session in which the client's desire to search for his/her biological parents is the issue. If the parents are opposed, support their right, since the child is a minor, and ask them to state their rationale. Affirm the client's right to search after he/she is 18 if he/she still desires to.

20. Hold a family session in which the client's desire to search for his/her biological parents is the issue. If the parents are opposed, support their right, since the child is a minor, and ask them to state their rationale. Affirm the client's right to search after he/she is 18 if he/she still desires to.

21. Affirm the parents' right to refuse to support a search for the client's biological parents at present, and assist the client in working to a feeling of acceptance of this decision.

14. Verbalize anxieties associated with the search for the biological parents. (22, 23, 24)

22. Locate an adult who is adopted and who would agree to meet with the client and the therapist to tell of his/her search experience and answer any questions that the client has.

23. Prepare the client for the search by probing and affirming his/her fears, hopes, and concerns. Develop a list of questions about the biological parents that he/she would like to have answered.

24. Ask the client and the parents to read *Searching for a Past* (Schooler) to expand their knowledge and understanding of the search process.

15. Create an album of life experiences that could be shared with the biological parents. (25)

25. Have the client review his/her "life book" filled with pictures and mementos; if he/she does not have one, help him/her construct one to add to the search/reunion process.

16. Begin the search for the biological parents. (26)

26. Refer the client to the agency that did his/her adoption or to an adoption agency that has post-adoption services to begin the search process.

17. Share any increased knowledge of the biological parents and their backgrounds that is attained from the search. (27)

27. Debrief the client on the information he/she receives from the search. Identify and support his/her feelings around what is revealed.

18. Verbalize and resolve feelings associated with not being able to contact the biological parents. (28)

28. Assist the client in working through his/her feelings of disappointment, anger, or loss connected to a dead end regarding possible contact with the biological parents.

19. Inform the adoptive parents of information discovered about the biological parents and feelings about it. (29)

29. Monitor the client's communication to the adoptive parents of information regarding the search to make sure it is occurring at the agreed-upon level.

20. Make a decision to pursue or not pursue a reunion with the biological parents. (24, 30)

24. Ask the client and the parents to read *Searching for a Past* (Schooler) to expand their knowledge and understanding of the search process.

30. Help the client reach a decision to pursue or postpone contact or reunion with the biological parents, reviewing the pros and cons of each alternative.

21. Identify and express expectations and feelings around impending reunion with the biological parents. (31, 32)

31. Prepare the client to have contact with the biological parents by examining his/her expectations to make them as realistic as possible and to seed and reinforce the message to let the relationship build slowly.

32. Role-play with the client a first meeting with the biological parents and process the experience.

22. Attend and participate in a meeting with the biological parents. (33)

33. Arrange for and conduct a meeting with the client and the biological parents facilitating a complete expression of feelings by all family members; explore with all parties the next possible steps.

23. Verbalize feelings regarding first contact with the biological parents and expectations regarding the future of the relationship. (34)

34. Process with the client his/her first contact with the biological parents and explore the next step he/she would like to make in terms of a future relationship.

24. Reassure the adoptive parents of love and loyalty to them that is not compromised by contact with the biological parents. (35)

35. Assist the client in creating a plan for further developing his/her new relationship with the biological parents, with emphasis on taking things slowly, keeping expectations realistic, and being sensitive to the feelings of the adoptive parents who have provided consistent love and nurturing.

25. Verbalize a realistic plan for a future relationship with the biological parents. (33, 36)

33. Arrange for and conduct a meeting with the client and the biological parents facilitating a complete expression of feelings by all family members; explore with all parties the next possible steps.

36. Conduct a family session with the client and the adoptive parents to update them on the meeting with the biological parents and the next possible steps. Offer appropriate affirmation and explore how the new family arrangement might work.

—. _____   —. _____
   _____   _____
—. _____   —. _____
   _____   _____
—. _____   —. _____
   _____   _____

DIAGNOSTIC SUGGESTIONS

Axis I: 309.0   Adjustment Disorder With Depressed Mood
              309.4   Adjustment Disorder With Mixed Disturbance of Emotions and Conduct
              303.90   Alcohol Dependence
              300.4   Dysthymic Disorder
              312.81   Conduct Disorder, Childhood-Onset Type
              312.82   Conduct Disorder, Adolescent-Onset Type
              313.81   Oppositional Defiant Disorder
              314.01   Attention-Deficit/Hyperactivity Disorder, Combined Type

              _____   _____

              _____   _____

Axis II: 799.9   Diagnosis Deferred
              V71.09   No Diagnosis

              _____   _____

              _____   _____

ANGER MANAGEMENT

BEHAVIORAL DEFINITIONS

1. Repeated angry outbursts that are out of proportion to the precipitating event.
2. Excessive screaming, cursing, or use of verbally abusive language when frustrated or stressed.
3. Frequent fighting, intimidation of others, and acts of cruelty or violence toward people or animals.
4. Verbal threats of harm to parents, adult authority figures, siblings, or peers.
5. Persistent pattern of destroying property or throwing objects when angry.
6. Consistent failure to accept responsibility for loss of control, accompanied by repeated pattern of blaming others for his/her anger control problems.
7. History of engaging in passive-aggressive behaviors (e.g., forgetting, pretending not to listen, dawdling, procrastinating, stubborn refusal to comply with reasonable requests or rules) to frustrate or annoy other family members, adults, or peers.
8. Strained interpersonal relationships with peers due to anger control problems and aggressive or destructive behaviors.
9. Underlying feelings of depression, anxiety, or insecurity that contribute to angry outbursts and aggressive behaviors.

—. _____
   _____
—. _____
   _____
—. _____
   _____

LONG-TERM GOALS

1. Express anger through appropriate verbalizations and healthy physical outlets.
2. Significantly reduce the intensity and frequency of angry verbal outbursts.
3. Terminate all acts of physical violence or cruelty toward people or animals and destruction of property.
4. Interact consistently with adult authority figures in a mutually respectful manner.
5. Markedly reduce the frequency of passive-aggressive behaviors by expressing anger and frustration through controlled, respectful, and direct verbalizations.
6. Resolve the core conflicts that contribute to the emergence of anger control problems.
7. Parents establish and maintain appropriate parent-child boundaries, setting firm, consistent limits when the client reacts in a verbally or physically aggressive or passive-aggressive manner.
8. Demonstrate marked improvement in the ability to listen and respond empathetically and respectfully to the thoughts, feelings, and wishes of others.

—. _____
   _____
—. _____
   _____
—. _____
   _____

SHORT-TERM OBJECTIVES

1. Identify situations, thoughts, feelings that trigger anger, angry verbal and/or behavioral actions and the targets of those actions. (1)

THERAPEUTIC INTERVENTIONS

1. Thoroughly assess the various stimuli (e.g., situations, people, thoughts) that have triggered the client's anger and the thoughts, feelings, and actions that have characterized his/her anger responses.

2. Cooperate with a medical evaluation to assess possible organic contributors to poor anger control. (2)

2. Refer the client to a physician for a complete physical exam to rule out organic contributors (e.g., brain damage, tumor, elevated testosterone levels) to poor anger control.

3. Complete psychological testing. (3)

3. Conduct or arrange for psychological testing to help in assessing whether a comorbid condition (e.g., depression, Attention-Deficit/Hyperactivity Disorder [ADHD]) is contributing to anger control problems; follow up accordingly with client and parents regarding treatment options.

4. Complete a substance abuse evaluation and comply with the recommendations offered by the evaluation findings. (4)

4. Arrange for a substance abuse evaluation and/or treatment for the client.

5. Cooperate with the recommendations or requirements mandated by the criminal justice system. (5, 6, 7)

5. Consult with criminal justice officials about the appropriate consequences for the client's destructive or aggressive behaviors (e.g., pay restitution, community service, probation, intensive surveillance).

6. Consult with parents, school officials, and criminal justice officials about the need to place the client in an alternative setting (e.g., foster home, group home, residential program, juvenile detention facility).

7. Encourage and challenge the parents not to protect the client from the natural or legal consequences of his/her destructive or aggressive behaviors.

▼ 6. Cooperate with a physician evaluation for possible treatment with psychotropic medications to assist in anger

8. Assess the client for the need for psychotropic medication to assist in control of anger; refer him/her to a physician for an evaluation

---

▼ indicates that the Objective/Intervention is consistent with those found in evidence-based treatments.

control and take medications consistently, if prescribed. (8, 9)

and prescription of medication, if needed. ▽

9. Monitor the client for prescription compliance, effectiveness, and side effects; provide feedback to the prescribing physician. ▽

▽ 7. Parents learn and implement Parent Management Training skills to recognize and manage aggressive behavior of the client. (10, 11, 12, 13, 14)

10. Use a Parent Management Training approach to teaching the parents how parent and child behavioral interactions can encourage or discourage positive or negative behavior and that changing key elements of those interactions (e.g., prompting and reinforcing positive behaviors) can be used to promote positive change (e.g., see *Living with Children* by Patterson). ▽

11. Teach parents how to specifically define and identify problem behaviors, identify their reactions to the behavior, determine whether the reaction encourages or discourages the behavior, and generate alternatives to the problem behavior. ▽

12. Teach parents how to implement key parenting practices consistently, including establishing realistic age-appropriate rules for acceptable and unacceptable behavior, prompting of positive behavior in the environment, use of positive reinforcement to encourage behavior (e.g., praise), use of clear direct instruction, time-out, and other loss-of-privilege practices for problem behavior, negotiation, and renegotiation (with adolescents). ▽

13. Assign parents home exercises in which they implement and record results of implementation exercises (e.g., "Clear Rules, Positive Reinforcement, Appropriate Consequences" in the *Adolescent Homework Planner,* 2nd ed. by Jongsma, Peterson, and McInnis); review in session, providing corrective feedback toward improved, appropriate, and consistent use of skills. ▽

14. Ask parents to read parent training manuals (e.g., *Parenting Through Change* by Forgatch) or watch videotapes demonstrating the techniques being learned in session (see Webster-Stratton, 1994). ▽

▽ 8. Participate in either individual or group therapy for anger management. (15)

15. Conduct an anger management group (closed enrollment, with peers), or a directive individual therapy focused on anger management. ▽

▽ 9. Keep a daily journal of persons, situations, and other triggers of anger, recording thoughts, feelings, and actions taken. (16)

16. Ask the client to keep a daily journal in which he/she documents persons, situations, and other triggers of anger, irritation, or disappointment (or assign "Anger Journal" in the *Adult Psychotherapy Homework Planner,* 2nd ed. by Jongsma); routinely process the journal toward helping the client understand contributions to generating his/her anger. ▽

▽10. Verbalize increased awareness of anger expression patterns, their possible origins, and their consequences. (17, 18, 19)

17. Assist the client in generating a list of anger triggers; process the list toward helping the client understand the causes and extent of his/her anger. ▽

18. Assist the client in identifying ways that key life figures (e.g.,

father, mother, teachers) have
expressed angry feelings and how
these experiences have positively
or negatively influenced the way
he/she handles anger. ▽

19. Ask the client to list ways anger
has negatively impacted his/her
daily life (e.g., injuring others or
self, legal conflicts, loss of respect
from self and others, destruction
of property) and health (e.g., vulnerability to illness, headaches);
process this list. ▽

▽11. Agree to learn alternative ways
to think about and manage
anger. (20, 21)

20. Assist the client in reconceptualizing anger as involving different
components (cognitive, physiological, affective, and behavioral) that
go through predictable phases
(e.g., demanding expectations not
being met leading to increased
arousal and anger leading to acting out) that can be managed. ▽

21. Assist the client in identifying the
positive consequences of managing anger (e.g., respect from
others and self, cooperation from
others, improved physical health);
ask the client to agree to learn
new ways to conceptualize and
manage anger. ▽

▽12. Learn and implement calming
strategies as part of a new way
to manage reactions to frustration. (22, 23)

22. Teach the client calming techniques (e.g., muscle relaxation,
paced breathing, calming imagery) as part of a tailored strategy
for responding appropriately to
angry feelings when they occur. ▽

23. Assign the client to implement
calming techniques in his/her
daily life when facing anger trigger situations; process the results,
reinforcing success and redirecting
failure. ▽

▽13. Identify, challenge, and replace anger-inducing self-talk with self-talk that facilitates a less angry reaction. (24, 25)

24. Explore the client's self-talk that mediates his/her angry feelings and actions (e.g., demanding expectations reflected in should, must, or have to statements); identify and challenge biases, assisting him/her in generating appraisals and self-talk that corrects for the biases and facilitates a more flexible and temperate response to frustration. ▽

25. Assign the client a homework exercise in which he/she identifies angry self-talk and generates alternatives that help moderate angry reactions; review; reinforce success, providing corrective feedback toward improvement. ▽

▽14. Learn and implement thought-stopping to manage intrusive unwanted thoughts that trigger anger. (26)

26. Assign the client to implement a "thought-stopping" technique on a daily basis between sessions (or assign "Making Use of the Thought-Stopping Technique" in the *Adult Psychotherapy Homework Planner,* 2nd ed. by Jongsma); review implementation; reinforce success, providing corrective feedback toward improvement. ▽

▽15. Verbalize feelings of anger in a controlled, assertive way. (27, 28)

27. Use instruction, modeling, and/or role-playing to teach the client assertive communication; if indicated, refer him/her to an assertiveness training class/group for further instruction. ▽

28. Instruct the client to practice assertion, problem-solving, and/or conflict resolution skills with group members or otherwise significant others. ▽

▽16. Learn and implement problem-solving and/or conflict resolution skills to manage interpersonal problems. (29, 30)

29. Conduct conjoint sessions to help the client implement assertion, problem-solving, and/or conflict resolution skills with group

members or otherwise significant others. ▽

30. Teach the client conflict resolution skills (e.g., empathy, active listening, "I messages," respectful communication, assertiveness without aggression, compromise); use modeling, role-playing, and behavior rehearsal to work through several current conflicts. ▽

▽17. Practice using new anger management skills in session with the therapist and during homework exercises. (31, 32, 33)

31. Assist the client in constructing and consolidating a client-tailored strategy for managing anger that combines any of the somatic, cognitive, communication, problem-solving, and/or conflict resolution skills relevant to needs (see *Treatment of Individuals with Anger Control Problems and Aggressive Behaviors* by Meichenbaum). ▽

32. Use any of several techniques, including relaxation, imagery, behavioral rehearsal, modeling, role-playing, or practice in increasing challenging situations to help the client consolidate the use of his/her new anger management skills. ▽

33. Monitor the client's reports of angry outbursts toward the goal of decreasing their frequency, intensity, and duration through the client's use of new anger management skills (or assign "Alternatives To Destructive Anger" in the *Adult Psychotherapy Homework Planner,* 2nd ed. by Jongsma); review progress, reinforcing success and providing corrective feedback toward improvement. ▽

▽18. Decrease the number, intensity, and duration of angry outbursts, while increasing the use of new skills for managing anger. (34)

▽19. Identify social supports that will help facilitate the implementation of anger management skills. (35)

▽20. Implement relapse prevention strategies for managing possible future trauma-related symptoms. (36, 37, 38, 39)

21. Read a book or treatment manual that supplements the therapy by improving understanding of anger and anger management. (40)

34. Encourage the client to discuss his/her anger management goals with trusted persons who are likely to support his/her change. ▽

35. Discuss with the client the distinction between a lapse and relapse, associating a lapse with an initial and reversible angry outburst and relapse with the choice to return routinely to the old pattern of anger. ▽

36. Identify and rehearse with the client the management of future situations or circumstances in which lapses back to anger could occur. ▽

37. Instruct the client to routinely use the new anger management strategies learned in therapy (e.g., calming, adaptive self-talk, assertion, conflict resolution) to respond to frustrations. ▽

38. Develop a "coping card" or other reminder on which new anger management skills and other important information (e.g., calm yourself, be flexible in your expectations of others, voice your opinion calmly, respect other's point of view) are recorded for the client's later use. ▽

39. Schedule periodic "maintenance sessions" to help the client maintain therapeutic gains. ▽

40. Assign the client to read material that educates him/her about anger and its management (e.g., *Overcoming Situational and General Anger: Client Manual* by Deffenbacher and McKay; *The Anger Control Workbook* by McKay;

suggest parents read *The Angry Child* by Murphy).

—. _____   —. _____
   _____   _____
—. _____   —. _____
   _____   _____
—. _____   —. _____
   _____   _____

DIAGNOSTIC SUGGESTIONS

Axis I: 312.34   Intermittent Explosive Disorder
                296.xx   Bipolar I Disorder
                296.89   Bipolar II Disorder
                312.8   Conduct Disorder
                310.1   Personality Change Due to Axis III Disorder
                309.81   Posttraumatic Stress Disorder

                _____ _____
                _____ _____

Axis II: 799.9   Diagnosis Deferred
                V71.09   No Diagnosis

                _____ _____
                _____ _____

ANXIETY

BEHAVIORAL DEFINITIONS

1. Excessive anxiety, worry, or fear that markedly exceeds the normal level for the client's stage of development.
2. High level of motor tension, such as restlessness, tiredness, shakiness, or muscle tension.
3. Autonomic hyperactivity (e.g., rapid heartbeat, shortness of breath, dizziness, dry mouth, nausea, diarrhea).
4. Hypervigilance, such as feeling constantly on edge, concentration difficulties, trouble falling or staying asleep, and a general state of irritability.
5. A specific fear that has become generalized to cover a wide area and has reached the point where it significantly interferes with the client's and the family's daily life.
6. Excessive anxiety or worry due to parent's threat of abandonment, overuse of guilt, denial of autonomy and status, friction between parents, or interference with physical activity.

__. _____
_____

__. _____
_____

__. _____
_____

LONG-TERM GOALS

1. Reduce overall frequency, intensity, and duration of the anxiety so that daily functioning is not impaired.
2. Stabilize anxiety level while increasing ability to function on a daily basis.

3. Resolve the core conflict that is the source of anxiety.
4. Enhance ability to effectively cope with the full variety of life's anxieties.

—. _____

   _____

   _____

—. _____

   _____

   _____

—. _____

   _____

SHORT-TERM OBJECTIVES

1. Describe current and past experiences with specific fears, prominent worries, and anxiety symptoms, including their impact on functioning and attempts to resolve them. (1, 2)

2. Complete questionnaires designed to assess fear, worry, and anxiety symptoms. (3)

THERAPEUTIC INTERVENTIONS

1. Actively build the level of trust with the client though consistent eye contact, active listening, unconditional positive regard, and warm acceptance to help increase his/her ability to identify and express concerns.

2. Assess the focus, excessiveness, and uncontrollability of the client's fears and worries, and the type, frequency, intensity, and duration of his/her anxiety symptoms (e.g., use *The Anxiety Disorders Interview Schedule for Children—Parent Version or Child Version* by Silverman and Albano, assign "Finding and Losing Your Anxiety" in the *Adolescent Psychotherapy Homework Planner,* 2nd ed. by Jongsma, Peterson, and McInnis).

3. Administer a patient-report measure to help assess the nature and degree of the client's fears, worries, and anxiety symptoms (e.g., *The Penn State Worry Questionnaire* by Meyer, Miller, Metzger, and Borkovec).

▽ 3. Cooperate with an evaluation by a physician for antianxiety medication. (4, 5)

4. Refer the client to a physician for a psychotropic medication consultation. ▽

5. Monitor the client's psychotropic medication compliance, side effects, and effectiveness; confer regularly with the physician. ▽

▽ 4. Verbalize an understanding of how thoughts, physical feelings, and behavioral actions contribute to anxiety and its treatment. (6, 7, 8)

6. Discuss how fears and worries typically involve excessive concern about unrealistic threats, various bodily expressions of tension, overarousal, and hypervigilance, and avoidance of what is threatening, which interact to maintain the problem (see *Helping Your Anxious Child* by Rapee, Spence, Cobham, and Wignall). ▽

7. Discuss how treatment targets fear, worry, anxiety symptoms, and avoidance to help the client manage thoughts and overarousal effectively while overcoming unnecessary avoidance. ▽

8. Assign the client to read psychoeducational sections of books or treatment manuals on fears, worry, and anxiety symptoms (e.g., see *Helping Your Anxious Child* by Rapee, Spence, Cobham, and Wignall). ▽

▽ 5. Learn and implement calming skills to reduce overall anxiety and manage anxiety symptoms. (9, 10, 11, 12)

9. Teach the client calming skills (e.g., progressive muscle relaxation, guided imagery, slow diaphragmatic breathing) and how to discriminate better between relaxation and tension; teach the client how to apply these skills to his/her daily life. ▽

▽ indicates that the Objective/Intervention is consistent with those found in evidence-based treatments.

10. Assign the client homework each session in which he/she practices calming daily; review and reinforce success while providing corrective feedback toward improvement. ▽

11. Assign the client to read about progressive muscle relaxation and other calming strategies in relevant books or treatment manuals (e.g., *New Directions in Progressive Relaxation Training* by Bernstein and Borkovec). ▽

12. Use biofeedback techniques to facilitate the client's success at learning relaxation skills. ▽

▽ 6. Verbalize an understanding of the role that fearful thinking plays in creating fears, excessive worry, and persistent anxiety symptoms. (13, 14, 15)

13. Discuss examples demonstrating that unrealistic fear or worry typically overestimates the probability of threats and underestimates the client's ability to manage realistic demands. ▽

14. Assist the client in challenging his/her fear or worry by examining the actual probability of the negative expectation occurring, the real consequences of it occurring, his/her ability to manage the likely outcome, the worst possible outcome, and his/her ability to accept it (see *Helping Your Anxious Child* by Rapee, Spence, Cobham, and Wignall). ▽

15. Help the client gain insight into the notion that fear and worry involve a form of avoidance of the problem, that this creates anxious arousal, and precludes resolution. ▽

▽ 7. Identify, challenge, and replace fearful self-talk with positive, realistic, and empowering self-talk. (16, 17, 18, 19)

16. Explore the client's schema and self-talk that mediate his/her fear response; challenge the biases; assist him/her in replacing the

distorted messages with reality-based alternatives and positive self-talk that will increase his/her self-confidence in coping with irrational fears or worries. ▽

17. Assign the client a homework exercise in which he/she identifies fearful self-talk and creates reality-based alternatives (or assign "Bad Thoughts Lead to Depressed Feelings" in the *Adolescent Psychotherapy Homework Planner,* 2nd ed. by Jongsma, Peterson, and McInnis); review and reinforce success, providing corrective feedback toward improvement. ▽

18. Teach the client to implement a thought-stopping technique (thinking of a stop sign and then a pleasant scene) for fears or worries that have been addressed but persist (or assign "Making Use of the Thought-Stopping Technique" in the *Adult Psychotherapy Homework Planner,* 2nd ed. by Jongsma); monitor and encourage the client's use of the technique in daily life between sessions. ▽

19. Assign the client to read about cognitive restructuring of fears or worries in relevant books or treatment manuals (e.g., *Helping Your Anxious Child* by Rapee, Spence, Cobham, and Wignall). ▽

▽ 8. Participate in imaginal exposure to the feared outcome of worries. (20, 21, 22, 23, 24)

20. Assign the client to read about "worry exposure" in books or treatment manuals on the treatment of worry or generalized anxiety (e.g., *Mastery of Your Anxiety and Worry—Client Guide* by Zinbarg, Craske, Barlow, and O'Leary). ▽

21. Direct and assist the client in constructing a hierarchy of two to three spheres of worry for use in exposure (e.g., fears of school failure, worries about relationship problems). ▽

22. Select initial exposures that have a high likelihood of being a success experience for the client; develop a plan for managing the negative affect engendered by exposure; mentally rehearse the procedure. ▽

23. Ask the client to vividly imagine worst-case consequences of fears or worries, holding them in mind until anxiety associated with them weakens (up to 30 minutes); generate reality-based alternatives to that worst case and process them (see *Mastery of Your Anxiety and Worry—Therapist Guide* by Craske, Barlow, and O'Leary). ▽

24. Assign the client a homework exercise in which he/she gradually allows exposure to the feared situation and records responses (see *Mastery of Your Anxiety and Worry—Client Guide* by Zinbarg, Craske, Barlow, and O'Leary or *Phobic and Anxiety Disorders in Children and Adolescents* by Ollendick and March); review, reinforce success, and provide corrective feedback toward improvement (or assign "Gradually Facing a Phobic Fear" in the *Adolescent Psychotherapy Homework Planner,* 2nd ed. by Jongsma, Peterson, and McInnis). ▽

▽ 9. Learn and implement new strategies for realistically addressing fears or worries. (25, 26)

25. Ask the client to develop a list of key conflicts that trigger fear or worry and process this list toward resolution (e.g., using problem solving, assertiveness, acceptance, cognitive restructuring). ▽

26. Assign the client a homework exercise in which he/she works on solving a current problem (see *Helping Your Anxious Child* by Rapee, Spence, Cobham, and Wignall); review, reinforce success, and provide corrective feedback toward improvement. ▽

▽10. Increase participation in daily social and academic activities. (27)

27. Encourage the client to strengthen his/her new nonavoidant approach by using distraction from anxious thoughts through increasing daily social and academic activities and other potentially rewarding experiences. ▽

▽11. Learn and implement relapse prevention strategies for managing possible future fears or worries. (28, 29, 30, 31)

28. Discuss with the client the distinction between a lapse and relapse, associating a lapse with an initial and reversible return of a fear, worry, anxiety symptom, or urges to avoid and relapse with the decision to return to a fearful and avoidant manner of dealing with the fear or worry. ▽

29. Identify and rehearse with the client the management of future situations or circumstances in which lapses could occur. ▽

30. Instruct the client to routinely use his/her newly learned skills in relaxation, cognitive restructuring, exposure, and problem-solving exposures as needed to address emergent fears or worries, building them into his/her life as much as possible. ▽

31. Develop a "coping card" or other reminder on which coping strategies and other important information (e.g., "Breathe deeply and relax," "Challenge unrealistic worries," "Use problem-solving") are recorded for the client's later use. ▽

▽12. Parents verbalize an understanding of the client's treatment plan and a willingness to participate in it with the client. (32)

32. If acceptable to the client and if possible, involve the client's parents in the treatment, having them participate in selective activities. ▽

▽13. Parents learn and implement constructive ways to respond to the client's fear and avoidance. (33)

33. Teach the parents skills in effectively responding to the client's fears and anxieties with calm reassurance and reward for successes and with calm persistence in prompting coping skills when needed; frame the family as an expert team. ▽

▽14. Parents learn and implement problem solving strategies, assertive communication, and other constructive ways to respond to their own anxieties. (34)

34. Teach and encourage parents to use the same nonavoidant skills the client is learning to manage and approach their own fears and worries, including problem solving conflicts and assertive communication (e.g., *Keys to Parenting Your Anxious Child* by Manassis). ▽

15. Explore a connection, symbolic or not, between present anxiety and past experiences. (35)

35. Explore with the client the influence of past experiences with loss, abandonment, or other anxiety-related developmental themes on current fears or worries; process toward resolution.

__. _____

_____

__. _____

_____

__. _____

_____

__. _____

_____

—. _____   —. _____
    _____   _____

DIAGNOSTIC SUGGESTIONS

Axis I: 300.02   Generalized Anxiety Disorder
                   300.00   Anxiety Disorder NOS
                   314.01   Attention-Deficit/Hyperactivity Disorder,
                               Combined Type

                   _____   _____
                   _____   _____

Axis II: V71.09   No Diagnosis

                   _____   _____
                   _____   _____

ATTENTION-DEFICIT/HYPERACTIVITY DISORDER (ADHD)

BEHAVIORAL DEFINITIONS

1. Short attention span; difficulty sustaining attention on a consistent basis.
2. Susceptibility to distraction by extraneous stimuli and internal thoughts.
3. Gives impression that he/she is not listening well.
4. Repeated failure to follow through on instructions or complete school assignments or chores in a timely manner.
5. Poor organizational skills as demonstrated by forgetfulness, inattention to details, and losing things necessary for tasks.
6. Hyperactivity as evidenced by a high energy level, restlessness, difficulty sitting still, or loud or excessive talking.
7. Impulsivity as evidenced by difficulty awaiting turn in group situations, blurting out answers to questions before the questions have been completed, and frequent intrusions into others' personal business.
8. Frequent disruptive, aggressive, or negative attention-seeking behaviors.
9. Tendency to engage in carelessness or potentially dangerous activities.
10. Difficulty accepting responsibility for actions; history of projecting blame for problems onto others; failing to learn from experience.
11. Low self-esteem and poor social skills.

—. _____

_____

—. _____

_____

—. _____

_____

LONG-TERM GOALS

1. Sustain attention and concentration for consistently longer periods of time.
2. Increase the frequency of on-task behaviors.
3. Demonstrate marked improvement in impulse control.
4. Regularly take medication as prescribed to decrease impulsivity, hyperactivity, and distractibility.
5. Parents and/or teachers successfully utilize a reward system, contingency contract, or token economy to reinforce positive behaviors and deter negative behaviors.
6. Parents set firm, consistent limits and maintain appropriate parent-child boundaries.
7. Improve self-esteem.
8. Develop positive social skills to help maintain lasting peer friendships.

—. _____

_____

—. _____

_____

—. _____

_____

SHORT-TERM OBJECTIVES	THERAPEUTIC INTERVENTIONS
1. Complete psychological testing to confirm the diagnosis of ADHD and/or rule out emotional factors. (1)	1. Arrange for psychological testing to confirm the presence of ADHD and/or rule out emotional problems that may be contributing to the client's inattentiveness, impulsivity, and hyperactivity; give feedback to the client and his/her parents regarding the testing results.
▽ 2. Take prescribed medication as directed by the physician. (2, 3)	2. Arrange for a medication evaluation for the client. ▽

▽ indicates that the Objective/Intervention is consistent with those found in evidence-based treatments.

3. Monitor the client for psycho-tropic medication prescription compliance, side effects, and effectiveness; consult with the prescribing physician at regular intervals. ▽

▽ 3. Parents and the client increase knowledge about ADHD symptoms. (4, 5, 6)

4. Educate the client's parents and siblings about the symptoms of ADHD. ▽

5. Assign the parents readings to increase their knowledge about symptoms of ADHD (e.g., *ADHD: A Clinical Workbook* by Barkley and Murphy; *ADHD and Teens* by Alexander-Roberts; *Teenagers with ADD* by Dendy-Zeigler). ▽

6. Assign the client readings to increase his/her knowledge about ADHD and ways to manage symptoms (e.g., *Adolescents and ADD* by Quinn). ▽

▽ 4. Parents develop and utilize an organized system to keep track of the client's school assign-ments, chores, and household responsibilities. (7, 8)

7. Assist the parents in developing and implementing an organi-zational system to increase the client's on-task behaviors and completion of school assign-ments, chores, or household responsibilities (e.g., using calen-dars, charts, notebooks, and class syllabi). ▽

8. Assist the parents in developing a routine schedule to increase the client's compliance with school, household, or work-related re-sponsibilities. ▽

▽ 5. Parents maintain communica-tion with the school to increase the client's compliance with completion of school assign-ments. (9)

9. Encourage the parents and teachers to maintain regular communication about the client's academic, behavioral, emotional, and social progress. ▽

6. Utilize effective study skills on a regular basis to improve academic performance. (10, 11)

7. Increase frequency of completion of school assignments, household, and work-related responsibilities. (8, 12, 13)

8. Implement effective test-taking strategies on a consistent basis to improve academic performance. (14)

9. Delay instant gratification in favor of achieving meaningful long-term goals. (15, 16)

10. Teach the client more effective study skills (e.g., clearing away distractions, studying in quiet places, scheduling breaks in studying).

11. Assign the client to read *13 Steps to Better Grades* (Silverman) to improve organizational and study skills.

8. Assist the parents in developing a routine schedule to increase the client's compliance with school, household, or work-related responsibilities.

12. Consult with the client's teachers to implement strategies to improve school performance (e.g., sitting in the front row during class, using a prearranged signal to redirect the client back to task, scheduling breaks from tasks, providing frequent feedback, calling on the client often, arranging for a listening buddy).

13. Encourage the parents and teachers to utilize a school contract and reward system to reinforce completion of the client's assignments (or employ the "Getting It Done" program in the *Adolescent Psychotherapy Homework Planner,* 2nd ed. by Jongsma, Peterson, and McInnis).

14. Teach the client more effective test-taking strategies (e.g., reviewing material regularly, reading directions twice, rechecking work).

15. Teach the client mediational and self-control strategies (e.g., "stop, listen, think, and act") to delay the need for instant gratification and inhibit impulses to achieve more meaningful, longer-term goals.

▽10. Implement Parent Management Training in which the client and his/her parents comply with the implementation of a reward/punishment system, contingency contract, and/or token economy. (17, 18, 19, 20, 21)

16. Assist the parents in increasing structure to help the client learn to delay gratification for longer-term goals (e.g., completing homework or chores before playing basketball). ▽

17. Use a Parent Management Training approach beginning with teaching the parents how parent and child behavioral interactions can encourage or discourage positive or negative behavior and that changing key elements of those interactions (e.g., prompting and reinforcing positive behaviors) can be used to promote positive change (e.g., see *Parenting the Strong-Willed Child* by Forehand and Long; *Living with Children* by Patterson). ▽

18. Teach the parents how to specifically define and identify problem behaviors, identify their reactions to the behavior, determine whether the reaction encourages or discourages the behavior, and generate alternatives to the problem behavior. ▽

19. Teach parents how to implement key parenting practices consistently, including establishing realistic age-appropriate rules for acceptable and unacceptable behavior; prompting of positive behavior in the environment; use of positive reinforcement to encourage behavior (e.g., praise); and use of clear direct instruction, time out, and other loss-of-privilege practices for problem behavior (or assign "Switching From Defense to Offense" in the *Adolescent Psychotherapy Homework Planner,* 2nd ed. by Jongsma, Peterson, and McInnis). ▽

20. Assign the parents home exercises in which they implement and record results of implementation exercises (or assign "Clear Rules, Positive Reinforcement, Appropriate Consequences" in the *Adolescent Psychotherapy Homework Planner,* 2nd ed. by Jongsma, Peterson, and McInnis); review in session, providing corrective feedback toward improved, appropriate, and consistent use of skills. ▽

21. Ask the parents to read parent training manuals (e.g., *Parenting Through Change* by Forgatch) or watch videotapes demonstrating the techniques being learned in session (see Webster-Stratton, 1994). ▽

▽11. Learn and implement social skills to reduce anxiety and build confidence in social interactions. (22, 23)

22. Use instruction, modeling, and role-playing to build the client's general social and/or communication skills. ▽

23. Assign the client to read about general social and/or communication skills in books or treatment manuals on building social skills (e.g., *Your Perfect Right* by Alberti and Emmons; *Conversationally Speaking* by Garner; the "Social Skills Exercise" in the *Adolescent Psychotherapy Homework Planner,* 2nd ed. by Jongsma, Peterson, and McInnis). ▽

▽12. Identify and implement effective problem-solving strategies. (24, 25)

24. Teach the client effective problem-solving skills (e.g., identifying the problem, brainstorming alternative solutions, selecting an option, implementing a course of action, evaluating). ▽

25. Utilize role-playing and modeling to teach the client how to implement effective problem-solving techniques in his/her daily life (or assign the "Stop, Think, and Act" exercise in the *Adolescent Psychotherapy Homework Planner,* 2nd ed. by Jongsma, Peterson, and McInnis). ▽

13. Increase verbalizations of acceptance of responsibility for misbehavior. (26, 27, 28)

26. Assign the client's parents to read material on resolving conflict with adolescents more effectively by placing more responsibility on them (e.g., *Negotiating Parent/ Adolescent Conflict* by Robin and Foster).

27. Firmly confront the client's impulsive behaviors, pointing out consequences for himself/herself and others.

28. Confront statements in which the client blames others for his/her annoying or impulsive behaviors and fails to accept responsibility for his/her actions.

14. Identify stressors or painful emotions that trigger increase in hyperactivity and impulsivity. (29, 30)

29. Explore and identify stressful events or factors that contribute to an increase in impulsivity, hyperactivity, and distractibility. Help the client and parents develop positive coping strategies (e.g., "stop, listen, think, and act," relaxation techniques, positive self-talk) to manage stress more effectively.

30. Explore possible stressors, roadblocks, or hurdles that might cause impulsive and acting-out behaviors to increase in the future. Identify coping strategies (e.g., "stop, listen, think, and act," guided imagery, utilizing "I messages" to communicate needs)

15. Increase the frequency of positive interactions with parents. (31, 32, 33)

16. Parents and the client regularly attend and actively participate in group therapy. (34)

17. Increase the frequency of socially appropriate behaviors with siblings and peers. (35, 36)

that the client and his/her family can use to cope with or overcome stressors, roadblocks, or hurdles.

31. Explore for periods of time when the client demonstrated good impulse control and engaged in fewer disruptive behaviors; process his/her responses and reinforce positive coping mechanisms that he/she used to deter impulsive or disruptive behaviors.

32. Instruct the parents to observe and record three to five positive behaviors by the client in between therapy sessions; reinforce positive behaviors and encourage him/her to continue to exhibit these behaviors.

33. Encourage the parents to spend 10 to 15 minutes daily of one-on-one time with the client to create a closer parent-child bond. Allow the client to take the lead in selecting the activity or task.

34. Encourage the client's parents to participate in an ADHD support group.

35. Give homework assignments where the client identifies 5 to 10 strengths or interests (or assign "Show Your Strengths" in the *Adolescent Psychotherapy Homework Planner,* 2nd ed. by Jongsma, Peterson, and McInnis); review the list in the following session and encourage him/her to utilize strengths or interests to establish friendships.

36. Assign the client the task of showing empathy, kindness, or sensitivity to the needs of others (e.g., allowing sibling or peer to take first turn in a video game, helping with a school fundraiser).

18. Identify and list constructive ways to utilize energy. (37)

37. Give a homework assignment where the client lists the positive and negative aspects of his/her high energy level; review the list in the following session and encourage him/her to channel energy into healthy physical outlets and positive social activities.

19. Express feelings through artwork. (38)

38. Instruct the client to draw a picture reflecting what it feels like to have ADHD; process content of the drawing with the therapist.

—. _____
   _____
—. _____
   _____
—. _____
   _____

—. _____
   _____
—. _____
   _____
—. _____
   _____

DIAGNOSTIC SUGGESTIONS

Axis I:	314.01	Attention-Deficit/Hyperactivity Disorder, Combined Type
	314.00	Attention-Deficit/Hyperactivity Disorder, Predominantly Inattentive Type
	314.01	Attention-Deficit/Hyperactivity Disorder, Predominantly Hyperactive-Impulsive Type
	314.9	Attention-Deficit/Hyperactivity Disorder NOS
	312.81	Conduct Disorder, Childhood-Onset Type
	312.82	Conduct Disorder, Adolescent-Onset Type
	313.81	Oppositional Defiant Disorder
	312.9	Disruptive Behavior Disorder NOS
	296.xx	Bipolar I Disorder
	_____	_____
	_____	_____
Axis II:	V71.09	No Diagnosis
	_____	_____
	_____	_____

AUTISM/PERVASIVE DEVELOPMENTAL DISORDER

BEHAVIORAL DEFINITIONS

1. Pervasive lack of interest in or responsiveness to other people.
2. Chronic failure to develop social relationships appropriate to the developmental level.
3. Lack of spontaneity and emotional or social reciprocity.
4. Significant delays in or total lack of spoken language development.
5. Impairment in sustaining or initiating conversation.
6. Oddities in speech and language as manifested by echolalia, pronominal reversal, or metaphorical language.
7. Inflexible adherence to repetition of nonfunctional rituals or stereotyped motor mannerisms.
8. Persistent preoccupation with objects, parts of objects, or restricted areas of interest.
9. Marked impairment or extreme variability in intellectual and cognitive functioning.
10. Extreme resistance or overreaction to minor changes in routines or environment.
11. Emotional constriction or blunted affect.
12. Recurrent pattern of self-abusive behaviors (e.g., head banging, biting or burning self).

—. _____
_____

—. _____
_____

—. _____
_____

LONG-TERM GOALS

1. Develop basic language skills and the ability to communicate simply with others.
2. Establish and maintain a basic emotional bond with primary attachment figures.
3. Achieve the educational, behavioral, and social goals identified on the individualized educational plan (IEP).
4. Family members develop acceptance of the client's overall capabilities and place realistic expectations on his/her behavior.
5. Engage in reciprocal and cooperative interactions with others on a regular basis.
6. Stabilize mood and tolerate changes in routine or environment.
7. Eliminate all self-abusive behaviors.
8. Attain and maintain the highest realistic level of independent functioning.

—. _____

_____

—. _____

_____

—. _____

_____

SHORT-TERM OBJECTIVES	THERAPEUTIC INTERVENTIONS
1. Cooperate with and complete all recommended evaluations and testing. (1, 2, 3, 4)	1. Arrange for an intellectual and cognitive assessment to gain greater insights into the client's strengths and weaknesses; provide feedback to the parents.
	2. Refer the client for a speech/language evaluation; consult with the speech/language pathologist about the evaluation findings.
	3. Arrange for a neurological evaluation or neuropsychological testing of the client to rule out organic factors.

2. Comply fully with the recommendations offered by the assessment(s) and individualized educational planning committee (IEPC). (5)

3. Comply with the move to an appropriate classroom setting. (6)

4. Comply with the move to an appropriate alternative residential placement setting. (7)

5. Attend speech and language therapy sessions. (8)

6. Increase the frequency of appropriate, spontaneous verbalizations toward the therapist, family members, and others. (9, 10, 11)

4. Arrange for a psychiatric evaluation of the client.

5. Attend an IEPC review to establish the client's eligibility for special education services, to update and revise educational interventions, and to establish new behavioral and educational goals.

6. Consult with the parents, teachers, and other appropriate school officials about designing effective learning programs, classroom assignments, or interventions that build on the client's strengths and compensate for weaknesses.

7. Consult with the parents, school officials, and mental health professionals about the need to place the client in an alternative residential setting (e.g., foster care, group home, residential program).

8. Refer the client to a speech/language pathologist for ongoing services to improve his/her speech and language abilities.

9. Actively build the level of trust with the client through consistent eye contact, frequent attention and interest, unconditional positive regard, and warm acceptance to facilitate increased communication.

10. Employ frequent use of praise and positive reinforcement to increase the client's initiation of verbalizations as well as acknowledgment of and responsiveness to others' verbalizations.

11. Provide the parents with encouragement, support, and reinforcement or modeling methods to foster the client's language development.

7. Decrease oddities or peculiarities in speech and language. (12)

8. Decrease the frequency and severity of temper outbursts and aggressive and self-abusive behaviors. (13, 14, 15, 16, 17)

9. Parents verbalize increased knowledge and understanding of autism and pervasive developmental disorders. (18)

12. In conjunction with the speech therapist, design and implement a response-shaping program using positive reinforcement principles to facilitate the client's language development and decrease oddities or peculiarities in speech and language.

13. Teach the parents behavior management techniques (e.g., time-out, response cost, overcorrection, removal of privileges) to decrease the client's idiosyncratic speech, excessive self-stimulation temper outbursts, and self-abusive behaviors.

14. Design a token economy for use in the home, classroom, or residential program to improve the client's social skills, anger management, impulse control, and speech/language abilities.

15. Develop a reward system or contingency contract to improve the client's social skills and anger control.

16. Teach the proper use of aversive therapy techniques to stop or limit the client's self-abusive or self-stimulating behaviors.

17. Counsel the parents to develop interventions to manage the client's self-abusive behaviors, including positive reinforcement, response cost, and, if necessary, physical restraint.

18. Educate the client's parents and family members about the maturation process in individuals with autism or pervasive developmental disorders and the challenges that this process presents.

10. Parents increase social support network. (19, 20)

19. Direct the parents to join the Autism Society of America to expand their social network, to gain additional knowledge of the disorder, and to give them support and encouragement.

20. Refer the client's parents to a support group for parents of autistic children.

11. Parents utilize respite care to reduce stress related to being caregiver(s). (21)

21. Refer the parents to, and encourage them to use, respite care for the client on a periodic basis.

12. Demonstrate essential self-care and independent living skills. (22, 23, 24)

22. Counsel the parents about teaching the client essential self-care skills (e.g., combing hair, bathing, brushing teeth).

23. Monitor and provide frequent feedback to the client regarding his/her progress toward developing self-care skills.

24. Use operant conditioning principles and response-shaping techniques to help the client develop self-help skills (e.g., dressing self, making bed, fixing sandwich) and improve personal hygiene.

13. Parent and siblings report feeling a closer bond with the client. (25, 26)

25. Conduct family therapy sessions to provide the parents and siblings with the opportunity to share and work through their feelings pertaining to the client's autism or pervasive developmental disorder.

26. Assign the client and his/her parents a task (e.g., swimming, riding a bike) that will help build trust and mutual dependence.

14. Increase the frequency of positive interactions with parents and siblings. (27, 28)

27. Encourage the family members to regularly include the client in structured work or play activities for 20 minutes each day.

28. Encourage detached parents to increase their involvement in the client's daily life, leisure activities, or schoolwork.

15. Channel strengths or areas of interest into a positive, constructive activity. (29, 30)

29. Redirect the client's preoccupation with a single object or restricted area of interest to turn it into a productive activity (e.g., learning to tune instruments, using interest with numbers to learn how to budget allowance money).

30. Employ applied behavior analysis in home, school, or residential setting to alter maladaptive behaviors. First, define and operationalize target behaviors. Next, select antecedents and consequences for specific behaviors. Then, observe and record the client's response to reinforcement interventions. Finally, analyze data to assess treatment effectiveness.

16. Increase the frequency of social contacts with peers. (31, 32)

31. Consult with the client's parents and teachers about increasing the frequency of the client's social contacts with his/her peers (working with student aide in class, attending Sunday school, participating in Special Olympics).

32. Refer the client to a summer camp program to foster social contacts.

17. Attend vocational training sessions. (33, 34)

33. Refer the client to a sheltered workshop or vocational training program to develop basic job skills.

34. Help the family to arrange an interview for the client's possible placement in a school-based vocational training program.

18. Attend a program to build skills for independent activities of daily living. (35)

35. Refer the client to a life or daily skills program that builds competency in budgeting, cooking, shopping, and other skills required to maintain an independent living arrangement.

19. Parents verbalize their fears regarding the client living independent of them. (36)

36. Help the parents and family process their concerns and fears about the client living independently from them.

20. Parents develop and implement a step program for moving the client toward establishing independent status. (37, 38, 39)

37. Work with the family and parents to develop a step program that will move the client toward working and living independently.

38. Coach and monitor the parents and the client in implementing a plan for the client to live independently.

39. Assist the family in finding a group home or supervised living program (e.g., an apartment with an on-site manager) for the client to establish his/her independence from the family.

__. _____
_____
__. _____
_____
__. _____
_____

__. _____
_____
__. _____
_____
__. _____
_____

DIAGNOSTIC SUGGESTIONS

Axis I:	299.00	Autistic Disorder
	299.80	Pervasive Developmental Disorder NOS
	299.80	Rett's Disorder
	299.10	Childhood Disintegrative Disorder
	299.80	Asperger's Disorder

307.3	Stereotypic Movement Disorder
295.xx	Schizophrenia
_____	_____
_____	_____

Axis II:

317	Mild Mental Retardation
319	Mental Retardation, Severity Unspecified
799.9	Diagnosis Deferred
V71.09	No Diagnosis
_____	_____
_____	_____

BLENDED FAMILY

BEHAVIORAL DEFINITIONS

1. Children from a previous union of respective parents are brought into a single family unit, resulting in interpersonal conflict, anger, and frustration.
2. Resistance and defiance on the part of a child toward his/her new stepparent.
3. Open conflict between siblings with different parents now residing as siblings in the same family system.
4. Overt or covert defiance of the stepparent by one or several siblings.
5. Verbal threats to the biological parent of going to live with the other parent, report abuse, and so on.
6. Interference from ex-spouse in the daily life of the new family system.
7. Anxiety and concern by both new partners regarding bringing their two families together.
8. No clear lines of communication or responsibilities assigned within the blended family, making for confusion, frustration, and unhappiness.
9. Internal conflicts regarding loyalty to the noncustodial parent result in distance from the stepparent.

—. _____
   _____
—. _____
   _____
—. _____
   _____

LONG-TERM GOALS

1. Achieve a reasonable level of family connectedness and harmony whereby members support, help, and are concerned for each other.

2. Become an integrated blended family system that is functional and in which members are bonded to each other.
3. Attain a level of peaceful coexistence where daily issues can be negotiated without becoming ongoing conflicts.
4. Accept the stepparent and/or stepsiblings and treat them with respect, kindness, and cordiality.
5. Establish a new family identity in which each member feels he/she belongs and is valued.
6. Accept the new blended family system as not inferior to the nuclear family, just different.
7. Establish a strong bond between the couple as a parenting team that is free from triangulation and is able to bring stabilization to the family.

—. _____

_____

—. _____

_____

—. _____

_____

SHORT-TERM OBJECTIVES

THERAPEUTIC INTERVENTIONS

1. Each family member openly shares thoughts and feelings regarding the blended family. (1)

1. Actively build the level of trust with each family member within family therapy sessions through consistent eye contact, active listening, unconditional positive regard, and acceptance to allow each family member to identify and express openly his/her thoughts and feelings regarding the blended family.

2. Attend and actively take part in family or sibling group sessions. (2, 3)

2. Conduct family, sibling, and marital sessions to address the issues of loss, conflict negotiation, parenting, stepfamily psycho-education, joining, rituals, and relationship building.

3. Utilize an exercise with a set of markers and a large sheet of drawing paper in a family session. The therapist indicates that everyone is going to make a drawing and begins by making a scribble line on the paper, then has each family member add to the line using a colored marker of his/her choice. When the drawing is complete, the family is given the chance to either interpret the drawing individually or develop a mutual story based on the drawing (see Lowe in *101 Favorite Play Therapy Techniques* by Kaduson and Schaefer).

3. Family members verbalize realistic expectations and rejection of myths regarding stepfamilies. (4, 5, 6)

4. Within a family session, ask each member to list his/her expectations for the new family. Members will share and process their lists with the whole family and the therapist.

5. Remind family members that "instant love" of new family members is a myth. It is unrealistic to expect children to immediately like (and certainly to love) the partner who is serving in the new-parent role.

6. Help family members accept the position that siblings from different biological families need not like or love one another, but that they should be mutually respectful and kind.

4. Family members identify losses/changes in each of their lives. (2, 7, 8)

2. Conduct family, sibling, and marital sessions to address the issues of loss, conflict negotiation, parenting, stepfamily psycho-education, joining, rituals, and relationship building.

7. Assign siblings to complete a list of losses and changes each has experienced for the last year and then for all years. Give empathetic confirmation while they share their lists in session and help them see the similarity in their experiences to those of the other siblings.

8. Ask the family to read *Changing Families: An Interactive Guide for Kids and Grownups* (Fassler, Lash, and Ives) to help them identify the changes within the family and give them ways to adjust and thrive.

5. Family members demonstrate increased skills in recognizing and expressing feelings. (9, 10, 11)

9. Have the family or siblings play The Ungame (Zakich; available from The Ungame Company) or The Talking, Feeling, and Doing Game (Gardner; available from Childswork/Childsplay) to promote family members' awareness of self and their feelings.

10. Provide education to the family on identifying, labeling, and expressing feelings appropriately.

11. Help the family practice identifying and expressing feelings by doing a feelings exercise (e.g., "I feel sad when _____," "I feel excited when _____") in a family session. The therapist models affirming and acknowledging each member as he/she shares during the exercise.

6. Family members verbalize expanded knowledge of stepfamilies. (12, 13, 14)

12. Suggest that the parents and teen read material to expand their knowledge of stepfamilies and their development (e.g., *Stepfamily Realities* by Newman; *Stepfamilies Stepping Ahead* by Burt).

13. Refer parents to the Stepfamily Association of America (1-800-735-0329) to obtain additional information and resources on stepfamilies.

14. Assign the parents to read *How to Win as a Stepfamily* (Visher and Visher) and process the key concepts they gather from the reading.

7. Family members demonstrate increased negotiating skills. (15, 16)

15. Train family members in building negotiating skills (e.g., problem identification, brainstorming solutions, evaluating pros and cons, compromising, agreeing on a selected solution, making an implementation plan) and have them practice these skills on issues that present in family sessions.

16. Ask siblings to specify their conflicts and suggest solutions (or assign the exercise "Negotiating a Peace Treaty" from the *Adolescent Psychotherapy Homework Planner,* 2nd ed. by Jongsma, Peterson, and McInnis).

8. Family members report a reduced level of tension between all members. (17, 18, 19)

17. Inject humor whenever appropriate in family or sibling sessions to decrease tensions and conflict and to model balance and perspective. Give positive feedback to members who create appropriate humor.

18. Hold a family sibling session in which each child lists and verbalizes an appreciation of each sibling's unique traits or abilities (or assign the exercise "Cloning the Perfect Sibling" from the *Adolescent Psychotherapy Homework Planner,* 2nd ed. by Jongsma, Peterson, and McInnis).

9. Family members report increased trust of each other. (20, 21)

10. Each parent takes primary role of discipline with own children. (22)

11. The parents attend a step-parenting didactic group to increase parenting skills. (23)

12. Family members attend weekly family meeting in the home to express feelings and voice issues. (24)

13. The parents create and institute new family rituals. (25, 26, 27)

19. Utilize a brief solution-focused intervention of reframing or normalizing the conflictual situation as a stage that the family needs to get through. Identify the next stage as the coming together stage, and talk about when they might be ready to move there and how they could start to head there (see *A Guide to Possibility Land* by O'Hanlon and Beadle).

20. Read and process with the family the story *Stone Soup* (Brown), focusing on the issues of risk, mistrust, and cooperation.

21. Read Dr. Seuss's *The Sneetches* in a family session to seed with members the folly of top dog, low dog, one-upmanship, and insider-outsider attitudes.

22. Encourage each parent to take the primary role in disciplining his/her own children and refrain from all negative references to ex-spouses.

23. Refer the parents to a parenting group for stepparents.

24. Assist the parents in implementing a once-a-week family meeting in which issues can be raised and resolved and where members are encouraged to share their thoughts, complaints, and compliments.

25. Encourage the parents to create and implement daily rituals (e.g., mealtimes, bedtime stories, household chores, time alone with parents, time together) in order to give structure and connection to the system.

26. Conduct a family session where rituals from both former families are examined. Then work with the family to retain the rituals that are appropriate and will work in the new system and create the necessary new ones to fill in any gaps.

27. Give the family the assignment to create birthday rituals for their new blended unit in a family session.

14. The parents identify and eliminate triangulation within the system. (28)

28. Provide education to the parents on patterns of interactions within families, focusing on the pattern of triangulation and its dysfunctional aspects.

15. The parents report a strengthening of their marital bond. (29, 30, 31)

29. Refer the couple to skills-based marital therapy based on strengthening avenues of responsibilities, communication, and conflict resolution (see *PREP—Fighting for Your Marriage* by Markman, Stanley, and Blumberg).

30. Work with the parents in conjoint sessions to deal with issues of time away alone, privacy, and individual space; develop specific ways for these things to regularly occur.

31. Hold conjoint sessions with the parents to process the issue of showing affection toward each other. Help the parents develop appropriate boundaries and ways of showing affection that do not give rise to unnecessary anger in their children.

16. The parents spend one-on-one time with each child. (32)

32. Work with the parents to build into each of their schedules one-on-one time with each child and stepchild in order to give each child undivided attention and to build and maintain relationships.

17. Family members report a slow development of bonds between each member. (33, 34, 35)

33. Refer the family members to an initiatives camp weekend to increase their skills in working cooperatively and conflict resolution and their sense of trust. Process the experience with the family in the next family session.

34. Complete and process with the siblings a cost-benefit analysis (see *Ten Days to Self-Esteem* by Burns) to evaluate the pluses and minuses of becoming a family or resisting. Use a positive outcome to move beyond resistance to begin the process of joining.

35. Emphasize and model in family, sibling, and couple sessions the need for family members to build their new relationships slowly, allowing everyone time and space to adjust and develop a level of trust with each other.

18. Family members report an increased sense of loyalty and connectedness. (33, 36, 37)

33. Refer the family members to an initiatives camp weekend to increase their skills in working cooperatively and conflict resolution and their sense of trust. Process the experience with the family in the next family session.

36. Conduct family sessions in which a genogram is developed for the entire new family system to show everyone how they are connected.

37. Give a family session assignment to design a family coat of arms on poster board. The coat of arms is to reflect where the family members came from and where they are now. Process this experience when completed, and then have the family display the poster at home.

—. _____   —. _____
   _____   _____
—. _____   —. _____
   _____   _____
—. _____   —. _____
   _____   _____

DIAGNOSTIC SUGGESTIONS

Axis I: 309.0   Adjustment Disorder With Depressed Mood
                  309.3   Adjustment Disorder With Disturbance of
                             Conduct
                  309.24   Adjustment Disorder With Anxiety
                  309.81   Posttraumatic Stress Disorder
                  300.4   Dysthymic Disorder
                  V62.81   Relational Problem NOS

                  _____   _____

                  _____   _____

Axis II: 799.9   Diagnosis Deferred
                  V71.09   No Diagnosis

                  _____   _____

                  _____   _____

CHEMICAL DEPENDENCE

BEHAVIORAL DEFINITIONS

 1. Self-report of almost daily use of alcohol or illicit drugs or regularly using until intoxicated.
 2. Caught or observed intoxicated and/or high on two or more occasions.
 3. Changing peer groups to one that is noticeably oriented toward regular use of alcohol and/or illicit drugs.
 4. Drug paraphernalia and/or alcohol found in the client's possession or in his/her personal area (e.g., bedroom, car, school locker, backpack).
 5. Marked change in behavior (e.g., isolation or withdrawal from family and close friends, loss of interest in activities, low energy, sleeping more, a drop in school grades).
 6. Physical withdrawal symptoms (shaking, seizures, nausea, headaches, sweating, anxiety, insomnia, and/or depression).
 7. Continued substance use despite persistent physical, legal, financial, vocational, social, or relationship problems that are directly caused by the substance use.
 8. Mood swings.
 9. Absent, tardy, or skipping school on a regular basis.
10. Poor self-image as evidenced by describing self as a loser or a failure, and rarely making eye contact when talking to others.
11. Predominately negative or hostile outlook on life and other people.
12. Has been caught stealing alcohol from a store, the home of friends, or parents.
13. Has been arrested for minor in possession, driving under the influence, or drunk and disorderly charges.
14. Positive family history of chemical dependence.

—. _____
    _____
—. _____
    _____

—. _____
_____

LONG-TERM GOALS

1. Confirm or rule out the existence of chemical dependence.
2. Maintain total abstinence from all mood-altering substances while developing an active recovery program.
3. Reestablish sobriety while developing a plan for addressing relapse issues.
4. Confirm and address chemical dependence as a family issue.
5. Develop the skills that are essential to maintaining a drug-free life.
6. Reestablish connections with relationships and groups that will support and enhance ongoing recovery from chemical dependence.
7. Develop an understanding of the pattern of relapse and strategies for coping effectively to help sustain long-term recovery.

—. _____
_____

—. _____
_____

—. _____
_____

SHORT-TERM OBJECTIVES	THERAPEUTIC INTERVENTIONS
1. Describe the type, amount, frequency, and history of substance abuse. (1)	1. Gather a complete drug/alcohol history from the client, including the amount and pattern of his/her use, signs and symptoms of use, and negative life consequences (e.g., social, legal, familial, vocational).
2. Complete psychological tests designed to assess the nature and severity of social anxiety and avoidance. (2)	2. Administer to the client an objective test of drug and/or alcohol abuse (e.g., Adolescent Substance Abuse Subtle Screening Inventory [SASSI-A2], Alcohol Severity Index, Michigan Alcohol Screening Test [MAST]); process the results with the client.

3. Participate in a medical examination to evaluate the effects of chemical dependence. (3)

▼ 4. Cooperate with an evaluation by a physician for psychotropic medication. (4, 5)

▼ 5. Identify the negative consequences of drug and/or alcohol abuse. (6)

▼ 6. Decrease the level of denial around using as evidenced by fewer statements about minimizing amount of use and its negative impact on life. (7, 8)

▼ 7. Make verbal "I statements" that reflect a knowledge and acceptance of chemical dependence. (9)

3. Refer the client for a thorough physical examination to determine any physical/medical consequences of chemical dependence.

4. Arrange for an evaluation for a prescription of psychotropic medications (e.g., serotonergic medications) or replacement pharmacotherapy (e.g., methadone, nicotine patches). ▼

5. Monitor the client for prescription compliance, side effects, and overall effectiveness of the medication; consult with the prescribing physician at regular intervals. ▼

6. Ask the client to make a list of the ways substance abuse has negatively impacted his/her life (or assign "Taking Your First Step" in the *Adolescent Psychotherapy Homework Planner,* 2nd ed. by Jongsma, Peterson, and McInnis); process these with him/her. ▼

7. Assign the client to ask two or three people who are close to him/her to write a letter to the therapist in which they identify how they saw the client's chemical dependence negatively impacting his/her life. ▼

8. Assign the client to complete a First-Step paper and then to process it with group, sponsor, or therapist to receive feedback. ▼

9. Model and reinforce statements that reflect the client's acceptance of his/her chemical dependence and its destructive consequences for self and others. ▼

▼ indicates that the Objective/Intervention is consistent with those found in evidence-based treatments.

▽ 8. Verbalize increased knowledge of chemical dependence and the process of recovery. (10, 11)

10. Assign the client to learn more about chemical dependency and the recovery process (e.g., through assignment of didactic lectures, reading, films); ask the client to identify key points. ▽

11. Assign the client to meet with an AA/NA member who has been working the 12-step program for several years and find out specifically how the program has helped him/her to stay sober (or assign "Welcome to Recovery" in the *Adolescent Psychotherapy Homework Planner,* 2nd ed. by Jongsma, Peterson, and Mc-Innis); afterward, process the meeting. ▽

▽ 9. Verbalize a commitment to abstain from the use of mood-altering drugs. (12)

12. Develop an abstinence contract with the client regarding the termination of the use of his/her drug of choice; process client's feelings related to the commitment. ▽

▽10. Attend Alcoholics Anonymous/Narcotics Anonymous (AA/NA) meetings as frequently as necessary to support sobriety. (13)

13. Recommend that the client attend AA or NA meetings and report on the impact of the meetings; process messages the client is receiving. ▽

▽11. Verbalize an understanding of personal, social, and family factors that can contribute to development of chemical dependence and pose risks for relapse. (14, 15)

14. Assess the client's intellectual, personality, and cognitive vulnerabilities, family history, and life stresses that contribute to his/her chemical dependence. ▽

15. Facilitate the client's understanding of his/her genetic and environmental risk factors that led to the development of chemical dependency and serve as risk factors for relapse. ▽

▼12. Identify the ways being sober could positively impact life. (16)

16. Ask the client to make a list of how being sober could positively impact his/her life; process the list. ▼

▼13. Identify and make changes in social relationships that will support recovery. (17, 18)

17. Review the negative influence of the client continuing his/her chemical dependence-related friendships ("drinking buddies") and assist him/her in making a plan to develop new sober relationships including "sobriety buddies"; revisit routinely and facilitate toward development of a new social support system. ▼

18. Assist the client in planning social and recreational activities that are free from association with substance abuse; revisit routinely and facilitate toward development of a new social support system. ▼

▼14. Identify projects and other social and recreational activities that sobriety will now afford and that will support sobriety. (18, 19)

18. Assist the client in planning social and recreational activities that are free from association with substance abuse; revisit routinely and facilitate toward development of a new social support system. ▼

19. Plan household, school-related, work-related, and/or other projects that can be accomplished to build the client's self-esteem and self-concept as clean and sober. ▼

▼15. Verbalize how living situation contributes to chemical dependence and acts as a hindrance to recovery. (20)

20. Evaluate the role of the client's living situation in fostering a pattern of chemical dependence; process coping skills with the client. ▼

▼16. Identify positive impact that sobriety will have on intimate and family relationships. (21)

21. Assist the client in identifying positive changes that will be made in family relationships during recovery. ▼

▽17. Agree to make amends to significant others who have been hurt by the life dominated by substance abuse. (22, 23)

22. Discuss the negative effects the client's substance abuse has had on family, friends, and work relationships and encourage a plan to make amends for such hurt. ▽

23. Elicit from the client a verbal commitment to make initial amends now to key individuals and further amends when working Steps Eight and Nine of AA program. ▽

▽18. Participate in family therapy. (24)

24. Conduct or refer the client to family therapy with the goal of strengthing family-client attachment and support of recovery goals. ▽

▽19. Participate in Voucher-Based Reinforcement program by routinely providing chemical-free urine screens. (25)

25. Enroll the client in a drug screening program that provides him/her with vouchers with increasing monetary value for each urine screen he/she passes. ▽

▽20. Identify, challenge, and replace destructive self-talk with positive, strength-building self-talk. (26, 27)

26. Explore the client's schema and self-talk that weaken his/her resolve to remain abstinent; challenge the biases and assist him/her in generating realistic self-talk that correct for the biases and build resilience. ▽

27. Rehearse situations in which the client identifies his/her negative self-talk and generates empowering alternatives; review and reinforce success. ▽

▽21. Learn and implement coping strategies to manage urges to lapse back into chemical use. (28)

28. Teach the client a "coping package" involving calming strategies (e.g., relaxation, breathing), thought stopping, positive self-talk, and attentional focusing skills (e.g., using distraction to cope with urges, staying focused on behavioral goals of abstinence) to manage urges to use chemical substances. ▽

▼22. Undergo gradual repeated exposure to triggers of urges to lapse back into chemical substance use. (29, 30)

29. Direct and assist the client in construction of a hierarchy of urge-producing cues to use substances. ▼

30. Select initial in vivo or role-played cue exposures that have a high likelihood of being a successful experience for the client; facilitate coping and cognitive restructuring within and after the exposure, use behavioral strategies (e.g., modeling, rehearsal, social reinforcement) to facilitate the exposure (or assign "Gradually Facing a Phobic Fear" in the *Adolescent Psychotherapy Homework Planner,* 2nd ed. by Jongsma, Peterson, and McInnis). ▼

▼23. Learn and implement personal skills to manage common day-to-day challenges without the use of substances. (31, 32)

31. Assess current skill in managing common everyday stressors (e.g., work, social, family role demands); use behavioral techniques (e.g., instruction, modeling, role-playing) to build social and/or communication skills to manage these challenges. ▼

32. Assign the client to read about general social skills in books or treatment manuals (e.g., *Your Perfect Right* by Alberti and Emmons; *Conversationally Speaking* by Garner); review the client's anxiety level in social situations and reiforce his/her attempts to reach out to others (or assign "Social Skills Exercise," "Greeting Peers," "Reach Out and Call," or "Show Your Strengths" in the *Adolescent Psychotherapy Homework Planner,* 2nd ed. by Jongsma, Peterson, and McInnis). ▼

▼24. Implement relapse prevention strategies for managing possible future situations with high-risk for relapse. (33, 34, 35, 36)

33. Discuss with the client the distinction between a lapse and relapse, associating a lapse with an initial and reversible use of a substance and relapse with the decision to return to a repeated pattern of abuse. ▼

34. Identify and rehearse with the client the management of future situations or circumstances in which lapses could occur (or assign "Keeping Straight" in the *Adolescent Psychotherapy Homework Planner,* 2nd ed. by Jongsma, Peterson, and McInnis). ▼

35. Instruct the client to routinely use strategies learned in therapy (e.g., using cognitive restructuring, social skills, exposure) while building social interactions and relationships. ▼

36. Recommend that the client read material on how to avoid relapse (e.g., *Staying Sober: A Guide to Relapse Prevention* by Gorski and Miller; *The Staying Sober Workbook* by Gorski). ▼

▼25. Develop a written aftercare plan that will support the maintenance of long-term sobriety. (37)

37. Assign and review the client's written aftercare plan to ensure it is adequate to maintain sobriety. ▼

__. _____

_____

__. _____

_____

__. _____

_____

__. _____

_____

__. _____

_____

__. _____

_____

DIAGNOSTIC SUGGESTIONS

Axis I:	303.90	Alcohol Dependence
	305.00	Alcohol Abuse
	304.30	Cannabis Dependence
	305.20	Cannabis Abuse
	304.20	Cocaine Dependence
	305.60	Cocaine Abuse
	304.80	Polysubstance Dependence
	291.2	Alcohol-Induced Persisting Dementia
	291.1	Alcohol-Induced Persisting Amnestic Disorder
	300.4	Dysthymic Disorder
	312.34	Intermittent Explosive Disorder
	309.81	Posttraumatic Stress Disorder
	304.10	Sedative, Hypnotic, or Anxiolytic Dependence

_____   _____

_____   _____

Axis II: V71.09   No Diagnosis

_____   _____

_____   _____

CONDUCT DISORDER/DELINQUENCY

BEHAVIORAL DEFINITIONS

1. Persistent refusal to comply with rules or expectations in the home, school, or community.
2. Excessive fighting, intimidation of others, cruelty or violence toward people or animals, and destruction of property.
3. History of stealing at home, at school, or in the community.
4. School adjustment characterized by disrespectful attitude toward authority figures, frequent disruptive behaviors, and detentions or suspensions for misbehavior.
5. Repeated conflict with authority figures at home, at school, or in the community.
6. Impulsivity as manifested by poor judgment, taking inappropriate risks, and failing to stop and think about consequences of actions.
7. Numerous attempts to deceive others through lying, conning, or manipulating.
8. Consistent failure to accept responsibility for misbehavior accompanied by a pattern of blaming others.
9. Little or no remorse for misbehavior.
10. Lack of sensitivity to the thoughts, feelings, and needs of other people.
11. Multiple sexual partners, lack of emotional commitment, and engaging in unsafe sexual practices.
12. Use of mood-altering substances on a regular basis.
13. Participation in gang membership and activities.

—. _____
   _____

—. _____
   _____

—. _____
   _____

LONG-TERM GOALS

1. Comply with rules and expectations in the home, school, and community consistently.
2. Eliminate all illegal and antisocial behavior.
3. Terminate all acts of violence or cruelty toward people or animals and the destruction of property.
4. Demonstrate marked improvement in impulse control.
5. Express anger in a controlled, respectful manner on a consistent basis.
6. Parents establish and maintain appropriate parent-child boundaries, setting firm, consistent limits when the client acts out in an aggressive or rebellious manner.
7. Demonstrate empathy, concern, and sensitivity for the thoughts, feelings, and needs of others on a regular basis.

—. _____

   _____

—. _____

   _____

—. _____

   _____

SHORT-TERM OBJECTIVES	THERAPEUTIC INTERVENTIONS
1. Identify situations, thoughts, and feelings that trigger angry feelings, problem behaviors, and the targets of those actions. (1)	1. Thoroughly assess the various stimuli (e.g., situations, people, thoughts) that have triggered the client's anger and the thoughts, feelings, and actions that have characterized his/her anger responses.
2. Cooperate with a medical evaluation to assess possible organic contributors to poor anger control. (2)	2. Refer the client to a physician for a complete physical exam to rule out organic contributors (e.g., brain damage, tumor, elevated testosterone levels) to poor anger control.

3. Complete psychological testing. (3)

3. Conduct or arrange for psychological testing to help in assessing whether a comorbid condition (e.g., depression, Attention-Deficit/Hyperactivity Disorder [ADHD]) is contributing to anger control problems; follow up accordingly with client and parents regarding treatment options.

4. Complete a substance abuse evaluation and comply with the recommendations offered by the evaluation findings. (4)

4. Arrange for a substance abuse evaluation and/or treatment for the client.

5. Cooperate with the recommendations or requirements mandated by the criminal justice system. (5, 6, 7)

5. Consult with criminal justice officials about the appropriate consequences for the client's destructive or aggressive behaviors (e.g., pay restitution, community service, probation, intensive surveillance).

6. Consult with parents, school officials, and criminal justice officials about the need to place the client in an alternative setting (e.g., foster home, group home, residential program, juvenile detention facility).

7. Encourage and challenge the parents not to protect the client from the natural or legal consequences of his/her destructive or aggressive behaviors.

▽ 6. Cooperate with a physician's evaluation for possible treatment with psychotropic medications to assist in anger and behavioral control and take medications consistently, if prescribed. (8)

8. Assess the client for the need for psychotropic medication to assist in control of anger; refer him/her to a physician for an evaluation for prescription medication, monitor prescription compliance, effectiveness, and side effects and provide feedback to the prescribing physician. ▽

▽ indicates that the Objective/Intervention is consistent with those found in evidence-based treatments.

▽ 7. Recognize and verbalize how feelings are connected to misbehavior. (9)

9. Actively build the level of trust with the client through consistent eye contact, active listening, unconditional positive regard, and warm acceptance to help increase his/her ability to identify and express feelings instead of acting them out; assist the client in making a connection between his/her feelings and reactive behaviors. ▽

▽ 8. Increase the number of statements that reflect the acceptance of responsibility for misbehavior. (10, 11, 12)

10. Firmly confront the client's antisocial behavior and attitude, pointing out consequences for himself/herself and others (or assign "My Behavior and Its Full Impact" or "Patterns of Stealing" in the *Adolescent Psychotherapy Homework Planner,* 2nd ed. by Jongsma, Peterson, and McInnis). ▽

11. Confront statements in which the client lies and/or blames others for his/her misbehaviors and fails to accept responsibility for his/her actions. ▽

12. Explore and process the factors that contribute to the client's pattern of blaming others (e.g., harsh punishment experiences, family pattern of blaming others). ▽

▽ 9. Agree to learn alternative ways to think about and manage anger and misbehavior. (13, 14)

13. Assist the client in reconceptualizing anger as involving different components (cognitive, physiological, affective, and behavioral) that go through predictable phases (e.g., demanding expectations not being met leading to increased arousal and anger leading to acting out) that can be managed. ▽

▽10. Learn and implement calming strategies as part of a new way to manage reactions to frustration. (15)

▽11. Identify, challenge, and replace self-talk that leads to anger and misbehavior with self-talk that facilitates a more constructive reaction. (16)

▽12. Learn and implement thought-stopping to manage intrusive unwanted thoughts that trigger anger and acting out. (17)

▽13. Verbalize feelings of frustration, disagreement, and anger in a controlled, assertive way. (18)

14. Assist the client in identifying the positive consequences of managing anger and misbehavior (e.g., respect from others and self, cooperation from others, improved physical health); ask the client to agree to learn new ways to conceptualize and manage anger and misbehavior. ▽

15. Teach the client calming techniques (e.g., muscle relaxation, paced breathing, calming imagery) as part of a tailored strategy for responding appropriately to angry feelings when they occur. ▽

16. Explore the client's self-talk that mediates his/her angry feelings and actions (e.g., demanding expectations reflected in should, must, or have to statements); identify and challenge biases, assisting him/her in generating appraisals and self-talk that corrects for the biases and facilitates a more flexible and temperate response to frustration. ▽

17. Assign the client to implement a "thought-stopping" technique on a daily basis between sessions (or assign "Making Use of the Thought-Stopping Technique" in the *Adult Psychotherapy Homework Planner,* 2nd ed. by Jongsma); review implementation; reinforce success, providing corrective feedback toward improvement. ▽

18. Use instruction, modeling, and/or role-playing to teach the client assertive communication; if indicated, refer him/her to an assertiveness training class/group for further instruction. ▽

▽14. Learn and implement problem-solving and/or conflict resolution skills to manage interpersonal problems constructively. (19)

▽15. Practice using new calming, communication, conflict resolution, and thinking skills in session with the therapist and during homework exercises. (20, 21)

▽16. Practice using new calming, communication, conflict resolution, and thinking skills in homework exercises. (22)

19. Teach the client conflict resolution skills (e.g., empathy, active listening, "I messages," respectful communication, assertiveness without aggression, compromise); use modeling, role-playing, and behavior rehearsal to work through several current conflicts. ▽

20. Assist the client in constructing and consolidating a client-tailored strategy for managing anger that combines any of the somatic, cognitive, communication, problem-solving, and/or conflict resolution skills relevant to his/her needs. ▽

21. Use any of several techniques, including relaxation, imagery, behavioral rehearsal, modeling, role-playing, or feedback of videotaped practice in increasingly challenging situations to help the client consolidate the use of his/her new anger management skills (see *Treatment of Individuals with Anger Control Problems and Aggressive Behaviors* by Meichenbaum). ▽

22. Assign the client homework exercises to help them practice newly learned calming, assertion, conflict-resolution, or cognitive restructuring skills as needed (or assign "Anger Control" in the *Adolescent Psychotherapy Homework Planner,* 2nd ed. by Jongsma, Peterson, and McInnis); review and process toward the goal of consolidation. ▽

▽17. Decrease the number, intensity, and duration of angry outbursts, while increasing the use of new skills for managing anger. (23)

▽18. Identify social supports that will help facilitate the implementation of new skills. (24)

▽19. Parents learn and implement Parent Management Training skills to recognize and manage problem behavior of the client. (25, 26, 27, 28, 29)

23. Monitor the client's reports of angry outbursts with the goal of decreasing their frequency, intensity, and duration through the client's use of new anger management skills (or assign "Alternatives to Destructive Anger" in the *Adult Psychotherapy Homework Planner,* 2nd ed. by Jongsma); review progress, reinforcing success and providing corrective feedback toward improvement. ▽

24. Encourage the client to discuss and/or use his/her new anger and conduct management skills with trusted peers, family, or otherwise significant others who are likely to support his/her change. ▽

25. Use a Parent Management Training approach beginning with teaching the parents how parent and child behavioral interactions can encourage or discourage positive or negative behavior and that changing key elements of those interactions (e.g., prompting and reinforcing positive behaviors) can be used to promote positive change (e.g., see *Parenting the Strong-willed Child* by Forehand and Long; *Living with Children* by Patterson). ▽

26. Teach the parents how to specifically define and identify problem behaviors, identify their reactions to the behavior, determine whether the reaction encourages or discourages the behavior, and generate alternatives to the problem behavior. ▽

27. Teach parents how to implement key parenting practices consistently, including establishing realistic age-appropriate rules for acceptable and unacceptable behavior; prompting of positive behavior in the environment; use of positive reinforcement to encourage behavior (e.g., praise); use of clear direct instruction, time out, and other loss-of-privilege practices for problem behavior. ▽

28. Assign the parents home exercises in which they implement and record results of implementation exercises (or assign "Clear Rules, Positive Reinforcement, Appropriate Consequences" in the *Adolescent Psychotherapy Homework Planner*, 2nd ed. by Jongsma, Peterson, and McInnis); review in session, providing corrective feedback toward improved, appropriate, and consistent use of skills. ▽

29. Ask the parents to read parent training manuals (e.g., *Parenting Through Change* by Forgatch) or watch videotapes demonstrating the techniques being learned in session (see Webster-Stratton, 1994). ▽

▽20. Increase compliance with rules at home and school. (30)

30. Design a reward system and/or contingency contract for the client and meet with school officials to reinforce identified positive behaviors at home and school and deter impulsive or rebellious behaviors. ▽

▽21. Parents verbalize appropriate boundaries for discipline to prevent further occurrences of abuse and to ensure the safety of the client and his/her siblings. (31)

31. Explore the client's family background for a history of neglect and physical or sexual abuse that may contribute to his/her behavioral problems; confront the client's parents to cease physically

abusive or overly punitive methods of discipline; implement the steps necessary to protect the client or siblings from further abuse (e.g., report abuse to the appropriate agencies; remove the client or perpetrator from the home). ▽

▽22. Identify and verbally express feelings associated with past neglect, abuse, separation, or abandonment. (32)

32. Encourage and support the client in expressing feelings associated with neglect, abuse, separation, or abandonment and help process (e.g., assign the task of writing a letter to an absent parent, use the empty-chair exercise). ▽

▽23. Increase verbalizations of empathy and concern for other people. (33)

33. Use role-playing and role-reversal techniques to help the client develop sensitivity to the feelings of others in reaction to his/her antisocial behaviors. ▽

▽24. Increase the frequency of responsible and positive social behaviors. (34, 35, 36)

34. Direct the client to engage in three altruistic or benevolent acts (e.g., read to a developmentally disabled student, mow grandmother's lawn) before the next session to increase his/her empathy and sensitivity to the needs of others. ▽

35. Assign homework designed to increase the client's empathy and sensitivity toward the thoughts, feelings, and needs of others (e.g., "Headed in the Right Direction" from the *Adolescent Psychotherapy Homework Planner,* 2nd ed. by Jongsma, Peterson, and McInnis). ▽

36. Place the client in charge of tasks at home (e.g., preparing and cooking a special dish for a family get-together, building shelves in the garage, changing oil in the car) to demonstrate confidence in his/her ability to act responsibly. ▽

▼25. Establish and maintain steady employment. (37, 38)

37. Refer the client to vocational training to develop basic job skills and find employment. ▼

38. Encourage and reinforce the client's acceptance of the responsibility of a job, the authority of a supervisor, and the employer's rules. ▼

▼26. Identify and verbalize the risks involved in sexually promiscuous behavior. (39)

39. Provide the client with sex education; discuss the risks involved with sexually promiscuous behaviors; and explore the client's feelings, irrational beliefs, and unmet needs that contribute to the emergence of sexually promiscuous behaviors. ▼

▼27. Parents participate in marital therapy. (40)

40. Assess the marital dyad for possible substance abuse, conflict, or triangulation that shifts the focus from marriage issues to the client's acting out behaviors; refer for appropriate treatment, if needed. ▼

—. _____

_____

—. _____

_____

—. _____

_____

—. _____

_____

—. _____

_____

—. _____

_____

DIAGNOSTIC SUGGESTIONS

Axis I:	312.81	Conduct Disorder, Childhood-Onset Type
	312.82	Conduct Disorder, Adolescent-Onset Type
	313.81	Oppositional Defiant Disorder
	312.9	Disruptive Behavior Disorder NOS
	314.01	Attention-Deficit/Hyperactivity Disorder, Predominantly Hyperactive-Impulsive Type
	314.9	Attention-Deficit/Hyperactivity Disorder NOS

	312.34	Intermittent Explosive Disorder
	V71.02	Child or Adolescent Antisocial Behavior
	V61.20	Parent-Child Relational Problem
	_____	_____
	_____	_____
Axis II:	799.9	Diagnosis Deferred
	V71.09	No Diagnosis
	_____	_____
	_____	_____

DEPRESSION

BEHAVIORAL DEFINITIONS

1. Sad or flat affect.
2. Preoccupation with the subject of death.
3. Suicidal thoughts and/or actions.
4. Moody irritability.
5. Isolation from family and/or peers.
6. Deterioration in academic performance.
7. Lack of interest in previously enjoyed activities.
8. Refusal to communicate openly.
9. Use of alcohol or street drugs to elevate mood.
10. Low energy.
11. Little or no eye contact.
12. Frequent verbalizations of low self-esteem.
13. Notably reduced or increased appetite.
14. Notably decreased or increased sleep.
15. Indecisiveness and poor concentration.
16. Feelings of hopelessness, worthlessness, or inappropriate guilt.
17. Unresolved grief issues.

—. _____
   _____
—. _____
   _____
—. _____
   _____

LONG-TERM GOALS

1. Elevate mood and show evidence of usual energy levels, activities, and socialization level.
2. Show a renewed typical interest in academic achievement, social involvement, and eating patterns, as well as occasional expressions of joy and zest for life.
3. Reduce irritability and increase normal social interaction with family and friends.
4. Acknowledge the depression verbally and resolve its causes, leading to normalization of the emotional state.
5. Develop healthy cognitive patterns and beliefs about self and the world that lead to alleviation and help prevent the relapse of depression symptoms.
6. Develop healthy interpersonal relationships that lead to alleviation and help prevent the relapse of depression symptoms.
7. Appropriately grieve the loss in order to normalize mood and to return to previous adaptive level of functioning.

—. _____

_____

—. _____

_____

—. _____

_____

SHORT-TERM OBJECTIVES

1. Describe current and past experiences with depression complete with its impact on functioning and attempts to resolve it. (1)

2. Verbally identify, if possible, the source of depressed mood. (2, 3)

THERAPEUTIC INTERVENTIONS

1. Assess current and past mood episodes including their features, frequency, intensity, and duration (e.g., Clinical Interview supplemented by the *Inventory to Diagnose Depression* by Zimmerman, Coryell, Corenthal, and Wilson).

2. Ask the client to make a list of what he/she is depressed about; process the list content.

3. Complete psychological testing to assess the depth of
   depression, the need for antidepressant medication, and
   suicide prevention measures. (4)

4. Verbalize any history of suicide attempts and any current
   suicidal urges. (5)

5. State no longer having thoughts
   of self-harm. (6, 7)

▽ 6. Take prescribed psychotropic
   medications responsibly at
   times ordered by physician.
   (8, 9)

▽ 7. Identify and replace depressive
   thinking that supports depression. (10, 11, 12, 13)

3. Encourage the client to share
   his/her feelings of depression in
   order to clarify them and gain
   insight as to causes.

4. Arrange for the administration
   of an objective assessment instrument for evaluating the client's
   depression and suicide risk (e.g.,
   Children's Depression Inventory;
   Beck Hopelessness Scale); evaluate results and give feedback to
   the client.

5. Explore the client's history and
   current state of suicidal urges and
   behavior (see Suicidal Ideation
   chapter in this *Planner* if suicide
   risk is present).

6. Assess and monitor the client's
   suicide potential.

7. Arrange for hospitalization,
   as necessary, when the client is
   judged to be harmful to self.

8. Evaluate the client's possible need
   for psychotropic medication and
   arrange for a physician to give
   him/her a physical examination
   to rule out organic causes for
   depression, assess need for anti-
   depressant medication, and order
   a prescription, if appropriate. ▽

9. Monitor and evaluate the client's
   psychotropic medication compliance, effectiveness, and side
   effects; communicate with prescribing physician. ▽

10. Assist the client in developing an
    awareness of his/her automatic
    thoughts that reflect a depresso-
    genic schemata. ▽

▽ indicates that the Objective/Intervention is consistent with those found in evidence-based
treatments.

11. Assign the client to keep a daily journal of automatic thoughts associated with depressive feelings (e.g., "Bad Thoughts Lead to Depressed Feeings" in the *Adolescent Psychotherapy Homework Planner,* 2nd ed. by Jongsma, Peterson, and McInnis; "Daily Record of Dysfunctional Thoughts" in *Cognitive Therapy of Depression* by Beck, Rush, Shaw, and Emery); process the journal material to challenge depressive thinking patterns and replace them with reality-based thoughts. ▽

12. Do "behavioral experiments" in which depressive automatic thoughts are treated as hypotheses/predictions, reality-based alternative hypotheses/predictions are generated, and both are tested against the client's past, present, and/or future experiences. ▽

13. Reinforce the client's positive, reality-based cognitive messages that enhance self-confidence and increase adaptive action (see "Positive Self-Talk" in the *Adult Psychotherapy Homework Planner,* 2nd ed. by Jongsma). ▽

▽ 8. Learn new ways to overcome depression through activity. (14, 15, 16)

14. Assist the client in developing coping strategies (e.g., more physical exercise, less internal focus, increased social involvement, more assertiveness, greater need sharing, more anger expression) for feelings of depression; reinforce success. ▽

15. Engage the client in "behavioral activation" by scheduling activities that have a high likelihood for pleasure and mastery (see "Identify and Schedule Pleasant

Activities" in the *Adult Psychotherapy Homework Planner,* 2nd ed. by Jongsma); use rehearsal, role-playing, or role reversal, as needed, to assist adoption in the client's daily life; reinforce success. ▽

16. Employ self-reliance training in which the client assumes increased responsibility for routine activities (e.g., cleaning, cooking, shopping); reinforce success. ▽

▽ 9. Identify important people in your life, past and present, and describe the quality, good and bad, of those relationships. (17)

17. Assess the client's "interpersonal inventory" of important past and present relationships and evidence of potentially depressive themes (e.g., grief, interpersonal disputes, role transitions, interpersonal deficits). ▽

▽10. Verbalize any unresolved grief issues that may be contributing to depression. (18)

18. Explore the role of unresolved grief issues as they contribute to the client's current depression (see Grief/Loss Unresolved chapter in this *Planner*). ▽

▽11. Learn and implement problem-solving and/or conflict resolution skills to resolve interpersonal problems. (19, 20, 21)

19. Teach the client conflict resolution skills (e.g., empathy, active listening, "I messages," respectful communication, assertiveness without aggression, compromise) to help alleviate depression; use modeling, role-playing, and behavior rehearsal to work through several current conflicts. ▽

20. Help the client resolve depression related to interpersonal problems through the use of reassurance and support, clarification of cognitive and affective triggers that ignite conflicts, and active problem-solving (or assign "Applying Problem-Solving to Interpersonal Conflict" in the *Adult Psychotherapy Homework Planner,* 2nd ed. by Jongsma). ▽

21. In conjoint sessions, help the client resolve interpersonal conflicts. ▽

▽12. Implement a regular exercise regimen as a depression reduction technique. (22, 23)

22. Develop and reinforce a routine of physical exercise for the client. ▽

23. Recommend that the client read and implement programs from *Exercising Your Way to Better Mental Health* (Leith). ▽

▽13. Learn and implement relapse prevention skills. (24)

24. Build the client's relapse prevention skills by helping him/her identify early warning signs of relapse, reviewing skills learned during therapy, and developing a plan for managing challenges. ▽

▽14. Increase assertive communication. (25)

25. Use modeling and/or role-playing to train the client in assertiveness; if indicated, refer him/her to an assertiveness training class/group for further instruction. ▽

15. Read books on overcoming depression. (26)

26. Recommend that the client read self-help books on coping with depression (e.g., *Feeling Good* by Burns); process material read.

16. State the connection between rebellion, self-destruction, or withdrawal and the underlying depression. (27, 28, 29)

27. Assess the client's level of self-understanding about self-defeating behaviors linked to the depression.

28. Interpret and confront the client's acting out behaviors as avoidance of the real conflict involving his/her unmet emotional needs and reflection of the depression.

29. Teach the client the connection between angry, irritable behaviors and feelings of hurt and sadness (or assign the exercise "Surface Behavior/Inner Feelings" in the *Adolescent Psychotherapy Homework Planner,* 2nd ed. by Jongsma, Peterson, and McInnis).

17. Express feelings of hurt, disappointment, shame, and anger that are associated with early life experiences. (30, 31)

30. Explore experiences from the client's childhood that contribute to current depressed state.

31. Encourage the client to share feelings of anger regarding pain inflicted on him/her in childhood that contribute to current depressed state.

18. Specify what in the past or present life contributes to sadness. (32)

32. Assist the client in identifying his/her unmet emotional needs and specifying ways to meet those needs (or assign the exercise "Unmet Emotional Needs—Identification and Satisfaction" from the *Adolescent Psychotherapy Homework Planner,* 2nd ed. by Jongsma, Peterson, and McInnis).

19. Express emotional needs to significant others. (33, 34)

33. Hold a family therapy session to facilitate the client's expression of conflict with family members.

34. Support the client's respectful expression of emotional needs while teaching family members and significant others to encourage, support, and tolerate the client's respectful expression of his/her thoughts and feelings.

20. Improve academic performance as evidenced by better grades and positive teacher reports. (35)

35. Challenge and encourage the client's academic effort; arrange for a tutor, if needed, to increase the client's sense of academic mastery.

21. Adjust sleep hours to those typical of the developmental stage. (36)

36. Monitor the client's sleep patterns and the restfulness of sleep.

22. Verbalize the amount and frequency of alcohol and/or drug use. (37, 38)

37. Assess the client for substance abuse as a means of coping with depressive feelings.

38. Refer the client for treatment or treat his/her substance abuse problems (see Chemical Dependence chapter in this *Planner*).

23. Describe the degree of sexual activity engaged in. (39)

39. Assess the client for sexual promiscuity as a means of trying to overcome depression; confront and treat sexual acting out (see Sexual Acting Out chapter in this *Planner*).

24. Identify the losses that have been experienced and the feelings associated with those losses. (40)

40. Assess the client for unresolved grief and loss issues; treat grief issues that underlie his/her depression (see Grief/Loss Unresolved chapter in this *Planner*).

__. _____

_____

__. _____

_____

__. _____

_____

__. _____

_____

__. _____

_____

__. _____

_____

DIAGNOSTIC SUGGESTIONS

Axis I:	309.0	Adjustment Disorder With Depressed Mood
	296.xx	Bipolar I Disorder
	296.89	Bipolar II Disorder
	300.4	Dysthymic Disorder
	301.13	Cyclothymic Disorder
	296.2x	Major Depressive Disorder, Single Episode
	296.3x	Major Depressive Disorder, Recurrent
	295.70	Schizoaffective Disorder
	310.1	Personality Change Due to Axis III Disorder
	V62.82	Bereavement
	_____	_____
	_____	_____
Axis II:	799.9	Diagnosis Deferred
	V71.09	No Diagnosis
	_____	_____
	_____	_____

DIVORCE REACTION

BEHAVIORAL DEFINITIONS

1. Infrequent contact or loss of contact with a parental figure due to separation or divorce.
2. Intense emotional outbursts (e.g., crying, yelling, swearing) and sudden shifts in mood due to significant change in the family system.
3. Excessive use of alcohol and drugs as a maladaptive coping mechanism to ward off painful emotions surrounding separation or divorce.
4. Strong feelings of grief and sadness combined with feelings of low self-worth, lack of confidence, social withdrawal, and loss of interest in activities that normally bring pleasure.
5. Feelings of guilt accompanied by the unreasonable belief of having behaved in some manner to cause the parents' divorce and/or failing to prevent the divorce from occurring.
6. Marked increase in frequency and severity of acting out, oppositional, and aggressive behaviors since the onset of the parents' marital problems, separation, or divorce.
7. Significant decline in school performance and lack of interest or motivation in school-related activities.
8. Pattern of engaging in sexually promiscuous or seductive behaviors to compensate for the loss of security or support within the family system.
9. Pseudomaturity as manifested by denying or suppressing painful emotions about divorce and often assuming parental roles or responsibilities.
10. Numerous psychosomatic complaints in response to anticipated separations, stress, or frustration.
11. Loss of contact with a positive support network due to a geographic move.

—. _____
   _____
   _____
—. _____
   _____

—. _____
_____

LONG-TERM GOALS

1. Accept the parents' separation or divorce with understanding and control of feelings and behavior.
2. Establish and/or maintain secure, trusting relationships with the parents.
3. Eliminate feelings of guilt and statements that reflect self-blame for the parents' divorce.
4. Elevate and stabilize mood.
5. Cease maladaptive pattern of engaging in sexually promiscuous or seductive behaviors to meet needs for affection, affiliation, and acceptance.
6. Refrain from using drugs or alcohol and develop healthy coping mechanisms to effectively deal with changes in the family system.
7. Create a strong, supportive social network outside of the immediate family to offset the loss of affection, approval, or support from within the family.
8. Parents establish and maintain a consistent, yet flexible, visitation arrangement that meets the client's emotional needs.
9. Parents establish and maintain appropriate parent-child boundaries in discipline and assignment of responsibilities.
10. Parents consistently demonstrate mutual respect for one another, especially in front of the children.

—. _____
_____

—. _____
_____

—. _____
_____

SHORT-TERM OBJECTIVES	THERAPEUTIC INTERVENTIONS
1. Tell the story of the parents' separation or divorce. (1, 2)	1. Actively build the level of trust with the client through consistent eye contact, active listening, unconditional positive regard, and warm acceptance to improve his/her ability to identify and

express feelings connected to parents' separation or divorce.

2. Explore, encourage, and support the client in verbally expressing and clarifying his/her feelings associated with the separation or divorce.

2. Identify and express feelings related to the parents' separation or divorce. (2, 3, 4)

2. Explore, encourage, and support the client in verbally expressing and clarifying his/her feelings associated with the separation or divorce.

3. Use the empty-chair technique to help the client express mixed emotions he/she feels toward both parents about the separation or divorce.

4. Ask the client to keep a journal in which he/she records experiences or situations that evoke strong emotions pertaining to the divorce. Review the journal in therapy sessions.

3. Describe how the parents' separation or divorce has impacted personal and family life. (5)

5. Develop a timeline where the client records significant developments that have positively or negatively impacted his/her personal and family life, both before and after the divorce. Allow the client to verbalize his/her feelings about the divorce and subsequent changes in the family system.

4. Express thoughts and feelings within the family system regarding parental separation or divorce. (6, 7, 8)

6. Assist the client in developing a list of questions about the parents' divorce, then suggest ways he/she could find possible answers for each question (e.g., asking parents directly, writing parents a letter).

7. Hold family therapy sessions to allow the client and siblings to express feelings about separation or divorce in presence of parent.

8. Encourage the parents to provide opportunities (e.g., family meetings) at home to allow the client and siblings to express feelings about separation/divorce and subsequent changes in family system.

5. Recognize and affirm self as not being responsible for the parents' separation or divorce. (9, 10)

9. Explore the factors contributing to the client's feelings of guilt and self-blame about parents' separation or divorce; assist him/her in realizing that his/her negative behaviors did not cause parents' divorce to occur.

10. Assist the client in realizing that he/she does not have the power or control to bring the parents back together.

6. Parents verbalize an acceptance of responsibility for the dissolution of the marriage. (11, 12)

11. Conduct family therapy sessions where parents affirm the client and siblings as not being responsible for separation or divorce.

12. Challenge and confront statements by parents that place blame or responsibility for separation or divorce on the children.

7. Identify positive and negative aspects of the parents' separation or divorce. (13)

13. Give a homework assignment in which the client lists both positive and negative aspects of parents' divorce; process the list in the next session and allow him/her to express different emotions.

8. Identify and verbalize unmet needs to the parents. (14, 15)

14. Give the parents the directive of spending 10 to 15 minutes of one-on-one time with the client and siblings on a regular daily basis to identify and meet the children's needs.

15. Assign the client homework in the middle stages of therapy to help him/her list unmet needs and identify steps he/she can take to meet those needs (or assign the "Unmet Emotional Needs—

9. Reduce the frequency and severity of acting out, oppositional, and aggressive behaviors. (16, 17)

10. Express feelings of anger about the parents' separation or divorce through controlled, respectful verbalizations and healthy physical outlets. (18, 19)

11. Parents verbally recognize how their guilt and failure to follow through with limits contributes to the client's acting out or aggressive behaviors. (20, 21)

12. Complete school and homework assignments on a regular basis. (22, 23)

Identification and Satisfaction" exercise from the *Adolescent Psychotherapy Homework Planner,* 2nd ed. by Jongsma, Peterson, and McInnis).

16. Empower the client by reinforcing his/her ability to cope with the divorce and make healthy adjustments.

17. Assist the client in making a connection between underlying painful emotions about divorce and angry outbursts or aggressive behaviors.

18. Assist the client in identifying appropriate and inappropriate ways for the client to express anger about parents' separation or divorce.

19. Teach relaxation and/or guided imagery techniques to help the client learn to control anger more effectively.

20. Encourage and challenge the parents not to allow guilt feelings about the divorce to interfere with the need to impose consequences for oppositional behaviors.

21. Assist the parents in establishing clearly defined rules, boundaries, and consequences for acting out, oppositional, or aggressive behaviors (see Anger Management and Oppositional Defiant chapters in this *Planner*).

22. Assist the parents in establishing a new study routine to help the client complete school or homework assignments.

23. Design and implement a reward system and/or contingency contract to reinforce completion of school and homework

13. Decrease the frequency of somatic complaints. (24)

14. Noncustodial parent verbally recognizes his/her pattern of overindulgence and begins to set limits on money and/or time spent in leisure or recreational activities. (25)

15. Noncustodial parent assigns household responsibilities and/or requires the client to complete homework during visits. (26)

16. Reduce the frequency of immature and irresponsible behaviors. (27, 28)

17. Parents cease making unnecessary, hostile, or overly critical remarks about the other parent in the presence of the children. (29)

18. Parents recognize and agree to cease the pattern of soliciting information about and/or sending messages to the other parent through the children. (30, 31)

assignments or good academic performance.

24. Refocus the client's discussion from physical complaints to emotional conflicts and the expression of feelings.

25. Encourage the noncustodial parent to set limits on the client's misbehavior and refrain from overindulging the client during visits.

26. Direct the noncustodial parent to assign a chore or have the client complete school or homework assignments during visits.

27. Teach how enmeshed or overly protective parents reinforce the client's immature or irresponsible behaviors by failing to set necessary limits.

28. Have the client and parents identify age-appropriate ways for the client to meet his/her needs for affiliation, acceptance, and approval. Process the list and encourage the client to engage in age-appropriate behaviors.

29. Confront and challenge the parents to cease making unnecessary hostile or overly critical remarks about the other parent in the presence of the client.

30. Counsel the parents about not placing the client in the middle by soliciting information about the other parent or sending messages about adult matters through the client to the other parent.

31. Challenge and confront the client about playing one parent against

the other to meet needs, obtain material goods, or avoid responsibility.

19. Disengaged or uninvolved parent follows through with recommendations to spend greater quality time with the client. (32, 33)

32. Hold individual and/or family therapy session to challenge and encourage the noncustodial parent to maintain regular visitation and involvement in the client's life.

33. Give a directive to the disengaged or distant parent to spend more time or perform a specific task with the client (e.g., go on an outing to the mall, assist the client with homework, work on a project around the home).

20. Identify and express feelings through artwork and music. (34, 35)

34. Direct the client to draw a variety of pictures that reflect his/her feelings about the divorce, family move, or change in schools.

35. Instruct the client to sing a song or play a musical instrument that reflects his/her feelings about separation or divorce, then have the client verbalize times when he/she experienced those feelings.

21. Increase participation in positive peer group, extracurricular, or school-related activities. (36)

36. Encourage the client to participate in school, extracurricular, or positive peer group activities to offset the loss of time spent with the parents.

22. Attend a support group for children of divorce. (37)

37. Refer the client to group therapy to help him/her share and work through feelings with other adolescents whose parents are divorcing.

23. Increase contacts with adults and build a support network outside the family. (38)

38. Identify a list of adult individuals (e.g., school counselor, neighbor, uncle or aunt, Big Brother or Big Sister, clergyperson) outside the family who the client can turn to for support and guidance to help cope with the divorce.

24. Identify and verbalize the feelings, irrational beliefs, stressors, and needs that contribute to sexually promiscuous or seductive behaviors. (39, 40)

39. Provide sex education and discuss the risks involved with sexually promiscuous or seductive behaviors.

40. Explore the client's feelings, irrational beliefs, stressors, and unmet needs that contribute to the emergence of sexually promiscuous or seductive behaviors.

25. Complete a substance abuse evaluation and comply with the recommendations offered by the evaluation findings. (41, 42, 43)

41. Arrange for substance abuse evaluation and/or treatment for the client (see Chemical Dependence chapter in this *Planner*).

42. Explore the client's underlying feelings of depression, insecurity, and rejection that led him/her to escape into substance abuse.

43. Assist the client in constructing and signing an agreement to refrain from using substances.

__. _____
  _____
__. _____
  _____
__. _____
  _____

__. _____
  _____
__. _____
  _____
__. _____
  _____

DIAGNOSTIC SUGGESTIONS

Axis I:	309.0	Adjustment Disorder With Depressed Mood
	309.24	Adjustment Disorder With Anxiety
	309.28	Adjustment Disorder With Mixed Anxiety and Depressed Mood
	309.3	Adjustment Disorder With Disturbance of Conduct
	309.4	Adjustment Disorder With Mixed Disturbance of Emotions and Conduct
	300.4	Dysthymic Disorder
	300.02	Generalized Anxiety Disorder

309.21   Separation Anxiety Disorder
313.81   Oppositional Defiant Disorder
300.81   Undifferentiated Somatoform Disorder

_____   _____

_____   _____

Axis II: 799.9   Diagnosis Deferred
                V71.09   No Diagnosis

_____   _____

_____   _____

EATING DISORDER

BEHAVIORAL DEFINITIONS

1. Refusal to consume the necessary calories to maintain body weight at or above a minimally normal weight for age and height—less than 85% of that expected.
2. Intense fear of gaining weight or becoming fat, even though underweight.
3. Recurrent episodes of binge eating (i.e., rapid consumption of large quantities of high-carbohydrate food) followed by self-induced vomiting and/or the use of laxatives to avoid weight gain.
4. Recurrent inappropriate conpensatory behavior to prevent weight gain, such as self-induced vomiting; misuse of laxatives, diuretics, enemas, or other medications; fasting; or excessive exercise.
5. Extreme weight loss (and amenorrhea in females) with refusal to maintain a minimal healthy weight.
6. Undue influence of body weight or shape in self-evaluation.
7. Persistent preoccupation with body image related to grossly inaccurate assessment of self as overweight.
8. Escalating fluid and electrolyte imbalance resulting from eating disorder.
9. Denial of seeing self as emaciated even when severely under recommended weight.

—. _____

_____

—. _____

_____

—. _____

_____

LONG-TERM GOALS

1. Restore normal eating patterns, body weight, balanced fluid and electrolytes, and a realistic perception of body size.
2. Terminate the pattern of binge eating and purging behavior with a return to normal eating of enough nutritious foods to maintain a healthy weight.
3. Develop healthy cognitive patterns and beliefs about self that lead to alleviation of the eating disorder and help prevent relapse.
4. Develop healthy interpersonal relationships that lead to alleviation and help prevent the relapse of the eating disorder.
5. Develop alternate coping strategies (e.g., feeling identification, problem-solving, assertiveness) to address emotional issues that could lead to relapse of the eating disorder.
6. Gain an awareness of the interconnectedness of low self-esteem and societal pressures with dieting, binge eating, and purging, in order to eliminate eating disorder behaviors.
7. Change the definition of the self so that it does not focus on weight, size, and shape as the primary criteria for self-acceptance.

—. _____

_____

—. _____

_____

—. _____

_____

SHORT-TERM OBJECTIVES	THERAPEUTIC INTERVENTIONS
1. Honestly describe the pattern of eating including types, amounts, and frequency of food consumed or hoarded. (1, 2, 3)	1. Establish rapport with the client toward building a therapeutic alliance.
	2. Assess the amount, type, and pattern of the client's food intake (e.g., too little food, too much food, binge eating, hoarding food).
	3. Compare the client's calorie consumption with the adult female rate of 1,600–2,400 calories per day to maintain body weight.

2. Describe any regular use of unhealthy weight control behaviors. (4, 5)

4. Assess for the presence of self-induced vomiting behavior by the client to purge himself/herself of calorie intake; monitor on an ongoing basis.

5. Assess for the client's misuse of laxatives, diuretics, enemas, or other medications; fasting; or excessive exercise; monitor on an ongoing basis.

3. Complete psychological tests designed to assess eating patterns and unhealthy weight-loss practices. (6)

6. Administer a measure of eating disorders to further assess its depth and breadth (e.g., self-induced vomiting; misuse of laxatives, diuretics, enemas, or other medications; fasting; excessive exercise) and/or to track treatment progress (e.g., *The Eating Disorders Inventory-2* by Garner, 1991).

▽ 4. Cooperate with a complete physical exam. (7)

7. Refer the client to a physician for a physical exam and stay in close consultation with the physician as to the client's medical condition and nutritional habits. ▽

▽ 5. Cooperate with a dental exam. (8)

8. Refer the client to a dentist for a dental exam. ▽

▽ 6. Cooperate with an evaluation by a physician for psychotropic medication. (9)

9. Assess the client's need for psychotropic medications (e.g., SSRIs); arrange for a physician to evaluate for and then prescribe psychotropic medications, if indicated. ▽

▽ 7. Take medications as prescribed and report effectiveness and side effects. (10)

10. Monitor the client's psychotropic medication prescription compliance, effectiveness, and side effects. ▽

▽ indicates that the Objective/Intervention is consistent with those found in evidence-based treatments.

▽ 8. Cooperate with admission to inpatient treatment if indicated. (11)

11. Refer the client for hospitalization, as necessary, if his/her weight loss becomes severe and physical health is jeopardized, if he/she is severely depressed, or suicidal. ▽

▽ 9. Verbalize an accurate understanding of how eating disorders develop. (12)

12. Discuss with the client a model of eating disorders development that includes concepts such as sociocultural pressures to be thin lead to vulnerability in some individuals to overvalue body shape and size in determining self-image, maladaptive eating habits (e.g., fasting, binging), maladaptive compensatory weight management behaviors (e.g., purging), and resultant feelings of low self-esteem (see *Overcoming Binge Eating* by Fairburn). ▽

▽10. Verbalize an understanding of the rationale and goals of treatment. (13, 14)

13. Discuss a rationale for treatment that includes using cognitive and behavioral procedures to break the cycle of thinking and behaving that promotes poor self-image, uncontrolled eating, and unhealthy compensatory actions while building physical and mental health-promoting eating practices. ▽

14. Assign the client to read psychoeducational chapters of books or treatment manuals on the the development and treatment of eating disorders (e.g., *Overcoming Binge Eating* by Fairburn). ▽

▽11. Keep a journal of food consumption. (15)

15. Assign the client to self-monitor and record food intake, purging, thoughts, and feelings (or assign "Reality: Food, Weight, Thoughts, and Feelings" in the *Adolescent Psychotherapy*

Homework Planner, 2nd ed. by Jongsma, Peterson, and McInnis, or "Daily Record of Dysfunctional Thoughts" in *Cognitive Therapy of Depression* by Beck, Rush, Shaw, and Emery); process the journal material to challenge maladaptive patterns of thinking and behaving, and replace them with adaptive alternatives. ▽

▽12. Establish regular eating patterns by eating at regular intervals and consuming at least the minimum daily calories necessary to progressively gain weight. (16, 17, 18)

16. Establish a minimum daily caloric intake for the client and assist him/her in meal planning. ▽

17. Establish healthy weight goals for the client per the Body Mass Index (BMI = pounds of body weight × 700/height in inches/ height in inches; normal range is 19 to 24 and below 17 is medically critical), the Metropolitan Height and Weight Tables, or some other recognized standard. ▽

18. Monitor the client's weight and give realistic feedback regarding body thinness. ▽

▽13. Attain and maintain balanced fluids and electrolytes as well as resumption of reproductive functions. (19, 20)

19. Monitor the client's fluid intake and electrolyte balance; give realistic feedback regarding progress toward the goal of balance. ▽

20. Refer the client back to the physician at regular intervals if fluids and electrolytes need monitoring due to poor nutritional habits. ▽

▽14. Identify and develop a hierarchy of situations that trigger unhealthy eating or weight-loss practices. (21, 22)

21. Assess the nature of any external cues (e.g., persons, objects, situations) and internal cues (thoughts, images, and impulses) that precipitate the client's uncontrolled eating and/or compensatory weight management behaviors. ▽

22. Direct and assist the client in construction of a hierarchy of high-risk internal and external triggers for uncontrolled eating and/or compensatory weight management behaviors. ▽

▽15. Identify, challenge, and replace self-talk and beliefs that promote the eating disorder. (15, 23, 24)

15. Assign the client to self-monitor and record food intake, purging, thoughts, and feelings (or assign "Reality: Food, Weight, Thoughts, and Feelings" in the *Adolescent Psychotherapy Homework Planner,* 2nd ed. by Jongsma, Peterson, and McInnis, or "Daily Record of Dysfunctional Thoughts" in *Cognitive Therapy of Depression* by Beck, Rush, Shaw, and Emery); process the journal material to challenge maladptive patterns of thinking and behaving, and replace them with adaptive alternatives. ▽

23. Assist the client in developing an awareness of his/her automatic thoughts and underlying assumptions, associated feelings, and actions that lead to maladaptive eating and weight control practices (e.g., poor self-image, distorted body image, perfectionism, fears of failure and/or rejection, fear of sexuality). ▽

24. Assist the client in the identification of negative cognitive messages (e.g., catastrophizing, exaggerating) that mediate his/her dysfunctional eating behavior, then train the client to establish realistic cognitive messages regarding food intake and body size (or assign the "Fears Beneath the Eating Disorder" exercise from the *Adolescent Psychotherapy Homework Planner,* 2nd ed. by Jongsma, Peterson, and McInnis). ▽

▽16. Participate in exposure exercises to build skills in managing urges to use maladaptive weight control practices. (25)

25. Conduct repeated exposure and ritual prevention to the client's high-risk situations (e.g., exposure to eating a high-carbohydrate food while resisting the urge to self-induce vomiting); select initial exposures that have a high likelihood of being a successful experience for the client; prepare and rehearse a plan for the session; do cognitive restructuring within and after the exposure; review/process the session with the client. ▽

▽17. Complete homework assignments involving behavioral experiments and/or exposure exercises. (26)

26. Assign the client a homework exercise in which he/she repeats the in-session behavioral experiment or exposure exercise between sessions and records responses; review the homework, doing cognitive restructuring, reinforcing success, and providing corrective feedback toward improvement. ▽

▽18. Discuss important people in your life, past and present, and describe the quality, good and bad, of those relationships. (27)

27. Conduct Interpersonal Therapy, assessing the client's "interpersonal inventory" of important past and present relationships and evidence of themes that may be supporting the eating disorder (e.g., interpersonal disputes, role transitions, interpersonal deficits). ▽

▽19. Learn and implement problem- solving and/or conflict resolution skills to resolve interpersonal problems. (28, 29, 30)

28. Teach the client conflict resolution skills (e.g., empathy, active listening, "I messages," respectful communication, assertiveness without aggression, compromise); use modeling, role-playing, and behavior rehearsal to work through several current conflicts. ▽

29. Help the client resolve interpersonal problems through the use of reassurance and support, clarification of cognitive and affective triggers that ignite conflicts, and active problem-solving. ▽

30. In conjoint sessions, help the client resolve interpersonal conflicts. ▽

▽20. Implement relapse prevention strategies for managing possible future anxiety symptoms. (31, 32, 33, 34)

31. Discuss with the client the distinction between a lapse and relapse, associating a lapse with an initial and reversible return of distress or urges to avoid and relapse with the decision to return to the cycle of maladaptive thoughts and actions (e.g., feeling anxious, binging, then purging). ▽

32. Identify and rehearse with the client the management of future situations or circumstances in which lapses could occur. ▽

33. Instruct the client to routinely use strategies learned in therapy (e.g., continued exposure to previous external or internal cues that arise) to prevent relapse. ▽

34. Schedule periodic "maintenance sessions" to help the client maintain therapeutic gains and adjust to life without the eating disorder. ▽

21. Verbalize the feelings of low self-esteem, depression, loneliness, anger, loss of control, need for nurturance, or lack of trust that underlie the eating disorder. (35)

35. Explore and process the client's emotional struggles and how the eating disorder may be an expression of these struggles or an unhealthy way of managing them.

22. Disclose to family members feelings of ambivalence regarding control and dependency and state how these feelings have affected eating patterns. (36)

36. Facilitate family therapy sessions that focus on owning feelings, clarifying messages, identifying control and separation conflicts, and developing age-appropriate boundaries.

23. Verbalize how fear of sexual identity and development has influenced severe weight loss. (37)

24. Identify the relationship between the fear of failure, the drive for perfectionism, and the roots of low self-esteem. (38)

25. Attend an eating disorder group. (39)

26. State a basis for positive identity that is not based on weight and appearance but on character, traits, relationships, and intrinsic value. (40)

37. Explore the client's fear regarding sexual development and control of sexual impulses; and how the fear relates to keeping himself/herself unattractively thin or fat; encourage acceptance of normal sexual thoughts, feelings, and desires.

38. Discuss the client's fear of failure and the role of perfectionism in the search for control and the avoidance of failure; normalize failure experiences as common and necessary for learning.

39. Refer the client to a support group for eating disorders.

40. Assist the client in identifying a basis for self-worth apart from body image by reviewing his/her talents, successes, positive traits, importance to others, and intrinsic spiritual value.

__. _____
   _____
__. _____
   _____
__. _____
   _____

__. _____
   _____
__. _____
   _____
__. _____
   _____

DIAGNOSTIC SUGGESTIONS

Axis I: 307.1   Anorexia Nervosa
             307.51   Bulimia Nervosa
             307.50   Eating Disorder NOS

             _____ _____
             _____ _____

Axis II: 799.9   Diagnosis Deferred
             V71.09   No Diagnosis

             _____ _____
             _____ _____

GRIEF/LOSS UNRESOLVED

BEHAVIORAL DEFINITIONS

1. Loss of contact with a parent due to the parent's death.
2. Loss of contact with a parent figure due to termination of parental rights.
3. Loss of contact with a parent due to the parent's incarceration.
4. Loss of contact with a positive support network due to a geographic move.
5. Loss of meaningful contact with a parent figure due to the parent's emotional abandonment.
6. Strong emotional response experienced when the loss is mentioned.
7. Lack of appetite, nightmares, restlessness, inability to concentrate, irritability, tearfulness, or social withdrawal that began subsequent to a loss.
8. Marked drop in school grades, and an increase in angry outbursts, hyperactivity, or clinginess when separating from parents.
9. Feelings of guilt associated with the unreasonable belief in having done something to cause the loss or not having prevented it.
10. Avoidance of talking at length or in any depth about the loss.

—. _____

_____

_____

—. _____

_____

_____

—. _____

_____

LONG-TERM GOALS

1. Begin a healthy grieving process around the loss.
2. Complete the process of letting go of the lost significant other.

3. Work through the grieving and letting-go process and reach the point of emotionally reinvesting in life.
4. Successfully grieve the loss within a supportive emotional environment.
5. Resolve the loss and begin reinvesting in relationships with others and in age-appropriate activities.
6. Resolve feelings of guilt, depression, or anger associated with loss and return to previous level of functioning.

—. _____
   _____

—. _____
   _____

—. _____
   _____

SHORT-TERM OBJECTIVES

THERAPEUTIC INTERVENTIONS

1. Develop a trusting relationship with the therapist as evidenced by the open communication of feelings and thoughts associated with the loss. (1, 2)

1. Actively build level of trust with the client through consistent eye contact, active listening, unconditional positive regard, and warm acceptance while asking him/her to identify and express feelings associated with the loss.

2. Ask the client to tell the story of the loss through drawing pictures of his/her experience.

2. Verbalize and experience feelings connected with the loss. (3, 4, 5)

3. Ask the client to write a letter to the lost person describing his/her feelings and read this letter to the therapist.

4. Assign the client to utilize *The Healing Your Grieving Heart Journal for Teens* (Wolfelt) to record his/her thoughts and feelings related to the loss.

5. Ask the client to collect and bring to a session various photos and other memorabilia related to the

3. Verbalize an understanding of
the process or journey of grief
that is unique for each individual. (6, 7, 8)

4. Attend a grief support group.
(9)

5. Identify those activities that
have contributed to the avoidance of feelings connected to
the loss. (10, 11)

6. Terminate the use of alcohol
and illicit drugs. (12)

lost loved one (or assign the "Create a Memory Album" exercise
from the *Adolescent Psychotherapy Homework Planner,* 2nd ed.
by Jongsma, Peterson, and Mc-
Innis).

6. Have the client read sections or
the entirety of the books *Common
Threads of Teenage Grief* (Tyson)
or *Straight Talk about Death for
Teenagers* (Grollman) and select
three to five key ideas from the
reading to discuss with the therapist.

7. Educate the client and his/her
parents about the grieving process
and assist the parents in how to
answer any of the client's questions.

8. Ask the client to watch *Terms of
Endearment, Ordinary People, My
Girl,* or a similar film that focuses
on loss and grieving, and then
discuss how various characters
coped with the loss and expressed
their grief.

9. Refer the client to a support
group for adolescents grieving
death or divorce in the family.

10. Ask the client to list how he/she
has avoided the pain of grieving and how that has negatively
impacted his/her life.

11. Explore the client's use of mood-
altering substances as a means
of grief avoidance (see Chemical
Dependence chapter in this
Planner).

12. Make a contract with the client
to abstain from all mood-altering
substances. Monitor for compliance by checking with the client
and parents and make a referral

for a substance abuse evaluation if he/she is unable to keep the contract.

7. Keep a daily journal of feelings of grief and their triggers. (4, 13)

4. Assign the client to utilize *The Healing Your Grieving Heart Journal for Teens* (Wolfelt) to record his/her thoughts and feelings related to the loss.

13. Assign the client to keep a daily grief journal of thoughts and feelings associated with the loss and how they were triggered. Review the journal in therapy sessions.

8. Verbalize questions about the loss and work to obtain answers for each. (14, 15, 16)

14. Assist the client in developing a list of questions about a specific loss, then try to direct him/her to resources (e.g., books, clergy, parent, counselor) for possible answers for each question.

15. Expand the client's understanding of death by reading *Lifetimes* (Mellonie and Ingpen) to him/her and discussing all questions that arise from the reading.

16. Assist the client in identifying a peer or an adult who has experienced a loss similar to the client's and has successfully worked his/her way through it. Work with the client to develop a list of questions that he/she would like to ask this person (e.g., "What was the experience like for you? What was the most difficult part? What did you find the most helpful?").

9. Verbalize an increase in understanding the process of grieving and letting go. (17, 18)

17. Assign the client to ask questions about grieving to a peer or adult who has successfully resolved a loss, or arrange a conjoint session to ask the questions. Process the experience.

18. Assign the client to interview a member of the clergy about death and to interview an adult who has experienced and successfully worked through the death of a loved one.

10. Identify positive things about the deceased loved one and/or the lost relationship and how these things may be remembered. (5, 19)

5. Ask the client to collect and bring to a session various photos and other memorabilia related to the lost loved one (or assign the "Create a Memory Album" exercise from the *Adolescent Psychotherapy Homework Planner,* 2nd ed. by Jongsma, Peterson, and McInnis).

19. Ask the client to list positive things about the deceased and how he/she plans to remember each one; process the list.

11. Decrease the expression of feelings of guilt and blame for the loss. (20, 21)

20. Explore the client's thoughts and feelings of guilt and blame surrounding the loss, replacing irrational thoughts with realistic thoughts.

21. Help the client lift the self-imposed curse he/she believes to be the cause for the loss by asking the person who is perceived as having imposed the curse to take it back or by role-playing a phone conversation for the client to apologize for the behavior he/she believes is the cause for the curse.

12. Verbalize and resolve feelings of anger or guilt focused on self, God, or the deceased loved one that block the grief process. (22, 23, 24)

22. Suggest an absolution ritual (e.g., dedicate time to a charity that the deceased loved one supported) for the client to implement to relieve the guilt or blame for the loss. Monitor the results and adjust as necessary.

23. Encourage and support the client in sessions to look angry, then act angry, and finally put words to the anger.

24. Assign the client to complete an exercise related to an apology or forgiveness (e.g., writing a letter asking for forgiveness from the deceased, using the empty-chair technique to apologize) and to process it with the therapist.

13. Say good-bye to the lost loved one. (25, 26)

25. Assign the client to write a good-bye letter to the deceased (or assign the "Grief Letter" exercise in the *Adolescent Psychotherapy Homework Planner,* 2nd ed. by Jongsma, Peterson, and McInnis).

26. Suggest the client visit the grave of the loved one with an adult to communicate feelings and say good-bye, perhaps by leaving the good-bye letter or drawing. Process the experience.

14. List how life will demonstrate that the loss is being resolved. (27)

27. Assist the client in developing a list of indicators that the loss is beginning to be resolved (e.g., sleeping undisturbed, feeling less irritable and tearful, experiencing more happy times, recalling the loss with good memories instead of just heartache, reinvesting in life interests).

15. Parents verbalize an increase in their understanding of how to be supportive during the grief process. (7, 28, 29)

7. Educate the client and his/her parents about the grieving process and assist the parents in how to answer any of the client's questions.

28. Train the parents in specific ways they can provide comfort, consolation, love, companionship, and support to the client in grief (e.g., bring up the loss occasionally for discussion, encourage the client to talk freely of the loss, encourage photographs of the loved one to be displayed, spend one-on-one

time with the client in quiet activities that may foster sharing of feelings, spend time with the client in diversion activities).

29. Assign the parents to read a book to help them become familiar with the grieving process (e.g., *The Grieving Teen* by Fitzgerald; *Learning to Say Good-Bye* by LeShan).

16. Parents increase their verbal openness about the loss. (30, 31, 32)

30. Refer the parents to a grief/loss support group.

31. Conduct family sessions where each member of the client's family talks about his/her experience related to the loss.

32. Assign the client and parents to play The Good Mourning Game (Bisenius and Norris), first in a family session and then later at home by themselves. Follow up the assignment by processing with the family members, focusing on what each learned about themselves and about others in the grieving process.

17. Parents facilitate the client's participation in grief healing rituals. (33, 34)

33. Assist the family in the development of new rituals to fill the void created by the loss.

34. Encourage the parents to allow the client to participate in the rituals and customs of grieving if the client is willing to be involved.

18. Participate in memorial services, funeral services, or other grieving rituals. (34)

34. Encourage the parents to allow the client to participate in the rituals and customs of grieving if the client is willing to be involved.

19. Verbalize an understanding of the grief anniversary reaction and state a plan to cope with it. (35)

35. Educate the client and parents in the area of anniversary dates, focusing on what to expect and ways to handle the feelings (e.g.,

reminisce about the loss with significant others, visit the grave site, celebrate the good memories with a dinner out).

20. Parents who are losing custody verbally say good-bye to the client. (36)

36. Conduct a session with the parents who are losing custody of the client to prepare them to say good-bye to the client in a healthy, affirmative way.

21. Attend and participate in a formal session to say good-bye to the parents whose parental rights are being terminated. (37)

37. Facilitate a good-bye session with the client and the parents who are losing custody, for the purpose of giving the client permission to move on with his/her life. If the parents who are losing custody or the current parents are not available, ask them to write a letter that can be read at the session, or conduct a role play in which the client says good-bye to each parent.

22. Verbalize positive memories of the past and hopeful statements about the future. (38)

38. Ask the client to make a record of his/her life in a book format, using pictures and other memorabilia, to help visualize his/her past, present, and future life (or assign the "Create a Memory Album" exercise from the *Adolescent Psychotherapy Homework Planner,* 2nd ed. by Jongsma, Peterson, and McInnis). When it is completed, have the client keep a copy and give another to the current parents.

__. _____

_____

__. _____

_____

__. _____

_____

__. _____

_____

__. _____

_____

__. _____

_____

DIAGNOSTIC SUGGESTIONS

Axis I: 296.2x   Major Depressive Disorder, Single Episode
296.3x   Major Depressive Disorder, Recurrent
V62.82   Bereavement
309.0   Adjustment Disorder With Depressed Mood
309.4   Adjustment Disorder With Mixed Disturbance of
Emotions and Conduct
300.4   Dysthymic Disorder

_____   _____

_____   _____

Axis II: 799.9   Diagnosis Deferred
V71.09   No Diagnosis

_____   _____

_____   _____

LOW SELF-ESTEEM

BEHAVIORAL DEFINITIONS

1. Verbalizes self-disparaging remarks, seeing self as unattractive, worthless, stupid, a loser, a burden, unimportant.
2. Takes blame easily.
3. Inability to accept compliments.
4. Refuses to take risks associated with new experiences, as she/he expects failure.
5. Avoids social contact with adults and peers.
6. Seeks excessively to please or receive attention/praise of adults and/or peers.
7. Unable to identify or accept positive traits or talents about self.
8. Fears rejection from others, especially peer group.
9. Acts out in negative, attention-seeking ways.
10. Difficulty saying no to others; fears not being liked by others.

___. _____
    _____

___. _____
    _____

___. _____
    _____

LONG-TERM GOALS

1. Elevate self-esteem.
2. Increase social interaction, assertiveness, confidence in self, and reasonable risk-taking.
3. Build a consistently positive self-image.
4. Demonstrate improved self-esteem by accepting compliments, by identifying

positive characteristics about self, by being able to say no to others, and by eliminating self-disparaging remarks.

5. See self as lovable and capable.
6. Increase social skill level.

—. _____
   _____

—. _____
   _____

—. _____
   _____

SHORT-TERM OBJECTIVES

THERAPEUTIC INTERVENTIONS

1. Verbalize an increased aware-ness of self-disparaging statements. (1, 2)

1. Confront and reframe the client's self-disparaging comments.

2. Assist the client in becoming aware of how he/she expresses or acts out (e.g., lack of eye contact, social withdrawal, expectation of failure or rejection) negative feel-ings about self.

2. Decrease frequency of negative self-statements. (3, 4, 5)

3. Refer the client to group therapy that is focused on ways to build self-esteem.

4. Ask the client to read *Reviving Ophelia* (Pipher) or selected parts and have him/her note 5 to 10 key points to discuss with the thera-pist.

5. Assign the client to read *Why Am I Afraid to Tell You Who I Really Am?* (Powell) and choose 5 to 10 key points to discuss with the therapist.

3. Decrease verbalized fear of rejection while increasing statements of self-acceptance. (6, 7, 8)

6. Ask the client to make one positive statement about him-self/herself daily and record it on a chart or in a journal.

4. Identify positive traits and talents about self. (9, 10, 11)

7. Assist the client in developing positive self-talk as a way of boosting his/her confidence and positive self-image.

8. Probe the parents' interactions with the client in family sessions and redirect or rechannel any patterns of interaction or methods of discipline that are negative or critical of the client.

9. Reinforce verbally the client's use of positive statements of confidence or identification of positive attributes about himself/herself.

10. Develop with the client a list of positive affirmations about himself/herself and ask that it be read three times daily.

11. Assign a mirror exercise in which the client looks daily into a mirror and then records all that he/she sees there. Repeat the exercise a second week, increasing the daily time to 4 minutes, and have the client look for and record only the positive things he/she sees. Have the client process what he/she records and what the experience was like with the therapist.

5. Identify and verbalize feelings. (12, 13, 14)

12. Have the client complete the exercise "Self-Esteem—What Is It—How Do I Get It?" from *Ten Days to Self-Esteem* (Burns) and then process the completed exercise with the therapist.

13. Use a therapeutic game (e.g., The Talking, Feeling, and Doing Game by Gardner, available from Creative Therapeutics; Let's See About Me, available from Childswork/Childsplay; or The Ungame by Zakich, available

from The Ungame Company) to promote the client becoming more aware of self and his/her feelings.

14. Educate the client in the basics of identifying and labeling feelings, and assist him/her in the beginning to identify what he/she is feeling.

6. Increase eye contact with others. (15, 16)

15. Focus attention on the client's lack of eye contact; encourage and reinforce increased eye contact within sessions.

16. Ask the client to increase eye contact with teachers, parents, and other adults; review and process reports of attempts and the feelings associated with them.

7. Identify actions that can be taken to improve self-image. (17, 18, 19)

17. Assign the client to read *Feed Your Head* (Hipp and Hanson) and to select five key ideas from the reading to process with the therapist.

18. Ask the client to draw representations of the changes he/she desires for himself/herself or his/her life situation; help the client develop a plan of implementation for the changes (or assign either the "Three Wishes Game" or the "Three Ways to Change Yourself" exercise from the *Adolescent Psychotherapy Homework Planner,* 2nd ed. by Jongsma, Peterson, and McInnis).

19. Utilize a brief solution-focused approach (O'Hanlon and Beadle) such as externalizing the problem by framing the difficulty as a stage or something that the client might grow out of or get over in order to depathologize the issue and open up new hopes and possibilities for action that might improve the client's self-esteem.

8. Identify and verbalize needs. (20, 21)

9. Identify instances of emotional, physical, or sexual abuse that have damaged self-esteem. (22)

10. Identify negative automatic thoughts and replace them with positive self-talk messages to build self-esteem. (23, 24)

11. Take responsibility for daily self-care and household tasks that are developmentally age-appropriate. (25)

12. Positively acknowledge and verbally accept praise or compliments from others. (26, 27)

20. Assist the client in identifying and verbalizing his/her emotional needs; brainstorm ways to increase the chances of his/her needs being met.

21. Conduct a family session in which the client expresses his/her needs to family and vice versa.

22. Explore for incidents of abuse (emotional, physical, or sexual) and how they have impacted feelings about self (see Sexual Abuse Victim and/or Physical/Emotional Abuse Victim chapters in this *Planner*).

23. Help the client identify his/her distorted negative beliefs about self and the world.

24. Help the client identify, and reinforce the use of, more realistic, positive messages about self and life events.

25. Help the client find and implement daily self-care and household or academic responsibilities that are age-appropriate. Monitor follow-through and give positive feedback when warranted.

26. Use neurolinguistic programming or reframing techniques in which messages about self are changed to assist the client in accepting compliments from others.

27. Ask the client to obtain three letters of recommendation from adults he/she knows but is not related to. The letters are to be sent directly to the therapist (the therapist provides three addressed, stamped envelopes) and then opened and read in session.

13. Parents identify specific activities for the client that will facilitate development of positive self-esteem. (28, 29)

28. Provide the parents with or have them purchase the book *Full Esteem Ahead!* (Loomans and Loomans) and have them look over the book and then select two to three ideas to implement. Have the parents process the results with the therapist.

29. Ask the parents to involve the client in esteem-building activities (Scouting, experiential camps, music, sports, youth groups, enrichment programs, etc.).

14. Parents verbalize realistic expectations and discipline methods for the client. (30, 31)

30. Explore parents' expectations of the client. Assist, if necessary, in making them more realistic.

31. Train the parents in the 3 R's (related, respectful, and reasonable) of discipline techniques (see *Raising Self-Reliant Children in a Self-Indulgent World* by Glenn and Nelson) in order to eliminate discipline that results in rebellion, revenge, or reduced self-esteem. Assist in implementation, and coach the parents as they develop and improve their skills using this method.

15. Parents attend a didactic series on positive parenting. (32)

32. Ask the parents to attend a didactic series on positive parenting, afterward processing how they can begin to implement some of these techniques.

16. Increase the frequency of speaking up with confidence in social situations. (33, 34, 35, 36)

33. Encourage the client to use the technique "Pretending to Know How" (see Theiss in *101 Favorite Play Therapy Techniques* by Kaduson and Schaefer) or "The Therapist on the Inside" (see Grigoryev in *101 Favorite Play Therapy Techniques*) on one identified task or problem area in the

next week. Follow up by processing the experience and results, and then have the client use the technique again on two new situations or problems, and so on.

34. Ask the client to read *How to Say No and Keep Your Friends* (Scott) and to process with the therapist how saying no can boost self-confidence and self-esteem.

35. Use role-playing and behavioral rehearsal to improve the client's assertiveness and social skills.

36. Encourage the client to attend an alternative camp or weekend experience to promote his/her personal growth in the areas of trust, self-confidence, and cooperation and in developing relationships with others.

17. Parents verbally reinforce the client's active attempts to build positive self-esteem. (32, 37)

32. Ask the parents to attend a didactic series on positive parenting, afterward processing how they can begin to implement some of these techniques.

37. Encourage the parents to seek out opportunities to praise, reinforce, and recognize the client's minor or major accomplishments.

__. _____

   _____

__. _____

   _____

__. _____

   _____

__. _____

   _____

__. _____

   _____

__. _____

   _____

DIAGNOSTIC SUGGESTIONS

Axis I:	300.4	Dysthymic Disorder
	314.01	Attention-Deficit/Hyperactivity Disorder, Predominantly Hyperactive-Impulsive Type
	300.23	Social Anxiety Disorder (Social Phobia)
	296.xx	Major Depressive Disorder
	307.1	Anorexia Nervosa
	309.21	Separation Anxiety Disorder
	300.02	Generalized Anxiety Disorder
	995.54	Physical Abuse of Child (Victim)
	995.53	Sexual Abuse of Child (Victim)
	995.52	Neglect of Child (Victim)
	303.90	Alcohol Dependence
	304.30	Cannabis Dependence
	_____	_____
	_____	_____
Axis II:	799.9	Diagnosis Deferred
	V71.09	No Diagnosis
	_____	_____
	_____	_____

MANIA/HYPOMANIA

BEHAVIORAL DEFINITIONS

1. Loud, overly friendly social style that oversteps social boundaries and shows poor social judgment (e.g., too trusting and self-disclosing too quickly).
2. Inflated sense of self-esteem and an exaggerated, euphoric belief in capabilities that denies any self-limitations or realistic obstacles but sees others as standing in the way.
3. Flight of ideas and pressured speech.
4. High energy and restlessness.
5. Disorganized impulsivity that does not foresee the consequences of the behavior.
6. A reduced need for sleep and a denial of emotional or physical pain.
7. A positive family history of affective disorder.
8. Verbal and/or physical aggression coupled with tantrum-like behavior (e.g., breaking things explosively) if wishes are blocked, which is in contrast to an earlier pattern of obedience and restraint.
9. Poor attention span and high susceptibility to distraction.
10. Lack of follow-through in projects even though the energy level is very high, since the behavior lacks discipline and goal-directedness.
11. Impulsive, self-defeating behaviors that reflect a lack of recognition of dangerous consequences (e.g., shoplifting, alcohol abuse, drug abuse, sexual promiscuity).
12. Outlandish dress and grooming.

___. _____
_____

___. _____
_____

___. _____
_____

LONG-TERM GOALS

1. Increase control over impulses, reduce energy level, and stabilize mood.
2. Decrease irritability and impulsivity, improve social judgment, and develop sensitivity to the consequences of behavior while having more realistic expectations of self.
3. Acknowledge the underlying depression and cope with feelings of fear of loss.
4. Talk about underlying feelings of low self-esteem or guilt and fears of rejection, dependency, and abandonment by significant others.

—. _____

    _____

—. _____

    _____

—. _____

    _____

SHORT-TERM OBJECTIVES	THERAPEUTIC INTERVENTIONS
1. Describe the nature of symptoms related to the mood disorder. (1, 2)	1. Conduct a thorough diagnostic interview to assess the client for pressured speech, flight of idea, euphoria, inflated self-esteem, impulsivity, lack of discipline, reduced sleep pattern, low frustration tolerance, and/or poor anger management.
	2. Administer or arrange for psychological testing to further assess the client for mania/hypomania; provide feedback to the client and parents.
2. Parents provide psychosocial history data regarding the client and his/her extended family, especially in regard to bipolar illness symptoms. (3)	3. Gather psychosocial history information from the client's parents to assess for patterns of mania in the client and bipolar illness in the client's extended family.

3. Identify stressors that precipitate manic behavior. (4)

4. Take psychotropic medications as directed. (5, 6)

5. Agree to impatient hospitalization to stabilize moods and reduce risk of harm to self or others. (7)

6. Parents and family members verbalize greater understanding about the nature of Bipolar Disorder. (8, 9)

7. Demonstrate trust in the therapeutic relationship by sharing fears about dependency, loss, and abandonment. (10, 11, 12, 13)

8. Differentiate between real and imagined losses, rejections, and abandonments. (14)

4. Explore the stressors that precipitate the client's manic behavior (e.g., school failure, social rejection, family trauma).

5. Arrange for a psychiatric examination of the client to evaluate the necessity for a prescription for mood-stabilizing medication (e.g., lithium carbonate).

6. Monitor the client's compliance with and reaction to the psychotropic medication (i.e., side effects and effectiveness).

7. Arrange for inpatient hospitalization if the client's unstable and erratic mood swings reach a point where he/she is dangerous to self and others.

8. Educate parents and family members about the nature, treatment, and prognosis of Bipolar Disorder.

9. Assign the parents to read *Bipolar Disorders* (Waltz) to educate them about the symptoms and treatment of Bipolar Disorder.

10. Pledge to be there consistently to help, listen to, and support the client.

11. Explore the client's fears of abandonment by sources of love and nurturance.

12. Probe real or perceived losses in the client's life.

13. Review ways for the client to replace the losses and put them in perspective.

14. Help the client differentiate between real and imagined, actual and exaggerated losses.

9. Identify the causes for low self-esteem and abandonment fears. (15, 16)

15. Explore the causes for the client's low self-esteem and abandonment fears in the family-of-origin history.

16. Hold family therapy sessions to explore and confront parental rejection or emotional abandonment of the client.

10. Decrease grandiose statements and express self more realistically. (17)

17. Confront the client's grandiosity and demandingness gradually but firmly.

11. Achieve mood stability, becoming slower to react with anger, less expansive, and more socially appropriate and sensitive. (18)

18. Set a goal with the client to attempt to control his/her impulses and to be more sensitive to the social impact of his/her behavior.

12. Identify instances of impulsive behavior that have led to negative consequences. (19, 20, 21, 22)

19. Assist the client in listing instances of impulsive behavior and the negative consequences that resulted from those behaviors.

20. Repeatedly focus on the consequences of behavior to reduce thoughtless impulsivity.

21. Facilitate impulse control by using role-playing, behavior rehearsal, and role reversal to increase sensitivity to the consequences of behavior.

22. Assign homework to the client designed to help the client understand that impulsive behavior has costly negative consequences for himself/herself and others (or assign the exercise "Action Minus Thought Equals Painful Consequences" from the *Adolescent Psychotherapy Homework Planner,* 2nd ed. by Jongsma, Peterson, and McInnis).

13. Parents reinforce positive behaviors while setting firm limits on hostility. (23, 24)

23. Meet with the parents to encourage them and teach them through modeling and role-playing to set firm limits on the client's angry rebellion while positively reinforcing the client's prosocial, measured behavior.

24. Assign the parents the task of listing rules and contingencies for the home (or assign the exercise "Clear Rules, Positive Reinforcement, Appropriate Consequences" from the *Adolescent Psychotherapy Homework Planner,* 2nd ed. by Jongsma, Peterson, and McInnis); process the completed assignment.

14. Accept the limits set on manipulative and hostile behaviors that attempt to control others. (25, 26)

25. Set limits on the client's manipulation or acting out by making rules and establishing clear consequences for breaking them.

26. Reinforce the parents in setting reasonable limits on the client's behavior and in expressing their commitment to love him/her unconditionally.

15. Speak more slowly and calmly while maintaining subject focus. (27, 28)

27. Provide structure and focus for the client's thoughts and actions by regulating the direction of conversation and establishing plans for behavior.

28. Verbally reinforce slower speech and more deliberate thought processes.

16. Dress and groom in a less attention-seeking manner. (29)

29. Encourage and reinforce appropriate dress and grooming.

17. Identify positive traits and behaviors that build genuine self-esteem. (30, 31)

30. Assist the client in identifying strengths and assets to build self-esteem and confidence.

31. Assign the client homework designed to increase his/her genuine self-esteem through the identification and listing of his/her positive character and personality traits (or assign the exercise "I Am a Good Person" from the *Adolescent Psychotherapy Homework Planner,* 2nd ed. by Jongsma, Peterson, and McInnis).

18. Verbalize the acceptance of and peace with dependency needs. (32, 33, 34)

32. Interpret the fear and insecurity underlying the client's braggadocio, hostility, and denial of dependency.

33. Hold family therapy sessions where the focus is on the client expressing his/her dependency needs and desire to become more independent in a reasonable manner.

34. Encourage the client to share feelings at a deeper level to facilitate openness, intimacy, and trust in relationships and to counteract denial, fear, and superficiality.

19. Identify and replace negative self-talk that produces fear and low self-esteem. (35, 36)

35. Assist the client in identifying negative cognitive messages that feed a fear of rejection and failure.

36. Assist the client in identifying positive, realistic thoughts that can replace the negative self-talk that nurtures low self-esteem and fear of failure or rejection.

—. _____

_____

—. _____

_____

—. _____

_____

—. _____

_____

—. _____

_____

—. _____

_____

DIAGNOSTIC SUGGESTIONS

Axis I:

296.xx	Bipolar I Disorder
296.89	Bipolar II Disorder
301.13	Cyclothymic Disorder
295.70	Schizoaffective Disorder
296.80	Bipolar Disorder NOS
310.1	Personality Change due to Axis III Disorder
314.01	Attention-Deficit/Hyperactivity Disorder, Predominantly Hyperactive-Impulsive Type

_____ _____

_____ _____

Axis II:

799.9	Diagnosis Deferred
V71.09	No Diagnosis

_____ _____

_____ _____

MEDICAL CONDITION

BEHAVIORAL DEFINITIONS

1. A diagnosis of a chronic illness that is not life threatening, but necessitates changes in living.
2. A diagnosis of an acute, serious illness that is life threatening.
3. A diagnosis of a chronic illness that eventually will lead to an early death.
4. Sad affect, social withdrawal, anxiety, loss of interest in activities, and low energy.
5. Suicidal ideation.
6. Denial of the seriousness of the medical condition.
7. Refusal to cooperate with recommended medical treatments.

—. _____

   _____

—. _____

   _____

—. _____

   _____

LONG-TERM GOALS

1. Accept the illness and adapt life to necessary changes.
2. Resolve emotional crisis and face terminal illness's implications.
3. Work through the grieving process and face the reality of own death with peace.
4. Accept emotional support from those who care without pushing them away in anger.
5. Resolve depression and find peace of mind despite the illness.
6. Live life to the fullest extent possible even though time may be limited.

7. Cooperate with the medical treatment regimen without passive-aggressive or active resistance.
8. Become as knowledgeable as possible about the diagnosed condition and about living as normally as possible.
9. Reduce fear, anxiety, and worry associated with the medical condition.

—. _____

_____

—. _____

_____

—. _____

_____

SHORT-TERM OBJECTIVES

THERAPEUTIC INTERVENTIONS

▽ 1. Describe history, symptoms, and treatment of the medical condition. (1, 2)

1. Gather a history of the facts regarding the client's medical condition, including symptoms, treatment, and prognosis. ▽

2. With the client's informed consent, contact the treating physician and family members for additional medical information regarding the client's diagnosis, treatment, and prognosis. ▽

▽ 2. Verbalize an understanding of the medical condition and its consequences. (3)

3. Encourage and facilitate the client in learning about the medical condition from which he or she suffers and its realistic course, including pain management options and chance for recovery. ▽

▽ 3. Comply with the medication regimen and necessary medical procedures, reporting any side effects or problems to physicians or therapists. (2, 4, 5, 6)

2. With the client's informed consent, contact the treating physician and family members for additional medical information regarding the client's diagnosis, treatment, and prognosis. ▽

▽ indicates that the Objective/Intervention is consistent with those found in evidence-based treatments.

4. Monitor and reinforce the client's compliance with the medical treatment regimen. ▽

5. Explore and address the client's misconceptions, fears, and situational factors that interfere with medical treatment compliance. ▽

6. Confront any manipulation, passive-aggressive, and denial mechanisms that block the client's compliance with the medical treatment regimen. ▽

▽ 4. Share feelings triggered by the knowledge of the medical condition and its consequences. (7)

7. Assist the client in identifying, sorting through, and verbalizing the various feelings generated by his/her medical condition. ▽

▽ 5. Family members share with each other feelings that are triggered by the client's medical condition. (8)

8. Meet with family members to facilitate their clarifying and sharing possible feelings of guilt, anger, helplessness, and/or sibling attention jealousy associated with the client's medical condition (or assign "Coping with a Sibling's Health Problems" in the *Adolescent Psychotherapy Homework Planner,* 2nd ed. by Jongsma, Peterson, and McInnis). ▽

▽ 6. Spend time with family and friends. (9)

9. Assess the effects of the medical condition on the client's social network (or assign "Effects of Physical Handicap or Illness on Self-Esteem and Peer Relations" in the *Adolescent Psychotherapy Homework Planner,* 2nd ed. by Jongsma, Peterson, and McInnis); facilitate the social support available through the client's family and friends. ▽

▽ 7. Identify and grieve the losses or limitations that have been experienced due to the medical condition. (10, 11, 12, 13)

10. Ask the client to list his/her perception of changes, losses, or limitations that have resulted from the medical condition. ▽

▽ 8. Decrease time spent focused on the negative aspects of the medical condition. (14, 15)

▽ 9. Verbalize acceptance of the reality of the medical condition and its consequences while decreasing denial. (16, 17)

▽10. Share fearful or depressed feelings regarding the medical condition and develop a plan for addressing them. (18, 19, 20)

11. Educate the client on the stages of the grieving process and answer any questions. ▽

12. Suggest that the client read a book on grief and loss (e.g., *Good Grief* by Westberg; *How Can It Be All Right When Everything Is All Wrong?* by Smedes; *When Bad Things Happen to Good People* by Kushner). ▽

13. Assign the client to keep a daily grief journal to be shared in therapy sessions. ▽

14. Suggest that the client set aside a specific time-limited period each day to focus on mourning the medical condition; after the time period is up, have the client resume regular daily activities with agreement to put off thoughts until next scheduled time. ▽

15. Challenge the client to focus his/her thoughts on the positive aspects of his/her life and time remaining, rather than on the losses associated with his/her medical condition; reinforce instances of such a positive focus. ▽

16. Gently confront the client's denial of the seriousness of his/her condition and of the need for compliance with medical treatment procedures. ▽

17. Reinforce the client's acceptance of his/her medical condition. ▽

18. Explore and process the client's fears associated with deterioration of physical health, death, and dying. ▽

19. Normalize the client's feelings of grief, sadness, or anxiety

associated with his/her medical condition; encourage verbal expression of these emotions. ▽

20. Assess the client for and treat his/her depression and anxiety using relevant cognitive, physiological, and/or behavioral aspects of treatments for those conditions (see Depression and Anxiety chapters in this *Planner*). ▽

▽11. Attend a support group of others diagnosed with a similar illness, if desired. (21)

21. Refer the client to a support group of others living with a similar medical condition. ▽

▽12. Parents and family members attend a support group, if desired. (22)

22. Refer family members to a community-based support group associated with the client's medical condition. ▽

▽13. Engage in social, productive, and recreational activities that are possible despite the medical condition. (23, 24)

23. Sort out with the client activities that can still be enjoyed alone and with others. ▽

24. Solicit a commitment from the client to increase his/her activity level by engaging in enjoyable and challenging activities; reinforce such engagement. ▽

▽14. Learn and implement stress-management skills. (25, 26, 27)

25. Teach the client deep muscle relaxation and deep breathing methods along with positive imagery to induce relaxation. ▽

26. Utilize electromyography (EMG) biofeedback to monitor, increase, and reinforce the client's depth of relaxation. ▽

27. Develop and encourage a routine of physical exercise for the client. ▽

▽15. Identify and replace negative self-talk and catastrophizing that is associated with the medical condition. (28, 29)

28. Assist the client in identifying the cognitive distortions and negative automatic thoughts that contribute to his/her negative attitude and hopeless feelings associated

with the medical condition (or assign "Bad Thoughts Lead to Depressed Feelings" in the *Adolescent Psychotherapy Homework Planner,* 2nd ed. by Jongsma, Peterson, and McInnis). ▽

29. Generate with the client a list of positive, realistic self-talk that can replace cognitive distortions and catastrophizing regarding his/her medical condition and its treatment. ▽

▽16. Implement positive imagery as a means of triggering peace of mind and reducing tension. (30)

30. Teach the client the use of positive, relaxing, healing imagery to reduce stress and promote peace of mind. ▽

▽17. Client and family identify the sources of emotional support that have been beneficial and additional sources that could be sought. (31, 32)

31. Probe and evaluate the client's, siblings', and parents' sources of emotional support. ▽

32. Encourage the parents and siblings to reach out for support from each other, church leaders, extended family, hospital social services, community support groups, and personal religious beliefs. ▽

▽18. Family members share any conflicts that have developed between them. (33, 34, 35)

33. Explore how each parent is dealing with the stress related to the client's illness and whether conflicts have developed between the parents because of differing response styles. ▽

34. Assess family conflicts using conflict resolution approach to addressing them. ▽

35. Facilitate a spirit of tolerance for individual difference in each person's internal resources and response styles in the face of threat. ▽

▽19. Family members verbalize an understanding of the one's own personal positive presence with the sick child. (36)

20. Implement faith-based activities as a source of comfort and hope. (37, 38, 39)

36. Stress the healing power in the family's constant presence with the ill child and emphasize that there is strong healing potential in creating a warm, caring, supportive, positive environment for the child. ▽

37. Draw out the parents' unspoken fears about the client's possible death; empathize with their panic, helplessness, frustration, and anxiety. Reassure them of their God's presence as the giver and supporter of life.

38. Encourage the client to rely upon his/her spiritual faith promises, activities (e.g., prayer, meditation, worship, music), and fellowship as sources of support.

39. Encourage the client to rely on faith-based promises of his/her God's love, presence, caring, and support to bring peace of mind.

__. _____   __. _____
    _____   _____
__. _____   __. _____
    _____   _____
__. _____   __. _____
    _____   _____

DIAGNOSTIC SUGGESTIONS

Axis I:	316	Psychological Symptoms Affecting Axis III Disorder
	309.0	Adjustment Disorder With Depressed Mood
	309.24	Adjustment Disorder With Anxiety
	309.28	Adjustment Disorder With Mixed Anxiety and Depressed Mood

309.3	Adjustment Disorder With Disturbance of Conduct
309.4	Adjustment Disorder With Mixed Disturbance of Emotions and Conduct
296.xx	Major Depressive Disorder
311	Depressive Disorder NOS
300.02	Generalized Anxiety Disorder
300.00	Anxiety Disorder NOS

_____   _____

_____   _____

Axis II: V71.09   No Diagnosis

_____   _____

_____   _____

MENTAL RETARDATION

BEHAVIORAL DEFINITIONS

1. Significantly subaverage intellectual functioning as demonstrated by an IQ score of approximately 70 or below on an individually administered intelligence test.
2. Significant impairments in academic functioning, communication, self-care, home living, social skills, and leisure activities.
3. Difficulty understanding and following complex directions in home, school, or community settings.
4. Short- and long-term memory impairment.
5. Concrete thinking or impaired abstract reasoning abilities.
6. Impoverished social skills as manifested by frequent use of poor judgment, limited understanding of the antecedents and consequences of social actions, and lack of reciprocity in peer interactions.
7. Lack of insight and repeated failure to learn from experience or past mistakes.
8. Low self-esteem as evidenced by frequent self-derogatory remarks (e.g., "I'm so stupid").
9. Recurrent pattern of acting out or engaging in disruptive behaviors without considering the consequences of the actions.

—. _____
_____

—. _____
_____

—. _____
_____

LONG-TERM GOALS

1. Achieve all academic goals identified on the client's individualized educational plan (IEP).
2. Function at an appropriate level of independence in home, residential, educational, or community settings.
3. Develop an awareness and acceptance of intellectual and cognitive limitations but consistently verbalize feelings of self-worth.
4. Parents and/or caregivers develop an awareness and acceptance of the client's intellectual and cognitive capabilities so that they place appropriate expectations on his/her functioning.
5. Consistently comply and follow through with simple directions in a daily routine at home, in school, or in a residential setting.
6. Significantly reduce the frequency and severity of socially inappropriate or acting out behaviors.

__. _____
   _____
__. _____
   _____
__. _____
   _____

SHORT-TERM OBJECTIVES

THERAPEUTIC INTERVENTIONS

1. Complete a comprehensive intellectual and cognitive assessment. (1)

1. Arrange for a comprehensive intellectual and cognitive assessment to determine the presence of Mental Retardation and gain greater insight into the client's learning strengths and weaknesses; provide feedback to the client, parents, and school officials.

2. Complete psychological testing. (2)

2. Arrange for psychological testing to assess whether emotional factors or Attention-Deficit/Hyperactivity Disorder (ADHD) are interfering with the client's intellectual and academic functioning; provide feedback to the client and parents.

3. Complete neuropsychological testing. (3)

3. Arrange for a neurological examination or neuropsychological testing to rule out possible organic factors that may be contributing to the client's intellectual or cognitive deficits.

4. Complete an evaluation by physical and occupational therapists. (4)

4. Refer the client to physical and occupational therapists to assess perceptual or sensory-motor deficits and determine the need for ongoing physical and/or occupational therapy.

5. Complete a speech/language evaluation. (5)

5. Refer the client to a speech/language pathologist to assess deficits and determine the need for appropriate therapy.

6. The client and his/her parents comply with recommendations made by a multidisciplinary evaluation team at school regarding educational interventions. (6, 7)

6. Attend an individualized educational planning committee (IEPC) meeting with the client's parents, teachers, and other appropriate professionals to determine his/her eligibility for special education services, design educational interventions, and establish goals.

7. Consult with the client, his/her parents, teachers, and other appropriate school officials about designing effective learning programs or interventions that build on the client's strengths and compensate for weaknesses.

7. Move to an appropriate residential setting. (8)

8. Consult with the client's parents, school officials, or mental health professionals about the client's need for placement in a foster home, group home, or residential program.

8. Attend a program focused on teaching basic job skills. (9)

9. Refer the client to a sheltered workshop or educational rehabilitation center to develop basic job skills.

9. Parents maintain regular communication with the client's teachers and other appropriate school officials. (10)

10. Parents, teachers, and caregivers implement a token economy in the classroom or placement setting. (11)

11. Parents increase praise and other positive reinforcement toward the client in regard to his/her academic performance or social behaviors. (12, 13)

12. Parents and family cease verbalizations of denial about the client's intellectual and cognitive deficits. (14, 15)

13. Parents recognize and verbally acknowledge their unrealistic expectations of or excessive pressure on the client. (16, 17)

14. Parents recognize and verbally acknowledge that their pattern of overprotectiveness interferes with the client's intellectual,

10. Encourage the parents to maintain regular communication with the client's teacher or school officials to monitor his/her academic, behavioral, emotional, and social progress.

11. Design a token economy for the classroom or residential program to reinforce on-task behaviors, completion of school assignments, good impulse control, and positive social skills.

12. Encourage the parents to provide frequent praise and other reinforcement for the client's positive social behaviors and academic performance.

13. Design a reward system or contingency contract to reinforce the client's adaptive or prosocial behaviors.

14. Educate the parents about the symptoms and characteristics of Mental Retardation.

15. Confront and challenge the parents' denial surrounding their child's intellectual deficits so they cooperate with recommendations regarding placement and educational interventions.

16. Conduct family therapy sessions to assess whether the parents are placing excessive pressure on the client to function at a level that he/she is not capable of achieving.

17. Confront and challenge the parents about placing excessive pressure on the client.

18. Observe parent-child interactions to assess whether the parents' overprotectiveness or infantilization of the client interferes with

emotional, and social development. (18, 19)

his/her intellectual, emotional, or
social development.

19. Assist the parents or caregivers
in developing realistic expectations of the client's intellectual
capabilities and level of adaptive
functioning.

15. Increase participation in
family activities or outings.
(20, 21, 22, 23, 24)

20. Encourage the parents and family
members to regularly include the
client in outings or activities (e.g.,
attending sporting events, going
ice skating, visiting a children's
museum).

21. Instruct family members to
observe positive behaviors by the
client between therapy sessions.
Reinforce positive behaviors and
encourage the client to continue
to exhibit these behaviors.

22. Assign the client a task in the
family (e.g., cooking a simple
meal, gardening) that is appropriate for his/her level of functioning
and provides him/her with a sense
of responsibility or belonging.

23. Place the client in charge of a
routine or basic task at home to
increase his/her self-esteem and
feelings of self-worth in the
family.

24. Assign homework designed to
promote the client's feelings of acceptance and a sense of belonging
in the family system, school setting, or community (or assign the
"You Belong Here" exercise from
the *Adolescent Psychotherapy
Homework Planner,* 2nd ed. by
Jongsma, Peterson, and Mc-
Innis).

16. Increase the frequency of responsible behaviors at school or residential program. (25)

17. Parents agree to and implement an allowance program that helps the client learn to manage money more effectively. (26)

18. Take a bath or shower, dress self independently, comb hair, wash hands before meals, and brush teeth on a daily basis. (27)

19. Parents consistently implement behavior management techniques to reduce the frequency and severity of temper outbursts or disruptive and aggressive behaviors. (28, 29)

20. Decrease frequency of impulsive, disruptive, or aggressive behaviors. (30, 31)

25. Consult with school officials or residential staff about the client performing a job (e.g., raising the flag, helping to run video equipment) to build self-esteem and provide him/her with a sense of responsibility.

26. Counsel the parents about setting up an allowance plan to increase the client's responsibilities and help him/her learn simple money management skills.

27. Design and implement a reward system to reinforce desired self-care behaviors, such as combing hair, washing dishes, or cleaning bedroom (or assign the parents to use the "Activities of Daily Living" program from the *Adolescent Psychotherapy Homework Planner,* 2nd ed. by Jongsma, Peterson, and McInnis).

28. Teach the parents effective behavior management techniques (e.g., time-outs, removal of privileges) to decrease the frequency and severity of the client's temper outbursts, acting out, and aggressive behaviors.

29. Encourage the parents to utilize natural, logical consequences for the client's inappropriate social or maladaptive behaviors.

30. Teach the client basic mediational and self-control strategies (e.g., "stop, listen, think, and act") to delay gratification and inhibit impulses.

31. Train the client in the use of guided imagery or relaxation techniques to calm himself/herself down and develop greater control of anger.

21. Recognize and verbally identify appropriate and inappropriate social behaviors. (32)

22. Increase the ability to identify and express feelings. (33, 34, 35)

32. Utilize role-playing and modeling in individual sessions to teach the client positive social skills. Reinforce new or emerging prosocial behaviors.

33. Educate the client about how to identify and label different emotions.

34. Tell the client to draw faces of basic emotions, then have him/her share times when he/she experienced the different emotions.

35. Teach the client effective communication skills (i.e., proper listening, good eye contact, "I statements") to improve his/her ability to express thoughts, feelings, and needs more clearly.

23. Express feelings of sadness, anxiety, and insecurity that are related to cognitive and intellectual limitations. (36, 37)

36. Assist the client in coming to an understanding and acceptance of the limitations surrounding his/her intellectual deficits and adaptive functioning.

37. Explore the client's feelings of depression, anxiety, and insecurity that are related to cognitive or intellectual limitations. Provide encouragement and support for the client.

24. Increase the frequency of positive self-statements. (38, 39)

38. Encourage the client to participate in the Special Olympics to build self-esteem.

39. Explore times when the client achieved success or accomplished a goal; reinforce positive steps that the client took to successfully accomplish goals.

25. Identify when it is appropriate to seek help with a task and when it is not. (40)

40. Assist the client in identifying appropriate and inappropriate times to ask for help; identify a list of acceptable resource people to whom the client can turn for support, help, and supervision when necessary.

26. Recognize and verbally identify appropriate and inappropriate sexual behaviors. (41)

41. Provide sex education to help the client identify and verbally recognize appropriate and inappropriate sexual urges and behaviors.

—. _____
   _____

—. _____
   _____

—. _____
   _____

—. _____
   _____

—. _____
   _____

—. _____
   _____

DIAGNOSTIC SUGGESTIONS

Axis I:	299.00	Autistic Disorder
	299.80	Rett's Disorder
	299.80	Asperger's Disorder
	299.10	Childhood Disintegrative Disorder
	_____	_____
	_____	_____
Axis II:	317	Mild Mental Retardation
	318.0	Moderate Mental Retardation
	318.1	Severe Mental Retardation
	318.2	Profound Mental Retardation
	319	Mental Retardation, Severity Unspecified
	V62.89	Borderline Intellectual Functioning
	799.9	Diagnosis Deferred
	V71.09	No Diagnosis
	_____	_____
	_____	_____

NEGATIVE PEER INFLUENCES

BEHAVIORAL DEFINITIONS

1. Strong susceptibility to negative peer influences that contribute to problems with authority figures at home, at school, and in the community; sexual promiscuity; or substance abuse problems.
2. Recurrent pattern of engaging in disruptive, negative attention-seeking behaviors at school or in the community to elicit attention, approval, or support from peers.
3. Excessive willingness to follow the lead of others in order to win approval or acceptance.
4. Propensity for taking ill-advised risks or engaging in thrill-seeking behavior in peer group settings.
5. Identification with negative peer group as a means to gain acceptance or elevate status and self-esteem.
6. Affiliation with negative peer groups or gangs to protect self from harm, danger, or perceived threats in the environment.
7. Tendency to gravitate toward negative peer groups because of underlying feelings of low self-esteem and insecurity.
8. Verbal report of being ostracized, teased, or mocked by peers at school or in the community.
9. History of rejection experiences within family system or peer group that contribute to the desire to seek out negative peer groups for belonging.
10. Social immaturity and pronounced deficits in the area of social skills.
11. Participation in substance abuse and other acting out behaviors to gain group acceptance.

—. _____
   _____

—. _____
   _____

—. _____
_____

LONG-TERM GOALS

1. Establish positive self-image and feelings of self-worth separate from affiliating with negative peer groups.
2. Achieve a sense of belonging and acceptance within the family and within positive peer groups by consistently engaging in socially appropriate behaviors.
3. Develop positive social skills necessary to establish and maintain positive, meaningful, and lasting peer friendships.
4. Resist negative peer group influences on a regular, consistent basis.
5. Terminate involvement with negative peer groups or gangs.
6. Eliminate all acting out behavior and delinquent acts.
7. Resolve the core conflicts that contribute to susceptibility to negative peer group influences.

—. _____
_____
—. _____
_____
—. _____
_____

SHORT-TERM OBJECTIVES

1. Describe the nature of peer relationships. (1, 2, 3)

THERAPEUTIC INTERVENTIONS

1. Explore the client's perception of the nature of his/her peer relationships as well as any areas of conflict; encourage and support him/her in expressing thoughts and feelings about peer relationships.

2. Gather a detailed psychosocial history of the client's development, family environment, and interpersonal relationships to gain

insight into the factors contributing to his/her desire to affiliate with negative peer groups.

3. Instruct the client to keep a daily journal in which he/she records both positive and negative experiences with peers that evoked strong emotions. Process excerpts from this journal in follow-up sessions to uncover factors that contribute to the desire to affiliate with negative peer groups, as well as to identify strengths that the client can use to build positive peer relationships.

2. Identify and verbalize needs that are met through involvement in negative peer groups. (4)

4. Assist the client in identifying the social-emotional needs that he/she attempts to meet through his/her involvement with negative peer groups (e.g., achieve sense of belonging and acceptance, elevate status, obtain material goods, seek protection).

3. Parents establish clearly defined rules and provide structure or boundaries to deter client from being highly susceptible to negative peer influences. (5, 6, 7)

5. Assist the parents in establishing clearly defined rules and boundaries, as well as providing greater structure, to deter the client from being highly susceptible to negative peer influences.

6. Encourage the parents to maintain regular communication with school officials to monitor the client's relationships with peers; encourage parents and teachers to follow through with firm, consistent limits if the client engages in acting out, disruptive, or aggressive behavior with peers at school.

7. Establish a contingency contract that identifies specific consequences that the client will receive if he/she engages in disruptive, acting out, or antisocial behaviors

with peers. Have the client repeat terms of contract to demonstrate understanding.

4. Parents and/or teachers implement a reward system to reinforce desired social behaviors. (8)

8. Design a reward system for parents and/or teachers to reinforce the client for engaging in specific, positive social behaviors and deter the need to affiliate with negative peer groups (e.g., introduce self to other individuals in positive peer group, display kindness, help another peer with academic or social problems).

5. Identify the negative consequences on self and others of participation with negative peer groups. (9, 10)

9. Have the client list between 5 and 10 negative consequences that his/her participation with negative peer groups has had on himself/herself and others.

10. Firmly confront the client about the impact of his/her involvement with negative peer groups, pointing out consequences for himself/herself and others.

6. Increase the number of statements that reflect acceptance of responsibility for negative social behavior. (11, 12, 13)

11. Challenge and confront statements by the client that minimize the impact that his/her involvement with negative peer groups has on his/her behavior.

12. Confront statements in which the client blames other peers for his/her acting out, disruptive, or anti-social behaviors and fails to accept responsibility for his/her actions.

13. Challenge the parents to cease blaming the client's misbehavior on his/her peers; instead, encourage parents to focus on the client and set limits for his/her negative social behaviors that occur while affiliating with peers.

7. Implement effective coping strategies to help resist negative peer influences. (14, 15, 16, 17)

14. Teach mediational and self-control techniques (e.g., "stop, listen, think, and act"; count to 10; walk away) to help the client successfully resist negative peer influences.

15. Utilize role-playing, modeling, or behavioral rehearsal techniques to teach the client more effective ways to resist negative peer influences, meet his/her social needs, or establish lasting, meaningful friendships (e.g., walk away, change subject, say "no," initiate conversations with positive peers, demonstrate empathy).

16. Assign the client to read *How to Say No and Keep Your Friends* (Scott) to teach him/her effective ways to resist negative peer influences and maintain friendships. Process reading with the client.

17. Explore times when the client was able to successfully resist negative peer influences and not engage in acting out, disruptive, or antisocial behaviors. Process the experiences and encourage him/her to use similar coping strategies to resist negative peer influences at present or in future.

8. Increase assertive behavior to deal more effectively with negative peer pressure. (18)

18. Teach the client effective communication and assertiveness skills (e.g., "I have to leave now"; "I can't afford to get into any more trouble") to help him/her successfully resist negative peer pressure.

9. Attend and regularly participate in group therapy sessions that focus on developing positive social skills. (19, 20)

19. Refer the client for group therapy to improve social skills and learn ways to successfully resist negative peer pressure; direct client to self-disclose at least two times in each group therapy session about his/her peer relationships.

20. Refer the client to a behavioral contracting group where he/she and other group members develop contracts each week to increase the frequency of positive peer interactions; review progress with the contracts each week and praise the client for achieving goals regarding peer interactions.

10. Identify and implement positive social skills that will help to improve peer relationships and establish friendships. (21, 22)

21. Teach positive social skills (e.g., introducing self to others, active listening, verbalizing empathy and concern for others, ignoring teasing) to improve peer relationships and increase chances of developing meaningful friendships (or use Skillstreaming: The Adolescent Kit [McGinnis and Goldstein; available from Childswork/Childsplay]).

22. Give the client a homework assignment of practicing newly learned positive social skills at least once each day between therapy sessions; review implementation, reinforcing success and redirecting for failure.

11. Increase involvement in positive social activities or community organizations. (23, 24)

23. Encourage the client to become involved in positive peer groups or community activities where he/she can gain acceptance and status (e.g., church or synagogue youth groups, YWCA or YMCA functions, school clubs, Boys Clubs or Girls Clubs).

24. Consult with school officials about ways to increase the client's socialization with positive peer groups at school (e.g., join school choir or newspaper staff, participate in student government, become involved in school fundraiser).

12. Increase frequency of positive interactions with peers. (25, 26, 27, 28)

25. Assign the client the task of initiating one social contact per day with other peers who are identified as being responsible, dependable, friendly, or well liked.

26. Direct the client to initiate three phone contacts per week to different individuals outside of the identified negative peer group.

27. Give the client a directive to invite a peer or friend (outside of negative peer group) for an overnight visit and/or set up an overnight visit at the other peer's or friend's home; process experience in follow-up session.

28. Give the client a homework assignment of engaging in three altruistic or benevolent acts with peers before the next therapy session. Process how others respond to acts of kindness, and encourage the client to engage in similar behavior in the future.

13. Identify and implement positive ways to meet needs other than through participation in negative peer group activities or gang involvement. (29, 30)

29. Brainstorm with the client more adaptive ways for him/her to meet needs for recognition/status, acceptance, material goods, and excitement other than through his/her involvement with negative peer groups or gangs (e.g., attend or participate in sporting events, secure employment, visit amusement park with youth group).

30. Assign the client to view the video entitled *Handling Peer Pressure and Gangs* (part of the Peace Talks series available through Wellness Reproductions & Publishing, LLC) to help the client resist negative peer influences or pressure to join a gang.

14. Identify and list resource people to whom the client can turn for support, comfort, and guidance. (31)

31. Help the client to identify a list of resource people, both peers and adults, at school or in the community to whom he/she can turn for support, comfort, or guidance when he/she is experiencing negative peer pressure and/or feels rejected by peers.

15. Identify and express feelings associated with past rejection experiences. (32, 33)

32. Explore the client's background in peer relationships to assess whether he/she feels rejected, ostracized, or unaccepted by many peers. Assist the client in identifying possible causes of rejection or alienation (e.g., hypersensitivity to teasing, target of scapegoating, poor social skills).

33. Use the empty-chair technique to help the client express his/her feelings of anger, hurt, and sadness toward individuals by whom he/she has felt rejected or alienated in the past.

16. Verbalize recognition of how underlying feelings of low self-esteem and insecurity are related to involvement with negative peer groups. (34, 35, 36, 37)

34. Assist the client in making a connection between underlying feelings of low self-esteem and insecurity and his/her gravitation toward negative peer groups to achieve a sense of belonging and acceptance.

35. Assist the client in identifying more constructive ways to build self-esteem and win approval other than affiliating with negative peer groups that influence him/her to act out and engage in antisocial behavior (e.g., try out for school play, attend a school dance, participate in sporting or recreational activities).

36. Instruct the client to identify 5 to 10 strengths or interests; review the list in follow-up session and

encourage the client to utilize his/her strengths to build self-esteem and increase positive peer interactions (or assign the "Show Your Strengths" exercise from the *Adolescent Psychotherapy Homework Planner,* 2nd ed. by Jongsma, Peterson, and McInnis).

37. Help the client to identify healthy risks that he/she can take in the near future to improve his/her self-esteem (e.g., try out for sports team, attend new social functions or gathering, initiate conversations with unfamiliar people outside of negative peer group); challenge the client to take three healthy risks before the next therapy session.

17. Overly rigid parents recognize how their strict or harsh enforcement of rules and boundaries contributes to the client's gravitation toward negative peer groups. (38, 39)

38. Explore whether the parents are overly rigid or strict in their establishment of rules and boundaries to the point where the client has little opportunity to socialize with peers and rebels by engaging in acting out behaviors with negative peer groups.

39. Encourage and challenge the overly rigid parents to loosen rules and boundaries to allow the client increased opportunities to engage in socially appropriate activities or positive peer group activities.

18. Parents recognize how their lack of supervision and failure to follow through with limits contributes to the client's affiliation with negative peer groups. (40)

40. Conduct family therapy session to explore whether the parents' lack of supervision and inability to establish appropriate parent-child boundaries contribute to the client's gravitation toward negative peer group influences.

19. Complete a substance abuse evaluation and comply with the recommendations offered by the evaluation findings. (41)

41. Conduct or arrange for a substance abuse evaluation and/or treatment for the client (see Chemical Dependence chapter in this *Planner*).

__. _____

__. _____

__. _____

__. _____

__. _____

__. _____

DIAGNOSTIC SUGGESTIONS

Axis I:	313.81	Oppositional Defiant Disorder
	312.82	Conduct Disorder, Adolescent-Onset Type
	312.9	Disruptive Behavior Disorder NOS
	314.01	Attention-Deficit/Hyperactivity Disorder, Predominantly Hyperactive-Impulsive Type
	314.9	Attention-Deficit/Hyperactivity Disorder NOS
	V71.02	Adolescent Antisocial Behavior
	V62.81	Relational Problem NOS
	_____	_____
	_____	_____
Axis II:	799.9	Diagnosis Deferred
	V71.09	No Diagnosis
	_____	_____
	_____	_____

OBSESSIVE-COMPULSIVE DISORDER (OCD)

BEHAVIORAL DEFINITIONS

1. Recurrent and persistent ideas, thoughts, or impulses that are viewed as intrusive, senseless, and time-consuming, or that interfere with the client's daily routine, school performance, or social relationships.
2. Failed attempts to ignore or control these thoughts or impulses or neutralize them with other thoughts and actions.
3. Recognition that obsessive thoughts are a product of his/her own mind.
4. Excessive concerns about dirt or unfounded fears of contracting a dreadful disease or illness.
5. Obsessions related to troubling aggressive or sexual thoughts, urges, or images.
6. Persistent and troubling thoughts about religious issues; excessive concern about morality and right or wrong.
7. Repetitive and intentional behaviors that are done in response to obsessive thoughts or increased feelings of anxiety or fearfulness.
8. Repetitive and excessive behavior that is done to neutralize or prevent discomfort or some dreadful situation; however, that behavior is not connected in any realistic way with what it is designed to neutralize or prevent.
9. Recognition of repetitive behaviors as excessive and unreasonable.
10. Cleaning and washing compulsions (e.g., excessive hand washing, bathing, showering, cleaning of household products).
11. Hoarding or collecting compulsions.
12. Checking compulsions (e.g., repeatedly checking to see if door is locked, rechecking homework to make sure it is done correctly, checking to make sure that no one has been harmed).
13. Compulsions about having to arrange objects or things in proper order (e.g., stacking coins in certain order, laying out clothes each evening at same time, wearing only certain clothes on certain days).

—. _____

   _____

—. _____

   _____

—. _____

   _____

LONG-TERM GOALS

1. Significantly reduce time involved with or interference from obsessions.
2. Significantly reduce frequency of compulsive or ritualistic behaviors.
3. Function daily at a consistent level with minimal interference from obsessions and compulsions.
4. Resolve key life conflicts and the emotional stress that fuels obsessive-compulsive behavior patterns.
5. Let go of key thoughts, beliefs, and past life events in order to maximize time free from obsessions and compulsions.

—. _____

   _____

—. _____

   _____

—. _____

   _____

SHORT-TERM OBJECTIVES

1. Describe the nature, history, and severity of obsessive thoughts and/or compulsive behavior. (1)

2. Comply with psychological testing evaluation to assess the nature and severity of the obsessive-compulsive problem. (2)

THERAPEUTIC INTERVENTIONS

1. Assess the nature, severity, and history of the obsessive-compulsive problems using clinical interview.

2. Arrange for psychological testing to further evaluate the nature and severity of the client's obsessive-compulsive problem (e.g., *The Children's Yale-Brown Obsessive Compulsive Scale* by Scahill and colleagues, 1997).

▽ 3. Cooperate with an evaluation by a physician for psychotropic medication. (3, 4)

3. Arrange for an evaluation for a prescription of psychotropic medications (e.g., serotonergic medications). ▽

4. Monitor the client for prescription compliance, side effects, and overall effectiveness of the medication; consult with the prescribing physician at regular intervals. ▽

▽ 4. Verbalize an understanding of the rationale for treatment of OCD. (5, 6)

5. Assign treatment participants to read psychoeducational chapters of books or treatment manuals on the rationale for exposure and ritual prevention therapy and/or cognitive restructuring for OCD (e.g., *Up and Down the Worry Hill* by Wagner; *Brain Lock: Free Yourself from Obsessive-Compulsive Behavior* by Schwartz; *Obsessive-Compulsive Disorder: Help for Children and Adolescents* by Waltz). ▽

6. Discuss how treatment serves as an arena to desensitize learned fear, reality test obsessional fears and underlying beliefs, and build confidence in managing fears without compulsions (see *Up and Down the Worry Hill* by Wagner). ▽

▽ 5. Identify, and replace biased, fearful self-talk and beliefs. (7)

7. Explore the client's schema and self-talk that mediate his/her obsessional fears and compulsive behavior, assist him/her in generating thoughts that correct for the biases (see *What to Do When Your Child has Obsessive-Compulsive Disorder* by Wagner; or *OCD in Children and Adolescents* by March and Mulle). ▽

▽ indicates that the Objective/Intervention is consistent with those found in evidence-based treatments.

▽ 6. Undergo repeated imaginal exposure to feared external and/or internal cues. (8, 9, 10)

8. Assess the nature of any external cues (e.g., persons, objects, situations) and internal cues (thoughts, images, and impulses) that precipitate the client's obsessions and compulsions. ▽

9. Direct and assist the client in construction of a hierarchy of feared internal and external fear cues. ▽

10. Select initial imaginal exposures to the internal and/or external OCD cues that have a high likelihood of being a successful experience for the client (or assign "Gradually Facing a Phobic Fear" in the *Adolescent Psychotherapy Homework Planner,* 2nd ed. by Jongsma, Peterson, and McInnis); do cognitive restructuring within and after the exposure (see *What to Do When Your Child has Obsessive-Compulsive Disorder* by Wagner; or *OCD in Children and Adolescents* by March and Mulle). ▽

▽ 7. Complete homework assignments involving in vivo exposure to feared external and/or internal cues. (11)

11. Assign the client a homework exercise in which he/she repeats the exposure to the internal and/or external OCD cues using restructured cognitions between sessions and records responses (or assign "Reducing the Strength of Compulsive Behaviors" in the *Adult Psychotherapy Homework Planner,* 2nd ed. by Jongsma); review during next session, reinforcing success and providing corrective feedback toward improvement (see *Up and Down the Worry Hill* by Wagner). ▽

▽ 8. Implement relapse prevention strategies for managing possible future anxiety symptoms. (12, 13, 14, 15)

12. Discuss with the client the distinction between a lapse and relapse, associating a lapse with an initial and reversible return of

symptoms, fear, or urges to avoid and relapse with the decision to return to fearful and avoidant patterns. ▽

13. Identify and rehearse with the client the management of future situations or circumstances in which lapses could occur. ▽

14. Instruct the client to routinely use strategies learned in therapy (e.g., continued exposure to previously feared external or internal cues that arise) to prevent relapse into obsessive-compulsive patterns. ▽

15. Schedule periodic "maintenance sessions" to help the client maintain therapeutic gains and adjust to life without OCD (see Hiss, Foa, and Kozak, 1994, for a description of relapse prevention strategies for OCD). ▽

▽ 9. Implement the use of the "thought-stopping" technique to reduce the frequency of obsessive thoughts. (16, 17)

16. Teach the client to interrupt obsessive thoughts using the "thought-stopping" technique of shouting STOP to himself/herself silently while picturing a red traffic signal and then thinking about a calming scene. ▽

17. Assign the client to implement the "thought-stopping" technique on a daily basis between sessions (or assign "Making Use of the Thought-Stopping Technique" in the *Adult Psychotherapy Homework Planner,* 2nd ed. by Jongsma); review. ▽

▽10. Implement a reward sytem and refocusing to resist urge to engage in compulsive behavior or talk about obsessive thoughts. (18)

18. Design a reward system to reinforce client for successfully resisting the urge to engage in compulsive behavior or openly share obsessive thoughts with others (see *OCD in Children*

and Adolescents by March and Mulle); encourage the use of refocusing techniques to distract the client from the thoughts or urges (or assign "Refocus Attention Away From Obsessions and Compulsions" in the *Adolescent Psychotherapy Homework Planner,* 2nd ed. by Jongsma, Peterson, and McInnis). ▽

▽11. Identify support persons or resources who can help the client manage obsessions/compulsions. (19, 20)

19. Encourage and instruct client to involve support person(s) or a "coach" who can help him/her resist urge to engage in compulsive behavior or take mind off obsessive thoughts. ▽

20. Refer the client and parents to support group(s) to help maintain and support the gains made in therapy. ▽

▽12. Identify key life conflicts that raise anxiety. (21)

21. Explore the client's life circumstances to help identify key unresolved conflicts that contribute to and/or exacerbate obsessions and compulsions. ▽

▽13. Parents provide appropriate support and establish effective boundaries surrounding the client's OCD symptoms. (22, 23, 24)

22. Hold family therapy sessions to identify specific, positive ways that the parents can help the client manage his/her obsessions or compulsions (e.g., parents refocus client's attention away from obsessions/compulsions by engaging in recreational activity or talking about other topics, parents encourage client to participate in feared activity). ▽

23. Encourage and instruct parents to remain calm, patient, and supportive when faced with the client's obsessions or compulsions; discourage parents from reacting strongly with anger or frustration. ▽

24. Challenge and confront the parents to cease giving long lectures or becoming locked in prolonged arguments with the client about how his/her OCD symptoms are irrational or unreasonable. ▽

▽ 14. Overly involved or protective parents identify how they reinforce the client's OCD symptoms. (25, 26)

25. Conduct family therapy sessions to assess the factors contributing to the emergence, maintenance, or exacerbation of OCD symptoms. ▽

26. Teach the parents how being overly protective or reassuring reinforces the client's OCD symptoms and interferes with his/her ability to manage the troubling or distressing thoughts, urges, or images. ▽

15. Verbalize and clarify feelings connected to key life concepts. (27)

27. Encourage, support, and assist the client in identifying and expressing feelings related to key unresolved life issues (or assign "Surface Behavior/Inner Feelings" in the *Adolescent Psychotherapy Homework Planner,* 2nd ed. by Jongsma, Peterson, and McInnis).

16. Decrease ruminations about death and other stressful or confusing life issues. (28)

28. Utilize a Rational Emotive Therapy approach and teach the client to analyze, attack, and destroy his/her self-defeating beliefs about death and other stressful life situations; monitor and offer appropriate encouragement.

17. Implement the Ericksonian task designed to interfere with OCD. (29)

29. Develop and design an Ericksonian task (e.g., if obsessed with a loss, give the client the task to visit, send a card, or bring flowers to someone who has lost someone) for the client that is centered around the obsession or compulsion and assess the results with the client.

OBSESSIVE-COMPULSIVE DISORDER (OCD)   175

18. Engage in a strategic ordeal to overcome OCD impulses. (30)

30. Create and sell a strategic ordeal that offers a guaranteed cure to help the client with the obsession or compulsion (e.g., instruct client to perform an aversive chore each time an obsessive thought or compulsive behavior occurs). Note that Haley emphasizes that the "cure" offers an intervention to achieve a goal and is not a promise to cure the client in beginning of therapy (see *Ordeal Therapy* by Haley).

19. Develop and implement a daily ritual that interrupts the current pattern of compulsions. (31)

31. Help the client create and implement a ritual (e.g., find a chore that the client finds necessary but very unpleasant, and have him/her do this chore each time he/she finds thoughts becoming obsessive); follow-up with the client on the outcome of its implementation and make any necessary adjustments.

___. _____   ___. _____
     _____   _____
___. _____   ___. _____
     _____   _____
___. _____   ___. _____
     _____   _____

DIAGNOSTIC SUGGESTIONS

Axis I: 300.3   Obsessive-Compulsive Disorder
               300.00   Anxiety Disorder NOS
               300.02   Generalized Anxiety Disorder
               296.xx   Major Depressive Disorder
               303.90   Alcohol Dependence
               304.10   Sedative, Hypnotic, or Anxiolytic Dependence

_____   _____

_____   _____

Axis II: 799.9   Diagnosis Deferred
          V71.09   No Diagnosis

_____   _____

_____   _____

OPPOSITIONAL DEFIANT

BEHAVIORAL DEFINITIONS

1. Displays a pattern of negativistic, hostile, and defiant behavior toward most adults.
2. Often acts as if parents, teachers, and other authority figures are the "enemy."
3. Erupts in temper tantrums (e.g., screaming, crying, throwing objects, thrashing on ground, refusing to move) in defiance of direction from an adult caregiver.
4. Consistently argues with adults.
5. Often defies or refuses to comply with reasonable requests and rules.
6. Deliberately annoys people and is easily annoyed by others.
7. Often blames others for own mistakes or misbehavior.
8. Consistently is angry and resentful.
9. Often is spiteful or vindictive.
10. Has experienced significant impairment in social, academic, or occupational functioning.

—. _____
   _____

—. _____
   _____

—. _____
   _____

LONG-TERM GOALS

1. Marked reduction in the intensity and frequency of hostile and defiant behaviors toward adults.

2. Terminate temper tantrums and replace with controlled, respectful compliance with directions from authority figures.
3. Begin to consistently interact with adults in a mutually respectful manner.
4. Bring hostile, defiant behaviors within socially acceptable standards.
5. Replace hostile, defiant behaviors toward adults with respect and cooperation.
6. Resolve the conflict that underlies the anger, hostility, and defiance.
7. Reach a level of reduced tension, increased satisfaction, and improved communication with family and/or other authority figures.
8. Parents learn and implement good child behavioral management skills.

—. _____

   _____

—. _____

   _____

—. _____

   _____

SHORT-TERM OBJECTIVES

1. Identify situations, thoughts, and feelings that trigger angry feelings, problem behaviors, and the targets of those actions. (1, 2, 3)

THERAPEUTIC INTERVENTIONS

1. Actively build the level of trust with the client through consistent eye contact, active listening, unconditional positive regard, and warm acceptance to help increase his/her disclosure of thoughts and feelings.

2. Explore the client's perception of his/her oppositional pattern toward rules and authority figures.

3. Thoroughly assess the various stimuli (e.g., situations, people, thoughts) that have triggered the client's anger and the thoughts, feelings, and actions that have characterized his/her anger responses.

2. Cooperate with a medical evaluation to assess possible general medical contributors to defiant behavior. (4)

3. Complete psychological testing. (5)

4. Complete a substance abuse evaluation and comply with the recommendations offered by the evaluation findings. (6)

▽ 5. Cooperate with a physician evaluation for possible treatment with psychotropic medications to assist in anger and behavioral control; take medications consistently, if prescribed. (7)

▽ 6. Agree to learn alternative ways to think about and manage anger and misbehavior. (8, 9)

4. Refer the client to a physician for a complete physical exam to rule out organic contributors (e.g., brain damage, tumor, elevated testosterone levels) to defiant behavior.

5. Conduct or arrange for psychological testing to help in assessing whether a comorbid condition (e.g., depression, Attention-Deficit/Hyperactivity Disorder [ADHD]) is contributing to behavior control problems; follow-up accordingly with client and parents regarding treatment options.

6. Arrange for a substance abuse evaluation and/or treatment for the client.

7. Assess the client for the need for psychotropic medication to assist in control of anger; refer him/her to a physician for an evaluation for prescription medication; monitor prescription compliance, effectiveness, and side effects; provide feedback to the prescribing physician. ▽

8. Assist the client in reconceptualizing anger as involving different components (cognitive, physiological, affective, and behavioral) that go through predictable phases (e.g., demanding expectations not being met leading to increased arousal and anger leading to acting out) that can be managed. ▽

▽ indicates that the Objective/Intervention is consistent with those found in evidence-based treatments.

9. Assist the client in identifying the positive consequences of managing anger and misbehavior (e.g., respect from others and self, cooperation from others, improved physical health); ask the client to agree to learn new ways to conceptualize and manage anger and misbehavior. ▽

▽ 7. Learn and implement calming strategies as part of a new way to manage reactions to frustration and defiance. (10)

10. Teach the client calming techniques (e.g., muscle relaxation, paced breathing, calming imagery) as part of a tailored strategy for responding appropriately to angry feelings and the urge to defy when they occur. ▽

▽ 8. Identify, challenge, and replace self-talk that leads to anger and misbehavior with self-talk that facilitates a more constructive reaction. (11)

11. Explore the client's self-talk that mediates his/her angry feelings and actions (e.g., demanding expectations reflected in should, must, or have to statements); identify and challenge biases, assisting him/her in generating appraisals and self-talk that corrects for the biases and facilitates a more flexible and temperate response to frustration. ▽

▽ 9. Learn and implement thought-stopping to manage intrusive unwanted thoughts that trigger anger and acting out. (12)

12. Assign the client to implement a "thought-stopping" technique on a daily basis to manage intrusive unwanted thoughts that trigger anger and acting out between sessions (or assign "Making Use of the Thought-Stopping Technique" in the *Adult Psychotherapy Homework Planner,* 2nd ed. by Jongsma); review implementation; reinforce success, providing corrective feedback toward improvement. ▽

▽10. Verbalize feelings of frustration, disagreement, and anger
in a controlled, assertive way.
(13)

▽11. Learn and implement problem-
solving and/or conflict
resolution skills to manage
interpersonal problems constructively. (14)

▽12. Practice using new calming,
communication, conflict resolution, and thinking skills in
session with the therapist and
during homework exercises.
(15, 16)

13. Use instruction, modeling, and/or
role-playing to teach the client
assertive communication; if
indicated, refer him/her to an
assertiveness training class/group
for further instruction. ▽

14. Teach the client conflict resolution skills (e.g., empathy, active
listening, "I messages," respectful communication, assertiveness
without aggression, compromise); use modeling, role-playing,
and behavior rehearsal to work
through several current conflicts.
▽

15. Assist the client in constructing
and consolidating a client-tailored
strategy for managing anger
that combines any of the somatic, cognitive, communication,
problem-solving, and/or conflict resolution skills relevant to
his/her needs (see *Treatment of
Individuals with Anger Control
Problems and Aggressive Behaviors*
by Meichenbaum). ▽

16. Use any of several techniques,
including relaxation, imagery,
behavioral rehearsal, modeling,
role-playing, or feedback of videotaped practice in increasingly
challenging situations, to help
the client consolidate the use of
his/her new anger and behavior
management skills. ▽

▽13. Practice using new calming,
communication, conflict resolution, and thinking skills in
homework exercises. (17)

17. Assign the client homework
exercises to help him/her practice
newly learned calming, assertion,
conflict resolution, or cognitive
restructuring skills as needed; review and process toward the goal
of consolidation. ▽

▼14. Parents learn and implement Parent Management Training skills to recognize and manage problem behavior of the client. (18, 19, 20, 21, 22)

18. Use a Parent Management Training approach beginning with teaching the parents how parent and child behavioral interactions can encourage or discourage positive or negative behavior and that changing key elements of those interactions (e.g., prompting and reinforcing positive behaviors) can be used to promote positive change (e.g., see *Parenting the Strong-Willed Child* by Forehand and Long; *Living with Children* by Patterson). ▼

19. Teach the parents how to specifically define and identify problem behaviors, identify their own reactions to the behavior, determine whether the reaction encourages or discourages the behavior, and generate alternatives to the problem behavior. ▼

20. Teach parents how to implement key parenting practices consistently, including establishing realistic age-appropriate rules for acceptable and unacceptable behavior; prompting of positive behavior in the environment; use of positive reinforcement to encourage behavior (e.g., praise); use of calm, clear, direct instruction, time out, and other loss-of-privilege practices for problem behavior (or assign "Switching from Defense to Offense in the *Adolescent Psychotherapy Homework Planner,* 2nd ed. by Jongsma, Peterson, and McInnis). ▼

21. Assign the parents home exercises in which they implement and record results of implementation exercises (or assign "Clear Rules,

Positive Reinforcement, Appropriate Consequences" in the *Adolescent Psychotherapy Homework Planner,* 2nd ed. by Jongsma, Peterson, and McInnis); review in session, providing corrective feedback toward improved, appropriate, and consistent use of skills. ▽

22. Ask the parents to read parent training manuals (e.g., *Parenting Through Change* by Forgatch) or watch and process videotapes demonstrating the techniques being learned in session (see Webster-Stratton, 1994). ▽

▽15. Decrease the frequency and intensity of hostile, negativistic, and defiant interactions with parents/adults. (23)

23. Track the frequency and intensity of negative, hostile feelings and defiant behaviors and problem-solve solutions (or assign "Stop Yelling" or "Filing a Complaint" in the *Adolescent Psychotherapy Homework Planner,* 2nd ed. by Jongsma, Peterson, and McInnis); implement plan toward decreasing frequency and intensity. ▽

▽16. Increase the frequency of civil, respectful interactions with parents/adults. (24, 25, 26)

24. Teach the client the principle of reciprocity, asking him/her to agree to treat everyone in a respectful manner for a 1-week period to see if others will reciprocate by treating him/her with more respect; track results, problem-solve, and revisit toward increasing respectful interactions. ▽

25. Use a therapeutic game (e.g., The Talking, Feeling, and Doing Game by Gardner, available from Creative Therapeutics; The Ungame by Zakich, available from The Ungame Company) to expand the client's ability to express feelings respectfully. ▽

26. Videotape a family session, using appropriate portions to show the family interaction patterns that are destructive; teach family members, using role-playing, role reversal, and modeling, to implement more respectful patterns. ▽

▽17. Learn how to identify what is wanted from parents and other adults. (27, 28)

27. Assist the client in becoming able to recognize feelings and wants, their connection to behavior, and how to express them in constructive, respectful ways. ▽

28. Assist the client in reframing complaints into requests for positive change (or assign the exercise "Filing a Complaint" or "If I Could Run My Family" from the *Adolescent Psychotherapy Homework Planner,* 2nd ed. by Jongsma, Peterson, and McInnis). ▽

18. Parents acknowledge their own conflicts that influence the client's misbehavior. (29)

29. In family sessions, expose the parental conflict that underlies the client's behavior; refer the parents to conjoint sessions to begin to resolve their issues of conflict.

19. Parents and child identify and work toward preferred relational patterns between family members. (30, 31, 32, 33, 34)

30. Use a family-system approach in individual sessions to assist the client in seeing the family from a different perspective and in moving toward disengaging from dysfunction.

31. Conduct family sessions during which the family system and its interactions are analyzed; develop and implement a strategic/structural/experiential intervention.

32. Facilitate a family session in which the family is sculpted (see *Peoplemaking* by Satir); process the experience with the family; then sculpt them as they would like to be.

33. Assist the parents in identifying and implementing new methods of intervention in the client's behaviors that focus on positive parenting (or assign the parents the exercise "Switching from Defense to Offense" from the *Adolescent Psychotherapy Homework Planner,* 2nd ed. by Jongsma, Peterson, and McInnis); monitor the parents' follow-through, coaching and giving encouragement as needed.

34. Monitor progress; give feedback, support, and praise as appropriate.

20. Increase involvement in cooperative activities at home and at school. (35)

35. Institute with the parents and teachers a system of positive consequences (see Selekman's *Solution-Focused Therapy with Children*) that promotes and encourages prosocial and cooperative behaviors (e.g., writing a card to a relative, mowing a neighbor's lawn, doing a good deed for an elderly neighbor as a consequence for bad behavior).

21. Parents learn and implement the Barkley method of oppositional child behavior control. (36)

36. Ask the parents to watch the video *Techniques for Working with Oppositional Defiant Disorder in Children* (Barkley) or read *Your Defiant Child* (Barkley and Benton) to increase understanding; facilitate implementation; monitor effectiveness.

22. Parents complete or rule out the emancipation of the child. (37, 38, 39)

37. Explore with the parents the options for placement of the client outside the home (e.g., with a relative, in foster care or respite care, emancipation).

38. Direct the parents to seek legal counsel on the process of emancipation.

39. Support the parents in their deci-
    sion to emancipate the client, and
    process the feelings they have
    regarding their decision.

__. _____   __. _____
    _____   _____
__. _____   __. _____
    _____   _____
__. _____   __. _____
    _____   _____

DIAGNOSTIC SUGGESTIONS

Axis I: 313.81   Oppositional Defiant Disorder
                 312.81   Conduct Disorder, Childhood-Onset Type
                 312.82   Conduct Disorder, Adolescent-Onset Type
                 312.9   Disruptive Behavior Disorder NOS
                 314.01   Attention-Deficit/Hyperactivity Disorder,
                             Predominantly Hyperactive-Impulsive Type
                 314.9   Attention-Deficit/Hyperactivity Disorder NOS
                 V62.81   Relational Problem NOS

                 _____   _____

                 _____   _____

Axis II: V71.09   No Diagnosis on Axis II

                 _____   _____

                 _____   _____

PANIC/AGORAPHOBIA

BEHAVIORAL DEFINITIONS

1. Complains of unexpected, sudden, debilitating panic symptoms (e.g., shallow breathing, sweating, heart racing or pounding, dizziness, depersonalization or derealization, trembling, chest tightness, fear of dying or losing control, nausea) that have occurred repeatedly, resulting in persisting concern about having additional attacks.
2. Demonstrates marked avoidance of activities or environments due to fear of triggering intense panic symptoms, resulting in interference with normal routine.
3. Acknowledges a persistence of fear in spite of the recognition that the fear is unreasonable.
4. Increasingly isolates self due to fear of traveling or leaving a "safe environment" such as home.
5. Avoids public places or environments with large groups of people such as malls or big stores.

—. _____
   _____
—. _____
   _____
—. _____
   _____

LONG-TERM GOALS

1. Reduce the frequency, intensity, and duration of panic attacks.
2. Reduce the fear that panic symptoms will recur without the ability to manage them.

3. Reduce the fear of triggering panic and eliminate avoidance of activities and environments thought to trigger panic.
4. Increase comfort in freely leaving home and being in a public environment.

—. _____
   _____
   _____

—. _____
   _____
   _____

—. _____
   _____
   _____

SHORT-TERM OBJECTIVES

THERAPEUTIC INTERVENTIONS

1. Describe the history and nature of the panic symptoms. (1, 2)

1. Assess the client's frequency, intensity, duration, and history of panic symptoms, fear, and avoidance (e.g., *The Anxiety Disorders Interview Schedule for Children— Parent Version or Child Version* by Silverman and Albano; "Panic Survey" in the *Adolescent Psychotherapy Homework Planner,* 2nd ed. by Jongsma, Peterson, and McInnis).

2. Assess the nature of any stimulus, thoughts, or situations that precipitate the client's panic.

2. Complete psychological tests designed to assess the depth of Agoraphobia and anxiety sensitivity. (3, 4)

3. Administer a fear survey to further assess the depth and breadth of agoraphobic responses (e.g., *The Mobility Inventory for Agoraphobia* by Chambless, Caputo, and Gracely).

4. Administer a measure of fear of anxiety symptoms to further assess its depth and breadth (e.g., *The Anxiety Sensitivity Index* by Reiss, Peterson, and Gursky).

⍱ 3. Cooperate with an evaluation by a physician for psychotropic medication. (5, 6)

5. Arrange for an evaluation for a prescription of psychotropic medications to alleviate the client's symptoms. ⍱

6. Monitor the client for prescription compliance, side effects, and overall effectiveness of the medication; consult with the prescribing physician at regular intervals. ⍱

⍱ 4. Verbalize an accurate understanding of panic attacks and Agoraphobia. (7, 8)

7. Discuss how panic attacks are "false alarms" of danger, not medically dangerous, and not a sign of weakness or craziness; they are common, but often lead to unnecessary avoidance. ⍱

8. Assign the client to read psycho-educational chapters of books or treatment manuals on panic disorders and Agoraphobia (e.g., *Mastery of Your Anxiety and Panic* by Barlow and Craske; *Don't Panic: Taking Control of Anxiety Attacks* by Wilson). ⍱

⍱ 5. Verbalize an understanding of the rationale for treatment of panic. (9, 10)

9. Discuss how exposure serves as an arena to desensitize learned fear, build confidence, and feel safer by building a new history of success experiences. ⍱

10. Assign the client to read about exposure-based therapy in chapters of books or treatment manuals on panic disorders and Agoraphobia (e.g., *Mastery of Your Anxiety and Panic* by Barlow and Craske; *Living with Fear* by Marks). ⍱

⍱ indicates that the Objective/Intervention is consistent with those found in evidence-based treatments.

▽ 6. Learn and implement calming and coping strategies to reduce overall anxiety and to manage panic symptoms. (11, 12, 13)

11. Teach the client progressive muscle relaxation as a daily exercise for general relaxation and train him/her in the use of coping strategies (e.g., staying focused on behavioral goals, muscular relaxation, evenly paced diaphragmatic breathing, positive self-talk) to manage symptom attacks. ▽

12. Teach the client to keep focus on external stimuli and behavioral responsibilities during panic rather than being preoccupied with internal focus on physiological changes. ▽

13. Assign the client to read about progressive muscle relaxation and paced diaphragmatic breathing in books or treatment manuals on Panic Disorder and Agoraphobia (e.g., *Mastery of Your Anxiety and Panic* by Barlow and Craske). ▽

▽ 7. Practice positive self-talk that builds confidence in the ability to endure anxiety symptoms without serious consequences. (14, 15)

14. Consistently reassure the client of no connection between panic symptoms and heart attack, loss of control over behavior, or serious mental illness ("going crazy"). ▽

15. Use modeling and behavioral rehearsal to train the client in positive self-talk that reassures him/her of the ability to endure anxiety symptoms without serious consequences. ▽

▽ 8. Identify, challenge, and replace fearful self-talk with reality-based, positive self-talk. (16, 17, 18)

16. Explore the client's schema and self-talk that mediate his/her fear response; challenge the biases; assist him/her in replacing the distorted messages with self-talk that neither overestimates the likelihood of catastrophic outcomes nor underestimates the ability to cope with panic symptoms. ▽

17. Assign the client to read about cognitive restructuring in books or treatment manuals on Panic Disorder and Agoraphobia (e.g., *Mastery of Your Anxiety and Panic* by Barlow and Craske). ▽

18. Assign the client a homework exercise in which he/she identifies fearful self-talk and creates reality-based alternatives; review and reinforce success, providing corrective feedback for failure (see *10 Simple Solutions to Panic* by Antony and McCabe; *Mastery of Your Anxiety and Panic* by Barlow and Craske; or assign "Bad Thoughts Lead to Depressed Feelings" in the *Adolescent Psychotherapy Homework Planner,* 2nd ed. by Jongsma, Peterson, McInnis). ▽

▽ 9. Participate in gradual repeated exposure to feared physical sensations until they are no longer frightening to experience. (19, 20, 21)

19. Teach the client a sensation exposure technique in which he/she generates feared physical sensations through exercise (e.g., breathes rapidly until slightly lightheaded, spins in chair briefly until slightly dizzy), then uses coping strategies (e.g., staying focused on behavioral goals, muscular relaxation, evenly paced diaphragmatic breathing, positive self-talk) to calm himself/herself down; repeat exercise until anxiety wanes (see *10 Simple Solutions to Panic* by Antony and McCabe; *Mastery of Your Anxiety and Panic—Therapist Guide* by Craske, Barlow, and Meadows). ▽

20. Assign the client to read about sensation (interoceptive) exposure in books or treatment manuals on

Panic Disorder and Agoraphobia (e.g., *Mastery of Your Anxiety and Panic* by Barlow and Craske; *10 Simple Solutions to Panic* by Antony and McCabe). ▽

21. Assign the client a homework exercise in which he/she does sensation exposures and records the experience (see *Mastery of Your Anxiety and Panic* by Barlow and Craske; *10 Simple Solutions to Panic* by Antony and McCabe; or "Panic Attack Rating Form" in the *Adolescent Psychotherapy Homework Planner,* 2nd ed. by Jongsma, Peterson, and McInnis); review and reinforce success, providing corrective feedback for failure. ▽

▽10. Participate in gradual repeated exposure to feared or avoided situations in which a symptom attack and its negative consequences are feared. (22, 23, 24, 25)

22. Direct and assist the client in construction of a hierarchy of anxiety-producing situations associated with the phobic response. ▽

23. Select initial exposures that have a high likelihood of being a successful experience for the client; develop a plan for managing the symptoms and rehearse the plan in imagination. ▽

24. Assign the client to read about situational (exteroceptive) exposure in books or treatment manuals on Panic Disorder and Agoraphobia (e.g., *Mastery of Your Anxiety and Panic* by Barlow and Craske; *Living With Fear* by Marks). ▽

25. Assign the client a homework exercise in which he/she does situational exposures and records responses (e.g., "Gradually Facing a Phobic Fear" in the *Adolescent Psychotherapy Homework Planner,* 2nd ed. by Jongsma, Peterson, and McInnis; see also *Mastery of*

▽11. Learn and implement relapse prevention strategies for managing possible future anxiety symptoms. (26, 27, 28, 29)

Your Anxiety and Panic by Barlow and Craske; *10 Simple Solutions to Panic* by Antony and McCabe); review and reinforce success, providing corrective feedback for failure. ▽

26. Discuss with the client the distinction between a lapse and relapse, associating a lapse with an initial and reversible return of symptoms, fear, or urges to avoid and relapse with the decision to return to fearful and avoidant patterns. ▽

27. Identify and rehearse with the client the management of future situations or circumstances in which lapses could occur. ▽

28. Instruct the client to routinely use strategies learned in therapy (e.g., cognitive restructuring, exposure), building them into his/her life as much as possible. ▽

29. Develop a "coping card" on which coping strategies and other important information (e.g., "Pace your breathing," "Focus on the task at hand," "You can manage it," "It will go away") are written for the client's later use. ▽

12. Verbalize the costs and benefits of remaining fearful and avoidant. (30)

30. Probe for the presence of secondary gain that reinforces the client's panic symptoms through escape or avoidance mechanisms; challenge the client to remain in feared situations and to use coping skills to endure.

13. Verbalize the separate realities of the irrationally feared object or situation and the emotionally painful experience from the past that has been evoked by the phobic stimulus. (31, 32)

31. Clarify and differentiate between the client's current irrational fear and past emotional pain.

32. Encourage the client's sharing of feelings associated with past traumas through active listening, positive regard, and questioning.

14. Commit self to not allowing panic symptoms to take control of life and lead to a consistent avoidance of normal responsibilities. (33)

15. Return for a follow-up session to track progress, reinforce gains, and problem-solve barriers. (34)

33. Support the client in following through with work, family, and social activities rather than escaping·or avoiding them to focus on panic.

34. Schedule a "maintenance session" for the client for 1 to 3 months after therapy ends.

—. _____

_____

—. _____

_____

—. _____

_____

—. _____

_____

—. _____

_____

—. _____

_____

DIAGNOSTIC SUGGESTIONS

Axis I:	300.01	Panic Disorder Without Agoraphobia
	300.21	Panic Disorder With Agoraphobia
	300.22	Agoraphobia Without History of Panic Disorder
	_____	_____
	_____	_____

Axis II:	799.9	Diagnosis Deferred
	V71.09	No Diagnosis
	_____	_____
	_____	_____

PARENTING

BEHAVIORAL DEFINITIONS

1. Express difficulty maintaining meaningful communication with their teen-ager.
2. Lack skills in setting age-appropriate and effective limits for their child.
3. Feel growing disconnection from their teen as he/she develops stronger bonds with a peer group.
4. Increasing conflict between spouses over how to parent/discipline their child.
5. A pattern of harsh, rigid, and demeaning behavior toward the child.
6. A pattern of physically and emotionally abusive parenting.
7. One parent is perceived as overindulgent, while the other is seen as too harsh.
8. Frequently struggle to control their emotional reactions to their child's misbehavior.
9. Have been told by others (e.g., school officials, court authorities, and/or friends) that their teen's behavior needs to be addressed.
10. Their adolescent child has become strongly oppositional toward any rules or limit setting.
11. Lack of knowledge regarding reasonable expectations for a child's behavior at a given developmental level.

—. _____
   _____

—. _____
   _____

—. _____
   _____

LONG-TERM GOALS

1. Achieve a level of competent, effective parenting.
2. Reach a realistic view and approach to parenting, given the child's developmental level.
3. Terminate ineffective and/or abusive parenting and implement positive, effective techniques.
4. Strengthen the parental team by resolving marital conflicts.
5. Establish and maintain a healthy functioning parental team.
6. Resolve own childhood or adolescent issues that prevent effective parenting.
7. Adopt appropriate expectations for their adolescent and themselves as parents.
8. Achieve a level of greater family connectedness.

—. _____

_____

—. _____

_____

—. _____

_____

SHORT-TERM OBJECTIVES

THERAPEUTIC INTERVENTIONS

1. Provide information on the marital relationship, child behavior expectations, and style of parenting. (1)

1. Engage the parents through the use of empathy and normalization of their struggles with parenting and obtain information on their marital relationship, child behavior expectations, and parenting style.

2. Identify specific marital conflicts and work toward their resolution. (2, 3)

2. Analyze the data received from the parents about their relationship and parenting and establish or rule out the presence of marital conflicts.

3. Conduct or refer the parents to marital/relationship therapy to resolve the conflicts that are preventing them from being effective parents.

3. Complete recommended evaluation instruments and receive the results. (4, 5, 6)

4. Administer or arrange for the parents to complete assessment instruments to evaluate their parenting strengths and weaknesses (e.g., the Parenting Stress Index [PSI]; the Parent-Child Relationship Inventory [PCRI]).

5. Share results of assessment instruments with the parents and identify issues to begin working on to strengthen the parenting team.

6. Assist the parents in identifying their strengths and begin to build the confidence and effectiveness level of the parental team (or assign "Evaluating the Strength of Your Parenting Team" in the *Adolescent Psychotherapy Homework Planner,* 2nd ed. by Jongsma, Peterson, and McInnis).

4. Express feelings of frustration, helplessness, and inadequacy that each experiences in the parenting role. (7, 8, 9)

7. Create a compassionate, empathetic environment where the parents become comfortable enough to let their guard down and express the frustrations of parenting.

8. Educate the parents on the full scope of parenting by using humor and normalization.

9. Help the parents reduce their unrealistic expectations of themselves.

5. Identify unresolved childhood issues that affect parenting and work toward their resolution. (10, 11)

10. Explore each parent's story of his/her childhood to identify any unresolved issues that are present and to identify how these issues are now affecting the ability to effectively parent.

11. Assist the parents in working through issues from childhood that are unresolved.

6. Decrease reactivity to the child's behaviors. (12, 13, 14)

12. Evaluate the level of the parental team's reactivity to the child's behavior and then help them to learn to respond in a more modulated, thoughtful, planned manner.

13. Help the parents become aware of the "hot buttons" they have that the child can push to get a quick negative response and how this overreactive response reduces their effectiveness as parents.

14. Role-play reactive situations with the parents to help them learn to thoughtfully respond instead of automatically reacting to their child's demands or negative behaviors.

7. Identify the child's personality/temperament type that causes challenges and develop specific strategies to more effectively deal with that personality/temperament type. (15, 16, 17)

15. Have the parents read *The Challenging Child* (Greenspan) and then identify which type of difficult behavior pattern their child exhibits; encourage implementation of several of the parenting methods suggested for that type of child.

16. Expand the parents' repertoire of intervention options by having them read material on parenting difficult children (e.g., *The Difficult Child* by Turecki and Tonner; *The Explosive Child* by Greene; *How to Handle A Hard-to-Handle Kid* by Edwards).

17. Support, empower, monitor, and encourage the parents in implementing new strategies for parenting their child, giving feedback and redirection as needed.

▽ 8. Learn and implement Parent Management Training skills to recognize and manage challenging problem behaviors in children. (18, 19, 20, 21, 22)

18. Use a Parent Management Training approach beginning with teaching the parents how parent and child behavioral interactions can encourage or discourage positive or negative behavior and that changing key elements of those interactions (e.g., prompting and reinforcing positive behaviors) can be used to promote positive change (e.g., see *Parenting the Strong-Willed Child* by Forehand and Long; *Living with Children* by Patterson). ▽

19. Teach the parents how to specifically define and identify problem behaviors, identify their reactions to the behavior, determine whether the reaction encourages or discourages the behavior, and generate alternatives to the problem behavior. ▽

20. Teach parents how to implement key parenting practices consistently, including establishing realistic age-appropriate rules for acceptable and unacceptable behavior, prompting of positive behavior in the environment, use of positive reinforcement to encourage behavior (e.g., praise), use of clear direct instruction, time out, and other loss-of-privilege practices for problem behavior. ▽

21. Assign the parents home exercises in which they implement and record results of implementation exercises (or assign "Clear Rules, Positive Reinforcement, Appropriate Consequences" in the

---

▽ indicates that the Objective/Intervention is consistent with those found in evidence-based treatments.

Adolescent Psychotherapy Home-work Planner, 2nd ed. by Jongsma, Peterson, and McInnis); review in session, providing corrective feedback toward improved, ap-propriate, and consistent use of skills. ▽

22. Ask the parents to read parent training manuals (e.g., *Parenting Through Change* by Forgatch) or watch videotapes demonstrat-ing the techniques being learned in session (see Webster-Stratton, 1994). ▽

9. Verbalize a sense of in-creased skill, effectiveness, and confidence in parenting. (17, 23, 24, 25)

17. Support, empower, monitor, and encourage the parents in implementing new strategies for parenting their child, giving feed-back and redirection as needed.

23. Train the parents or refer them to structured training in effective parenting methods (e.g., *1-2-3 Magic* by Phelan; *Parenting with Love and Logic* by Cline and Fay).

24. Educate the parents on the nu-merous key differences between boys and girls, such as rate of development, perspectives, im-pulse control, and anger, and how to handle these differences in the parenting process.

25. Have the children complete the "Parent Report Card" (Berg-Gross) and then give feedback to the parents; support areas of parenting strength and identify weaknesses that need to be bol-stered.

10. Partners express verbal support of each other in the parenting process. (26, 27)

26. Assist the parental team in identifying areas of parenting weaknesses; help the parents im-prove their skills and boost their confidence and follow-through.

27. Help the parents identify and implement specific ways they can support each other as parents and in realizing the ways children work to keep the parents from cooperating in order to get their way (or assign "Evaluating the Strength of Your Parenting Team" in the *Adolescent Psychotherapy Homework Planner,* 2nd ed. by Jongsma, Peterson, and McInnis).

11. Decrease outside pressures, demands, and distractions that drain energy and time from the family. (28, 29)

28. Give the parents permission to not involve their child and themselves in too numerous activities, organizations, or sports.

29. Ask the parents to provide a weekly schedule of their entire family's activities and then evaluate the schedule with them, looking for which activities are valuable and which can possibly be eliminated to create a more focused and relaxed time to parent.

12. Develop skills to talk openly and effectively with the children. (30, 31)

30. Use modeling and role-play to teach the parents to listen more than talk to their child and to use open-ended questions that encourage openness, sharing, and ongoing dialogue.

31. Ask the parents to read material on parent-child communication (e.g., *How to Talk So Kids Will Listen and Listen So Kids Will Talk* by Faber and Mazlish; *Parent Effectiveness Training* by Gordon); help them implement the new communication style in daily dialogue with their children and to see the positive responses each child had to it.

13. Parents verbalize a termination of their perfectionist expectations of the child. (32, 33)

32. Point out to the parents any unreasonable and perfectionist expectations of their child they hold and help them to modify these expectations.

33. Help the parents identify the negative consequences/outcomes that perfectionist expectations have on a child and on the relationship between the parents and the child.

14. Verbalize an increased awareness and understanding of the unique issues and trials of parenting adolescents. (34, 35, 36)

34. Provide the parents with a balanced view of the impact that adolescent peers have on their child.

35. Teach the parents the concept that adolescence is a time of "normal psychosis" (see *Turning Points* by Pittman) in which the parents need to "ride the adolescent rapids" (see *Preparing for Adolescence: How to Survive the Coming Years of Change* by Dobson) until both survive.

36. Assist the parents in coping with the issues and reducing their fears regarding negative peer groups, negative peer influences, and losing their influence to these groups.

15. Increase the gradual letting go of their adolescent in constructive, affirmative ways. (37)

37. Guide the parents in identifying and implementing constructive, affirmative ways they can allow and support the healthy separation of their adolescent.

16. Parents and child report an increased feeling of connectedness between them. (38, 39)

38. Assist the parents in removing and resolving any barriers that prevent or limit connectedness between family members and in identifying activities that will promote connectedness (or assign "One-on-One" in the *Adolescent Psychotherapy Homework Planner,* 2nd ed. by Jongsma, Peterson, and McInnis).

39. Plant the thought with the parents that just "hanging out at home" or being around/available is what quality time is about.

17. Develop and implement realistic and age-appropriate expectations for their child. (40, 41)

40. Have the parents read books to help them develop appropriate limits and expectations for their adolescent (e.g., *Between Parent and Teenager* by Ginott; *Get Out of My Life, But First Could You Take Me and Cheryl to the Mall?* by Wolf; *Grounded for Life* by Tracy; *Parents, Teens, and Boundaries* by Bluestein).

41. Assist the parents in developing appropriate and realistic expectations based on their adolescent's age and level of maturity (or assign "Transitioning from Parenting a Child to Parenting a Teen" in the *Adolescent Psychotherapy Homework Planner,* 2nd ed. by Jongsma, Peterson, and McInnis).

__. _____   __. _____

_____   _____

__. _____   __. _____

_____   _____

__. _____   __. _____

_____   _____

DIAGNOSTIC SUGGESTIONS

Axis I:	309.3	Adjustment Disorder With Disturbance of Conduct
	309.4	Adjustment Disorder With Mixed Disturbance of Emotions and Conduct
	V61.21	Neglect of Child
	V61.20	Parent-Child Relational Problem
	V61.1	Partner Relational Problem

	V61.21	Physical Abuse of Child
	V61.21	Sexual Abuse of Child
	313.81	Oppositional Defiant Disorder
	312.9	Disruptive Behavior Disorder NOS
	312.82	Conduct Disorder, Adolescent-Onset Type
	314.01	Attention-Deficit/Hyperactivity Disorder, Combined Type

_____   _____

_____   _____

Axis II:	301.7	Antisocial Personality Disorder
	301.6	Dependent Personality Disorder
	301.81	Narcissistic Personality Disorder
	301.83	Borderline Personality Disorder
	799.9	Diagnosis Deferred
	V71.09	No Diagnosis

_____   _____

_____   _____

PEER/SIBLING CONFLICT

BEHAVIORAL DEFINITIONS

1. Frequent, overt, intense fighting (verbal and/or physical) with peers and/or siblings.
2. Projects responsibility for conflicts onto others.
3. Believes that he/she is treated unfairly and/or that parents favor sibling(s) over himself/herself.
4. Peer and/or sibling relationships are characterized by bullying, defiance, revenge, taunting, and incessant teasing.
5. Has virtually no friends, or a few who exhibit similar socially disapproved behavior.
6. Exhibits a general pattern of behavior that is impulsive, intimidating, and unmalleable.
7. Behaviors toward peers are aggressive and lack discernible empathy for others.
8. Parents are hostile toward the client, demonstrating a familial pattern of rejection, quarreling, and lack of respect or affection.

—. _____
   _____

—. _____
   _____

—. _____
   _____

LONG-TERM GOALS

1. Form respectful, trusting peer and sibling relationships.
2. Develop healthy mechanisms for handling anxiety, tension, frustration, and anger.

3. Obtain the skills required to build positive peer relationships.
4. Terminate aggressive behavior and replace with assertiveness and empathy.
5. Compete, cooperate, and resolve conflict appropriately with peers and siblings.
6. Parents acquire the necessary parenting skills to model respect, empathy, nurturance, and lack of aggression.

—. _____

   _____

—. _____

   _____

—. _____

   _____

SHORT-TERM OBJECTIVES	THERAPEUTIC INTERVENTIONS
1. Describe relationship with siblings and friends. (1, 2)	1. Actively build a level of trust with client through consistent eye contact, active listening, unconditional positive regard, and warm acceptance to help increase the client's ability to identify and express feelings.
	2. Explore the client's perception of the nature of his/her relationships with siblings and peers; assess the degree of denial regarding conflict and projection of the responsibility for conflict onto others.
2. Decrease the frequency and intensity of aggressive actions toward peers or siblings. (3, 4)	3. Instruct the parents and teachers in social learning techniques of ignoring the client's aggressive acts, except when there is danger of physical injury, while making a concerted effort to attend to and praise all nonaggressive, cooperative, and peaceful behavior.

4. Use The Anger Control Game (Berg) or a similar game to expose the client to new, constructive ways to manage aggressive feelings.

3. Identify verbally and in writing how he/she would like to be treated by others. (5, 6, 7, 8)

5. Play with the client and/or family The Helping, Sharing, Caring Game (Gardner) to develop and expand feelings of respect for self and others.

6. Play with the client The Social Conflict Game (Berg) to assist him/her in developing behavior skills to decrease interpersonal antisocialism with others.

7. Ask the client to list the problems that he/she has with siblings and to suggest concrete solutions (or assign the client and parents the exercise "Negotiating a Peace Treaty" from the *Adolescent Psychotherapy Homework Planner,* 2nd ed. by Jongsma, Peterson, and McInnis).

8. Educate the client about feelings, concentrating on how others feel when they are the focus of aggressive actions and then asking how the client would like to be treated by others.

4. Recognize and verbalize the feelings of others as well as her/his own. (8, 9, 10)

8. Educate the client about feelings, concentrating on how others feel when they are the focus of aggressive actions and then asking how the client would like to be treated by others.

9. Refer the client to a peer therapy group whose objectives are to increase social sensitivity and behavioral flexibility through the use of group exercises (strength bombardment, trusting, walking, expressing negative feelings, etc.).

10. Use The Talking, Feeling, and Doing Game (Gardner; available from Creative Therapeutics) to increase the client's awareness of self and others.

5. Increase socially appropriate behavior with peers and siblings. (6, 11)

6. Play with the client The Social Conflict Game (Berg) to assist him/her in developing behavior skills to decrease interpersonal antisocialism with others.

11. Conduct or refer the client to a behavioral contracting group therapy in which contracts for positive peer interaction are developed each week and reviewed. Positive reinforcers are verbal feedback and small concrete rewards.

6. Participate in peer group activities in a cooperative manner. (12, 13)

12. Direct the parents to involve the client in cooperative activities (e.g., sports, Scouting).

13. Refer the client to an alternative summer camp that focuses on self-esteem and cooperation with peers.

7. Identify feelings associated with the perception that parent(s) have special feelings of favoritism toward a sibling. (14)

14. Ask the client to complete the exercise "Joseph, His Amazing Technicolor Coat, and More" from the *Adolescent Psychotherapy Homework Planner,* 2nd ed. (Jongsma, Peterson, and McInnis) to help the client work through his/her perception that his/her parents have a favorite child.

8. Respond positively to praise and encouragement as evidenced by smiling and expressing gratitude. (15, 16)

15. Use role-playing, modeling, and behavior rehearsal to teach the client to become open and responsive to praise and encouragement.

16. Assist the parents in developing their ability to verbalize affection and appropriate praise to the client in family sessions.

9. Family members decrease the frequency of quarreling and messages of rejection. (17, 18, 19)

10. Verbalize an understanding of the pain that underlies the anger. (20)

11. Implement a brief solution to sibling conflict that has had success in the past. (21, 22)

12. Parents attend a didactic series on positive parenting. (23)

13. Parents implement a behavior modification plan designed

17. Work with the parents in family sessions to reduce parental aggression, messages of rejection, and quarreling within the family.

18. Assign the parents to read *Between Parent and Teenager* (Ginott), especially the chapters "Jealousy" and "Children in Need of Professional Help." Process the reading, identifying key changes in family structure or personal interactions that will need to occur to decrease the level of rivalry.

19. Assign the parents to read *Siblings Without Rivalry* (Faber and Mazlish) and process key concepts with the therapist; ask the parents to choose two suggestions from the reading and implement them with their children.

20. Probe for rejection experiences with family and friends as the causes for the client's anger.

21. Reframe the family members' rivalry as a stage that they will get through with support, or (if appropriate) normalize the issue of the rivalry as something that occurs in all families to varying degrees (see *A Guide to Possibility Land* by O'Hanlon and Beadle).

22. Probe the client and parents to find "time without the problem," "exceptions," or "the ending or stopping pattern" (see *A Guide to Possibility Land* by O'Hanlon and Beadle).

23. Refer the parents to a positive parenting class.

24. Assist the parents in developing and implementing a behavior

to increase the frequency of cooperative social behaviors. (24, 25, 26)

modification plan in which the client's positive interaction with peers and siblings is reinforced immediately with tokens that can be exchanged for preestablished rewards. Monitor and give feedback as indicated.

25. Conduct weekly contract sessions with the client and the parents in which the past week's behavior modification contract is reviewed and revised for the following week. Give feedback and model positive encouragement when appropriate.

26. Institute with the client's parents and teachers a system of positive consequences (see *Solution-Focused Therapy with Children* by Selekman) for the client's misbehavior in order to promote prosocial behaviors (e.g., writing a card to a relative, mowing a neighbor's lawn, doing two good deeds for elderly neighbors, assisting a parent for a day with house-hold projects).

14. Family members engage in conflict resolution in a respectful manner. (27, 28)

27. Read and process in a family therapy session the fable "Raising Cain" or "Cinderella" from *Friedman's Fables* (Friedman).

28. Confront disrespectful expression of feelings in family sessions and use modeling, role-playing, and behavior rehearsal to teach cooperation, respect, and peaceful resolution of conflict.

15. Parents terminate alliances with children that foster sibling conflict. (29, 30, 31)

29. Assist the parents in identifying specific things they could do within their home (e.g., creating separate rooms, eating at the dinner table) or to alter the family

procedures (e.g., not putting one child in charge of the other) to reduce sibling conflict. Help the parents identify and make all changes and monitor their effectiveness after implementation.

30. Ask the parents to read *How to End the Sibling Wars* (Bieniek) and coach them on implementing several of the suggestions; follow up by monitoring, encouraging, and redirecting as needed.

31. Hold family therapy sessions to assess dynamics and alliances that may underlie peer or sibling conflict.

16. Family members verbalize increased cooperation and respect for one another. (32, 33)

32. Refer the family to an experiential or alternative weekend program (i.e., ropes course, cooperative problem-solving, trust activities). Afterward, process the experience with the family members, focusing on two to three specific things gained in terms of cooperation, respect, and trust.

33. Explore with the siblings to find an appropriate common point they would like to change in the family (e.g., amount of allowance, later bedtime/curfew) and then conduct a family session in which the siblings work together to negotiate the issue with the parents. Coach both sides in negotiating and move the parents to accept this point on a specific condition of decreased conflict between siblings.

17. Verbalize an acceptance of differences between siblings rather than being critical of each person's uniqueness. (34)

34. Hold a family sibling session in which each child lists and verbalizes an appreciation of each sibling's unique traits or abilities

(or assign the exercise "Cloning the Perfect Sibling" from the *Adolescent Psychotherapy Homework Planner,* 2nd ed. by Jongsma, Peterson, and McInnis).

18. Complete the recommended psychiatric or psychological testing/evaluation. (35)

19. Comply with the recommendations of the mental health evaluations. (36)

35. Assess and refer the client for a psychiatric or psychological evaluation.

36. Facilitate and monitor client and the parents in implementing the recommendations of the evaluations.

—. _____

_____

—. _____

_____

—. _____

_____

—. _____

_____

—. _____

_____

—. _____

_____

DIAGNOSTIC SUGGESTIONS

Axis I:	313.81	Oppositional Defiant Disorder
	312.81	Conduct Disorder, Childhood-Onset Type
	312.82	Conduct Disorder, Adolescent-Onset Type
	312.9	Disruptive Behavior Disorder NOS
	314.01	Attention-Deficit/Hyperactivity Disorder, Predominantly Hyperactive-Impulsive Type
	314.9	Attention-Deficit/Hyperactivity Disorder NOS
	V62.81	Relational Problem NOS
	V71.02	Child or Adolescent Antisocial Behavior
	315.00	Reading Disorder
	315.9	Learning Disorder NOS
	_____	_____
	_____	_____
Axis II:	799.9	Diagnosis Deferred
	V71.09	No Diagnosis
	_____	_____
	_____	_____

PHYSICAL/EMOTIONAL ABUSE VICTIM

BEHAVIORAL DEFINITIONS

1. Confirmed self-report or account by others of having been assaulted (e.g., hitting, burning, kicking, slapping, torture) by an older person.
2. Bruises or wounds as evidence of victimization.
3. Self-reports of being injured by a supposed caregiver coupled with feelings of fear and social withdrawal.
4. Significant increase in the frequency and severity of aggressive behaviors toward peers or adults.
5. Recurrent and intrusive distressing recollections of the abuse.
6. Feelings of anger, rage, or fear when in contact with the perpetrator.
7. Frequent and prolonged periods of depression, irritability, anxiety, and/or apathetic withdrawal.
8. Sleep disturbances (e.g., difficulty falling asleep, night terrors, recurrent distressing nightmares).
9. Running away from home to avoid further physical assaults.

—. _____
   _____
—. _____
   _____
—. _____
   _____

LONG-TERM GOALS

1. Terminate the physical abuse.
2. Escape from the environment where the abuse is occurring and move to a safe haven.

3. Rebuild sense of self-worth and overcome the overwhelming sense of fear, shame, and sadness.
4. Resolve feelings of fear and depression while improving communication and the boundaries of respect within the family.
5. Caregivers establish limits on the punishment of the client such that no physical harm can occur and respect for his/her rights is maintained.
6. Client and his/her family eliminate denial, putting the responsibility for the abuse on the perpetrator and allowing the victim to feel supported.
7. Reduce displays of aggression that reflect abuse and keep others at an emotional distance.
8. Build self-esteem and a sense of empowerment as manifested by an increased number of positive self-descriptive statements and greater participation in extracurricular activities.

—. _____

_____

—. _____

_____

—. _____

_____

SHORT-TERM OBJECTIVES

1. Tell the entire account of the most recent abuse. (1, 2, 3)

THERAPEUTIC INTERVENTIONS

1. Actively build the level of trust with the client through consistent eye contact, active listening, unconditional positive regard, and warm acceptance to help him/her increase the ability to identify and express facts and feelings about the abuse.

2. Explore, encourage, and support the client in verbally expressing and clarifying the facts associated with the abuse.

3. Assign the client to complete the "Take the First Step" exercise from the *Adolescent Psychotherapy Homework Planner,* 2nd ed. (Jongsma, Peterson, and McInnis)

2. Identify the nature, frequency, and duration of the abuse. (2, 4, 5)

3. Agree to actions taken to protect self and provide boundaries against any future abuse or retaliation. (6, 7, 8)

4. Identify and express the feelings connected to the abuse. (9)

in which he/she can read a story of a teenager who was abused and shared it with a trusted adult.

2. Explore, encourage, and support the client in verbally expressing and clarifying the facts associated with the abuse.

4. Report physical abuse to the appropriate child protection agency, criminal justice officials, or medical professionals.

5. Consult with the family, a physician, criminal justice officials, or child protection case managers to assess the veracity of the physical abuse charges.

6. Assess whether the perpetrator or the client should be removed from the client's home.

7. Implement the necessary steps (e.g., removal of the client from the home, removal of the perpetrator from the home) to protect the client and other children in the home from further physical abuse.

8. Reassure the client repeatedly of concern and caring on the part of the therapist and others who will protect him/her from any further abuse.

9. Explore, encourage, and support the client in expressing and clarifying his/her feelings toward the perpetrator and himself/herself (or assign the homework exercise "My Thoughts and Feelings" in the *Adolescent Psychotherapy Homework Planner,* 2nd ed. by Jongsma, Peterson, and McInnis).

5. Terminate verbalizations of denial or making excuses for the perpetrator. (10, 11, 12)

10. Actively confront and challenge denial within the perpetrator and the entire family system.

11. Confront the client about making excuses for the perpetrator's abuse and accepting blame for it.

12. Reassure the client that he/she did not deserve the abuse but that he/she deserves respect and a controlled response even in punishment situations.

6. Perpetrator takes responsibility for the abuse. (13, 14)

13. Reinforce any and all client statements that put responsibility clearly on the perpetrator for the abuse, regardless of any misbehavior by the client.

14. Hold a family therapy session in which the client and/or therapist confront the perpetrator with the abuse.

7. Perpetrator asks for forgiveness and pledges respect for disciplinary boundaries. (15)

15. Conduct a family therapy session in which the perpetrator apologizes to the client and/or other family member(s) for the abuse.

8. Perpetrator agrees to seek treatment. (16, 17, 18)

16. Require the perpetrator to participate in a child abusers' psychotherapy group.

17. Refer the perpetrator for a psychological evaluation and treatment.

18. Evaluate the possibility of substance abuse with the perpetrator or within the family; refer the perpetrator and/or family member(s) for substance abuse treatment, if indicated.

9. Parents and caregivers verbalize the establishment of appropriate disciplinary boundaries to ensure protection of the client. (19, 20)

19. Counsel the client's family about appropriate disciplinary boundaries.

20. Ask the parents/caregivers to list appropriate means of discipline

or correction; reinforce reasonable actions and appropriate boundaries that reflect respect for the rights and feelings of the child.

10. Family members identify the stressors or other factors that may trigger violence. (21, 22)

21. Construct a multigenerational family genogram that identifies physical abuse within the extended family to help the perpetrator recognize the cycle of violence.

22. Assess the client's family dynamics and explore for the stress factors or precipitating events that contributed to the emergence of the abuse.

11. Nonabusive parent and other key family members verbalize support and acceptance of the client. (23)

23. Elicit and reinforce support and nurturance of the client from the nonabusive parent and other key family members.

12. Reduce the expressions of rage and aggressiveness that stem from feelings of helplessness related to physical abuse. (24, 25)

24. Assign the client to write a letter expressing feelings of hurt, fear, and anger to the perpetrator; process the letter.

25. Interpret the client's generalized expressions of anger and aggression as triggered by feelings toward the perpetrator.

13. Decrease the statements of being a victim while increasing the statements that reflect personal empowerment. (26, 27)

26. Empower the client by identifying sources of help against abuse (e.g., phone numbers to call, a safe place to run to, asking for temporary alternate protective placement).

27. Assist the client in writing his/her thoughts and feelings regarding the abuse (or assign the exercise "Letter of Empowerment" in the *Adolescent Psychotherapy Homework Planner,* 2nd ed. by Jongsma, Peterson, and McInnis).

14. Increase the frequency of positive self-descriptive statements. (28, 29)

28. Assist the client in identifying a basis for self-worth by reviewing his/her talents, importance to others, and intrinsic spiritual value.

29. Reinforce positive statements that the client has made about himself/herself and the future.

15. Express forgiveness of the perpetrator and others connected with the abuse while insisting on respect for own right to safety in the future. (15, 30, 31)

15. Conduct a family therapy session in which the perpetrator apologizes to the client and/or other family member(s) for the abuse.

30. Assign the client to write a forgiveness letter and/or complete a forgiveness exercise in which he/she verbalizes forgiveness to the perpetrator and/or significant family member(s) while asserting the right to safety. Process this letter.

31. Assign the client a letting-go exercise in which a symbol of the abuse is disposed of or destroyed. Process this experience.

16. Increase socialization with peers and family. (32, 33, 34)

32. Encourage the client to make plans for the future that involve interacting with his/her peers and family.

33. Encourage the client to participate in positive peer groups or extracurricular activities.

34. Refer the client to a victim support group with other children to assist him/her in realizing that he/she is not alone in this experience.

17. Increase the level of trust of others as shown by increased socialization and a greater number of friendships. (35, 36, 37)

35. Facilitate the client expressing loss of trust in adults and relate this loss to the perpetrator's abusive behavior and the lack of protection provided.

36. Assist the client in making discriminating judgments that allow for trust of some people rather than distrust of all.

18. Verbalize how the abuse has affected feelings toward self. (38, 39)

37. Teach the client the share-check method of building trust, in which a degree of shared information is related to a proven level of trustworthiness.

38. Assign the client to draw pictures that represent how he/she feels about himself/herself.

39. Ask the client to draw pictures of his/her own face that represent how he/she felt about himself/herself before, during, and after the abuse occurred.

19. Verbalize instances of aggressive behavior toward peers and/or authority figures. (40)

40. Assess the client for adopting the aggressive manner that he/she has been exposed to in the home (see Anger Management chapter in this *Planner*).

20. Recognize how aggressive behavior impacts other people's feelings. (41)

41. Use role-playing and role reversal techniques to sensitize the client to the feelings of the target of his/her anger.

21. Acknowledge the use of alcohol and/or drugs as an escape from the pain and anger resulting from abuse. (42, 43)

42. Assess the client's use and abuse of alcohol or illicit drugs or refer him/her for a substance abuse evaluation and treatment if indicated (see Chemical Dependence chapter in this *Planner*).

43. Interpret the client's substance abuse as a maladaptive coping behavior for his/her feelings related to abuse.

___. _____

___. _____

___. _____

DIAGNOSTIC SUGGESTIONS

Axis I:	309.81	Posttraumatic Stress Disorder
	308.3	Acute Stress Disorder
	995.54	Physical Abuse of Child (Victim)
	300.4	Dysthymic Disorder
	296.xx	Major Depressive Disorder
	300.02	Generalized Anxiety Disorder
	307.47	Nightmare Disorder
	313.81	Oppositional Defiant Disorder
	312.81	Conduct Disorder, Childhood-Onset Type
	300.6	Depersonalization Disorder
	300.15	Dissociative Disorder NOS
	_____	_____
	_____	_____
Axis II:	799.9	Diagnosis Deferred
	V71.09	No Diagnosis
	_____	_____
	_____	_____

POSTTRAUMATIC STRESS
DISORDER (PTSD)

BEHAVIORAL DEFINITIONS

1. Exposure to threats of death or serious injury, or subjection to actual injury, that resulted in an intense emotional response of fear, helplessness, or horror.
2. Intrusive, distressing thoughts or images that recall the traumatic event.
3. Disturbing dreams associated with the traumatic event.
4. A sense that the event is recurring, as in illusions or flashbacks.
5. Intense distress when exposed to reminders of the traumatic event.
6. Physiological reactivity when exposed to internal or external cues that symbolize the traumatic event.
7. Avoidance of thoughts, feelings, or conversations about the traumatic event.
8. Avoidance of activity, places, or people associated with the traumatic event.
9. Inability to recall some important aspect of the traumatic event.
10. Lack of interest and participation in formerly meaningful activities.
11. A sense of detachment from others.
12. Inability to experience the full range of emotions, including love.
13. A pessimistic, fatalistic attitude regarding the future.
14. Sleep disturbance.
15. Irritability or angry outbursts.
16. Lack of concentration.
17. Hypervigilance.
18. Exaggerated startle response.
19. Symptoms have been present for more than 1 month.
20. Sad or guilty affect and other signs of depression.
21. Verbally and/or physically violent threats or behavior.

__. _____

_____

—. _____
_____
_____

—. _____
_____

LONG-TERM GOALS

1. Recall the traumatic event without becoming overwhelmed with negative emotions.
2. Interact normally with friends and family without irrational fears or intrusive thoughts that control behavior.
3. Return to pretrauma level of functioning without avoiding people, places, thoughts, or feelings associated with the traumatic event.
4. Display a full range of emotions without experiencing loss of control.
5. Develop and implement effective coping skills that allow for carrying out normal responsibilities and participating in relationships and social activities.

—. _____
_____
_____

—. _____
_____
_____

—. _____
_____

SHORT-TERM OBJECTIVES

THERAPEUTIC INTERVENTIONS

1. Describe the history and nature of PTSD symptoms. (1, 2)

1. Establish rapport with the client toward building a therapeutic alliance.

2. Assess the client's frequency, intensity, duration, and history of PTSD symptoms and their impact on functioning (e.g., *The Anxiety Disorders Interview Schedule for Children—Parent Version or Child Version* by Silverman and Albano).

2. Complete psychological tests designed to assess and or track the nature and severity of PTSD symptoms. (3)

3. Administer or refer the client for administration of psychological testing to assess for the presence or strength of PTSD symptoms (e.g., Clinician-Administered PTSD Scale–Child and Adolescent Version [CAPS-C] by Nader, Blake, Kriegler, and Pynoos).

3. Describe the traumatic event in as much detail as possible. (4)

4. Gently and sensitively explore the client's recollection of the facts of the traumatic incident and his/her emotional reactions at the time (or assign "Impact of Frightening or Dangerous Event" in the *Adolescent Psychotherapy Homework Planner,* 2nd ed. by Jongsma, Peterson, and McInnis).

4. Verbalize the symptoms of depression, including any suicidal ideation. (5)

5. Assess the client's depth of depression and suicide potential and treat appropriately, taking the necessary safety precautions as indicated (see Depression and Suicidal Ideation chapters in this *Planner*).

5. Provide honest and complete information for a chemical dependence biopsychosocial history. (6)

6. Conduct or arrange for a complete chemical dependence evaluation that assesses substance abuse history, frequency and nature of drugs used, peer use, physiological dependence signs, family use, and consequences.

6. Verbalize a recognition that mood-altering chemicals were used as the primary coping mechanism to escape from stress or pain, and that their use resulted in negative consequences. (7, 8)

7. Explore how the client's substance abuse was used as a coping mechanism for the fear, guilt, and rage associated with the trauma.

8. Refer the client for treatment for chemical dependence (see Chemical Dependence chapter in this *Planner*).

▼ 7. Cooperate with an evaluation by a physician for psychotropic medication. (9, 10)

9. Assess the client's need for medication (e.g., selective serotonin reuptake inhibitors) and arrange for prescription, if appropriate. ▼

10. Monitor and evaluate the client's psychotropic medication prescription compliance and the effectiveness of the medication on his/her level of functioning. ▼

▼ 8. Participate in individual or group therapy sessions focused on PTSD. (11)

11. Conduct group or individual therapy sessions based on Multimodality Trauma Treatment (see "Cognitive-behavioral psychotherapy for children and adolescents with Posttraumatic Stress Disorder following a single-incident stressor" by March, Amaya-Jackson, Murray, and Schulte in *Journal of the American Academy of Child and Adolescent Psychiatry*, 1998, vol. 37, 585–93). ▼

▼ 9. Verbalize an accurate understanding of PTSD and how it develops. (12, 13)

12. Discuss a biopsychosocial model of PTSD including that it results from exposure to trauma, results in intrusive recollection, unwarranted fears, anxiety, and a vulnerability to other negative emotions such as shame, anger, and guilt; normalize the client's experiences (see "Traumatic Stress Disorders" by Davidson and March in *Psychiatry, Vol. 2* by Tasman, Kay, and Lieberman [eds.]). ▼

13. Assign the client to read psychoeducational chapters of books or treatment manuals on PTSD that explain its features and development (e.g., *It Happened to Me* by Carter). ▼

▼ indicates that the Objective/Intervention is consistent with those found in evidence-based treatments.

▽10. Verbalize an understanding of the rationale for treatment of PTSD. (14, 15)

14. Discuss how coping skills, cognitive restructuring, and exposure help build confidence, desensitize and overcome fears, and see one's self, others, and the world in a less fearful and/or depressing way. ▽

15. Assign the client to read about anxiety management, stress inoculation, cognitive restructuring, and/or exposure-based therapy in chapters of books or treatment manuals on PTSD (e.g., *The PTSD Workbook* by Williams and Poijula). ▽

▽11. Learn and implement calming and coping strategies to manage challenging situations related to trauma. (16, 17)

16. Teach the client strategies from Anxiety Management Training or Stress Inoculation Training such as relaxation, breathing control, covert modeling (i.e., imagining the successful use of the strategies) and/or role-playing (i.e., with therapist or trusted other) for managing fears until a sense of mastery is evident (see *Cognitive Behavioral Psychotherapy* by Francis and Beidel, or *Clinical Handbook for Treating PTSD* by Meichenbaum). ▽

17. Assign the client to read about calming and coping strategies in books or treatment manuals on PTSD (e.g., *The PTSD Workbook* by Williams and Poijula). ▽

▽12. Learn and implement anger management techniques. (18)

18. Teach the client anger management techniques such as taking time out, engaging in physical exercise and relaxation, and expressing feelings assertively (see Anger Management chapter in this *Planner*). ▽

▼13. Identify, challenge, and replace fearful self-talk with reality-based, positive self-talk. (19, 20, 21)

19. Explore the client's schema and self-talk that mediate his/her trauma-related fears; identify and challenge biases; assist him/her in generating appraisals that correct for the biases and build confidence. ▼

20. Assign the client to read about cognitive restructuring in books or treatment manuals on social anxiety (e.g., *The PTSD Workbook* by Williams and Poijula). ▼

21. Assign the client a homework exercise in which he/she identifies fearful self-talk and creates reality-based alternatives (or assign "Bad Thoughts Lead to Depressed Feelings" in the *Adolescent Psychotherapy Homework Planner,* 2nd ed. by Jongsma, Peterson, and McInnis); review and reinforce success, providing corrective feedback for failure. ▼

▼14. Participate in imaginal and in vivo exposure to trauma-related memories. (22, 23, 24, 25)

22. Direct and assist the client in constructing a detailed narrative description of the trauma(s) for imaginal exposure; construct a fear and avoidance hierarchy of feared and avoided trauma-related stimuli for in vivo exposure. ▼

23. Have the client undergo imaginal exposure to the trauma by having them describe a traumatic experience at an increasing but client-chosen level of detail, repeating until associated anxiety reduces and stabilizes; record the session, having the client listen to it between sessions (see *Posttraumatic Stress Disorder* by Resick and Calhoun). ▼

24. Assign the client a homework exercise in which he/she repeats the narrative exposure or does in vivo exposure to environmental stimuli as rehearsed in therapy (or assign "Gradually Facing a Phobic Fear" in the *Adolescent Psychotherapy Homework Planner,* 2nd ed. by Jongsma, Peterson, and McInnis); review and reinforce progress (see *Posttraumatic Stress Disorder* by Resick and Calhoun). ▽

25. Assign the client to read about exposure therapy (e.g., *The PTSD Workbook* by Williams and Poijula). ▽

▽15. Learn and implement thought-stopping to manage intrusive unwanted thoughts. (26)

26. Teach the client thought-stopping in which he/she internally voices the word "stop" and/or imagines something representing the concept of stopping (e.g., a stop sign or light) immediately upon noticing unwanted trauma or otherwise negative unwanted thoughts (or assign "Making Use of the Thought-Stopping Technique" in the *Adult Psychotherapy Homework Planner,* 2nd ed. by Jongsma). ▽

▽16. Learn and implement guided self-dialogue to manage maladaptive thoughts, feelings, and urges. (27)

27. Teach the client a guided self-dialogue procedure in which he/she learns to recognize maladaptive self-talk brought on by encounters with trauma-related stimuli; teach him/her to challenge biases, cope with engendered feelings, and overcome avoidance (see *Posttraumatic Stress Disorder* by Resick and Calhoun). ▽

▽ 17. Implement relapse prevention strategies for managing possible future trauma-related symptoms. (28, 29, 30, 31)

28. Discuss with the client the distinction between a lapse and relapse, associating a lapse with an initial and reversible return of symptoms, fear, or urges to avoid and relapse with the decision to return to fearful and avoidant patterns. ▽

29. Identify and rehearse with the client the management of future situations or circumstances in which lapses could occur. ▽

30. Instruct the client to routinely use strategies learned in therapy (e.g., using cognitive restructuring, social skills, and exposure) while building social interactions and relationships. ▽

31. Develop a "coping card" or other reminder on which coping strategies and other important information (e.g., "Pace your breathing," "Focus on the task at hand," "You can manage it," "It will go away") are recorded for the client's later use. ▽

18. Cooperate with eye movement desensitization and reprocessing (EMDR) technique to reduce emotional reaction to the traumatic event. (32)

32. Utilize the EMDR technique to reduce the client's emotional reactivity to the traumatic event.

19. Implement a regular exercise regimen as a stress release technique. (33, 34)

33. Develop and encourage a routine of physical exercise for the client.

34. Recommend that the client read and implement programs from *Exercising Your Way to Better Mental Health* (Leith).

20. Sleep without being disturbed by dreams of the trauma. (35)

35. Monitor the client's sleep pattern and encourage use of relaxation, positive imagery, and sleep hygiene as aids to sleep (see Sleep Disturbance chapter in this *Planner*).

21. Participate in conjoint and/or family therapy sessions. (36)

36. Conduct family and conjoint sessions to facilitate healing of hurt caused by the client's symptoms of PTSD.

22. Participate in group support therapy sessions focused on sustaining recovery from PTSD. (37)

37. Refer the client to or conduct group therapy sessions where the focus is on sharing traumatic events and their effects with other PTSD survivors.

23. Verbalize hopeful and positive statements regarding the future. (38)

38. Reinforce the client's positive, reality-based cognitive messages that enhance self-confidence and increase adaptive action.

__. _____

__. _____

__. _____

__. _____

__. _____

__. _____

DIAGNOSTIC SUGGESTIONS

Axis I:

309.81	Posttraumatic Stress Disorder
309.xx	Adjustment Disorder
995.54	Physical Abuse of Child (Victim)
995.53	Sexual Abuse of Child (Victim)
308.3	Acute Stress Disorder
296.xx	Major Depressive Disorder
_____	_____
_____	_____

Axis II:

799.9	Diagnosis Deferred
V71.09	No Diagnosis on Axis II
_____	_____
_____	_____

PSYCHOTICISM

BEHAVIORAL DEFINITIONS

1. Bizarre thought content (delusions of grandeur, persecution, reference, influence, control, somatic sensations, or infidelity).
2. Illogical form of thought or speech (loose association of ideas in speech; incoherence; illogical thinking; vague, abstract, or repetitive speech; neologisms; perseverations; clanging).
3. Perception disturbance (hallucinations, primarily auditory but occasionally visual or olfactory).
4. Disturbed affect (blunted, none, flattened, or inappropriate).
5. Lost sense of self (loss of ego boundaries, lack of identity, blatant confusion).
6. Diminished volition (inadequate interest, drive, or ability to follow a course of action to its logical conclusion; pronounced ambivalence or cessation of goal-directed activity).
7. Relationship withdrawal (withdrawal from involvement with the external world and preoccupation with egocentric ideas and fantasies; alienation feelings).
8. Poor social skills (misinterpretation of the actions or motives of others; maintaining emotional distance from others; feeling awkward and threatened in most social situations; embarrassment of others by failure to recognize the impact of own behavior).
9. Inadequate control over sexual, aggressive, or frightening thoughts, feelings, or impulses (blatantly sexual or aggressive fantasies; fears of impending doom; acting out sexual or aggressive impulses in an unpredictable and unusual manner, often directed toward family and friends).
10. Psychomotor abnormalities (a marked decrease in reactivity to the environment; various catatonic patterns such as stupor, rigidity, excitement, posturing, or negativism; unusual mannerisms or grimacing).

__. _____

_____

—. _____

  _____

—. _____

  _____

LONG-TERM GOALS

1. Control or eliminate active psychotic symptoms such that supervised functioning is positive and medication is taken consistently.
2. Significantly reduce or eliminate hallucinations and/or delusions.
3. Eliminate acute, reactive psychotic symptoms and return to normal functioning in affect, thinking, and relating.
4. Interact appropriately in social situations and improve the reality-based understanding of and reaction to the behaviors and motives of others.
5. Attain control over disturbing thoughts, feelings, and impulses.

—. _____

  _____

—. _____

  _____

—. _____

  _____

SHORT-TERM OBJECTIVES

1. Describe thoughts about self and others; history, content, nature, and frequency of hallucinations or delusions; fantasies and fears. (1, 2)

2. Establish trust and therapeutic alliance to begin to express feelings and discuss the nature of psychotic symptoms. (3)

THERAPEUTIC INTERVENTIONS

1. Assess the pervasiveness of the client's thought disorder through a clinical interview.

2. Determine if the client's psychosis is of a brief, reactive nature or long-term with prodromal and reactive elements.

3. Provide supportive therapy characterized by genuine warmth, understanding, and acceptance to reduce the client's distrust, alleviate fears, and promote openness.

3. Cooperate with psychological testing to assess severity and type of psychosis. (4)

4. Administer or arrange for psychological testing to assess the client's severity and type of psychosis; provide feedback to the client and parents.

4. Family members and client provide psychosocial history of the client and the extended family. (5)

5. Explore the client's personal and family history for serious mental illness and significant traumas or stressors.

5. Accept and understand that the distressing thought disorder symptoms are due to mental illness. (6)

6. Explain to the client the nature of the psychotic process, its biochemical component, and the confusing effect on rational thought.

6. Take antipsychotic medications consistently with or without supervision. (7, 8)

7. Arrange for the administration of appropriate antipsychotic medications to the client.

8. Monitor the client for medication compliance and redirect if he/she is noncompliant.

7. Move to appropriate hospital or residential setting. (9)

9. Arrange for an appropriate level of residential or hospital care if the client may be harmful to self or others or unable to care for his/her own basic needs.

8. Verbally identify the stressors that contributed to the reactive psychosis. (10, 11, 12, 13)

10. Probe the external or internal stressors that may account for the client's reactive psychosis.

11. Explore the client's feelings about the stressors that triggered the psychotic episodes.

12. Assist the client in identifying threats in the environment and develop a plan with the family to reduce these stressors.

13. Explore the client's history for significant separations, losses, or traumas.

9. Family members verbalize increased understanding of and knowledge about the client's illness and treatment. (14)

10. Family members increase positive support of the client to reduce the chances of acute exacerbation of the psychotic episode. (15, 16)

11. Parents increase frequency of communicating to the client with direct eye contact, clear language, and complete thoughts. (17, 18)

12. Parents terminate hostile, critical responses to the client and increase their statements of praise, optimism, and affirmation. (19, 20)

13. Family members share their feelings of guilt, frustration, and fear associated with the client's mental illness. (21)

14. Arrange for family therapy sessions to educate the family regarding the client's illness, treatment, and prognosis.

15. Encourage the parents to involve the client in here-and-now-based social and recreational activities (e.g., intramural sports, after-school enrichment programs, YMCA structured programs).

16. Encourage the parents to look for opportunities to praise and reinforce the client for engaging in responsible, adaptive, and pro-social behaviors.

17. Assist the family in avoiding double-bind messages that are inconsistent and contradictory, resulting in increased anxiety, confusion, and psychotic symptoms in the client.

18. Confront the parents in family therapy when their communication is indirect and disjointed, leaving the client confused and anxious.

19. Hold family therapy sessions to reduce the atmosphere of criticism and hostility toward the client and promote an understanding of the client and his/her illness.

20. Support the parents in setting firm limits without hostility on the client's inappropriate aggressive or sexual behavior.

21. Encourage the family members to share their feelings of frustration, guilt, fear, or depression surrounding the client's mental illness and behavior patterns.

14. Stay current with school work, completing assignments and interacting appropriately with peers and teachers. (22, 23)

22. Arrange for and/or encourage ongoing academic training while the client is receiving psychological treatment.

23. Contact school personnel (having obtained the necessary confidentiality releases) to educate them regarding the client's unusual behavior and his/her need for an accepting, supportive environment.

15. Verbalize an understanding of the underlying needs, conflicts, and emotions that support the irrational beliefs. (24)

24. Probe the client's underlying needs and feelings (e.g., inadequacy, rejection, anxiety, guilt) that contribute to internal conflict and irrational beliefs.

16. Think more clearly as demonstrated by logical, coherent speech. (25, 26)

25. Gently confront the client's illogical thoughts and speech to refocus disordered thinking.

26. Assist in restructuring the client's irrational beliefs by reviewing reality-based evidence and misinterpretation.

17. Report a diminishing or absence of hallucinations and/or delusions. (27, 28, 29)

27. Encourage the client to focus on the reality of the external world as opposed to distorted fantasy.

28. Differentiate for the client between the sources of stimuli from self-generated messages and the reality of the external world.

29. Interpret the client's inaccurate perceptions or bizarre associations as reflective of unspoken fears of rejection or losing control.

18. Demonstrate control over inappropriate thoughts, feelings, and impulses by verbalizing a reduced frequency of occurrence. (28, 30, 31)

28. Differentiate for the client between the sources of stimuli from self-generated messages and the reality of the external world.

30. Set firm limits on the client's inappropriate aggressive or sexual

behavior that emanates from a lack of impulse control or a misperception of reality.

31. Monitor the client's daily level of functioning (i.e., reality orientation, personal hygiene, social interactions, affect appropriateness) and give feedback that either redirects or reinforces the behavior.

19. Begin to show limited social functioning by responding appropriately to friendly encounters. (32, 33)

32. Use role-playing and behavioral rehearsal of social situations to explore and teach the client alternative positive social interactions with family and friends.

33. Reinforce socially and emotionally appropriate responses to others.

20. Family members accept a referral to a support group. (34)

34. Refer family members to a community-based support group designed for the families of psychotic clients.

___. _____
_____
___. _____
_____
___. _____
_____

___. _____
_____
___. _____
_____
___. _____
_____

DIAGNOSTIC SUGGESTIONS

Axis I:	297.1	Delusional Disorder
	298.8	Brief Psychotic Disorder
	295.xx	Schizophrenia
	295.30	Schizophrenia, Paranoid Type
	295.70	Schizoaffective Disorder
	295.40	Schizophreniform Disorder
	296.xx	Bipolar I Disorder
	296.89	Bipolar II Disorder

296.24	Major Depressive Disorder, Single Episode With Psychotic Features
296.34	Major Depressive Disorder, Recurrent With Psychotic Features
310.1	Personality Change Due to Axis III Disorder

_____   _____

_____   _____

Axis II: 799.9   Diagnosis Deferred
             V71.09   No Diagnosis

_____   _____

_____   _____

RUNAWAY

BEHAVIORAL DEFINITIONS

1. Running away from home for a day or more without parental permission.
2. Pattern of running to the noncustodial parent, relative, or friend when conflicts arise with the custodial parent or guardian.
3. Running away from home and crossing state lines.
4. Running away from home overnight at least twice.
5. Running away at least one time without returning within 48 hours.
6. Poor self-image and feelings of worthlessness and inadequacy.
7. Chaotic, violent, or abusive home environment.
8. Severe conflict with parents.
9. Victim of physical, sexual, or emotional abuse.

—. _____
_____

—. _____
_____

—. _____
_____

LONG-TERM GOALS

1. Develop a closer, more caring relationship with the parents.
2. Reduce the level, frequency, and degree of family conflicts.
3. Attain the necessary skills to cope with family stress without resorting to the flight response.
4. Caregivers terminate any abuse of the client and establish a nurturing family environment with appropriate boundaries.
5. Eliminate the runaway behavior.

6. Begin the process of healthy separation from the family.
7. Parents demonstrate acceptance and respect for the client.

—. _____

_____

—. _____

_____

—. _____

_____

SHORT-TERM OBJECTIVES

1. Verbalize the emotions causing a need to escape from the home environment. (1, 2)

2. Identify and implement alternative reactions to conflictual situations. (3, 4)

3. Increase communication with and the expressed level of understanding of the parents. (5, 6)

THERAPEUTIC INTERVENTIONS

1. Actively build the level of trust with the client in individual sessions through consistent eye contact, active listening, unconditional positive regard, and warm acceptance to help him/her increase the ability to identify and express feelings.

2. Facilitate the client's expression of emotions that prompt the runaway behavior.

3. Ask the client to list all possible constructive ways of handling conflictual situations and process the list with the therapist.

4. Train the client in alternative ways of handling conflictual situations (e.g., being assertive with his/her wishes or plans, staying out of conflicts that are parents' issues) and assist him/her in implementing them into his/her daily life.

5. Conduct family therapy sessions with the client and his/her parents to facilitate healthy, positive communications.

4. Parents and client express acceptance of and responsibility for their share of the conflict between them. (7)

5. Parents terminate physical and/or sexual abuse of the client. (8, 9)

6. Parents acknowledge chemical dependence problem and accept referral for treatment. (10)

7. Parents identify unresolved issues with their parents and begin to move toward resolving each issue. (11, 12)

8. Parents decrease messages of rejection. (13)

6. Assign the client to attend a problem-solving psychoeducation group.

7. Assist the parents and the client in each accepting responsibility for their share of the conflicts in the home.

8. Explore for the occurrence of physical or sexual abuse to the client with the client and his/her family.

9. Arrange for the client to be placed in respite care or in another secure setting, if necessary, while the family works in family therapy to resolve conflicts that have led to abuse or neglect of the client.

10. Evaluate the parents for chemical dependence and its effect on the client; refer parents for treatment if necessary.

11. Hold a family session in which a detailed genogram is developed with a particular emphasis on unresolved issues between the client's parents and their own parents. Then assist the client's parents in coming to see the importance of resolving these issues before change can possibly occur in their own family system.

12. Facilitate sessions with the client's parents to assist in working through past unresolved issues with their own parents.

13. Help the client's parents identify and alter parenting techniques, interactions, or other messages that communicate rejection to the client.

9. Parents attend a didactic group focused on teaching positive parenting skills. (14)

14. Refer the parents to a class that teaches positive and effective parenting skills.

10. Parents identify and implement ways they can make the client feel valued and cherished within the family. (14, 15, 16)

14. Refer the parents to a class that teaches positive and effective parenting skills.

15. Assign the parents to read books on parenting (e.g., *Parent Effectiveness Training* [P.E.T.] by Gordon; *Raising Self-Reliant Children in a Self-Indulgent World* by Glenn and Nelsen); process what they have learned from reading the material assigned.

16. Assist the parents in identifying ways to make the client feel more valued (e.g., work out age-appropriate privileges with the client, give the client specific responsibilities in the family, ask for client's input on family decisions) as an individual and as part of the family; elicit a commitment from the parents for implementation of client-affirming behaviors.

11. Identify own needs in the family that are unsatisfied. (17)

17. Ask the client to make a list of his/her needs in the family that are not met. Process the list in an individual session and at an appropriate later time in a family therapy session.

12. Identify ways that unmet needs might be satisfied by means outside the family. (18)

18. Assist the client in identifying how he/she might meet his/her own unmet needs (e.g., obtain a Big Brother or Big Sister, find a job, develop a close friendship). Encourage the client to begin to meet those unmet needs that would be age-appropriate to pursue.

13. Verbalize hurt and angry feelings connected to the family and how it functions. (19, 20, 21)

19. Assign the client to write a description of how he/she perceives his/her family dynamics and then to keep a daily journal of

incidents that support or refute his/her perception (or assign the exercise "Home by Another Name" or "Undercover Assignment" from the *Adolescent Psychotherapy Homework Planner,* 2nd ed. by Jongsma, Peterson, and McInnis).

20. Assist the client in identifying specific issues of conflict he/she has with the family (or assign the "Airing Your Grievance" exercise from the *Adolescent Psychotherapy Homework Planner,* 2nd ed. by Jongsma, Peterson, and McInnis).

21. Support and encourage the client when he/she begins to appropriately verbalize anger or other negative feelings.

14. Identify and implement constructive ways to interact with the parents. (22)

22. Help the client identify and implement specific constructive ways (e.g., avoiding involvement or siding on issues between parents, stating his/her own feelings directly to the parents on issues involving him/her) to interact with the parents. Confront the client when he/she is not taking responsibility for himself/herself in family conflicts.

15. Verbalize fears associated with becoming more independent. (23)

23. Explore the client's fears surrounding becoming more independent and responsible for himself/herself.

16. Parents identify and implement ways to promote the client's maturity and independence. (24)

24. Help the parents find ways to assist in the advancement of the client's maturity and independence (e.g., give the client age-appropriate privileges, encourage activities outside of home, require the client to be responsible for specific jobs or tasks in the home).

17. Verbalize an understanding of various emotions and express them appropriately. (25)

18. Identify specifically how own acting out behavior rescues the parents from facing their own problems. (26, 27)

19. Family members verbally agree to and then implement the structural or strategic recommendations of the therapist for the family. (28, 29)

20. Complete psychiatric or other recommended evaluations. (30)

25. Educate the client (e.g., using a printed list of feeling adjectives) in how to identify and label feelings and in the value of expressing them in appropriate ways.

26. Assist the client in becoming more aware of her/his role in the family and how it impacts the parents.

27. Facilitate family therapy sessions with the objective of revealing underlying conflicts in order to release the client from being a symptom bearer.

28. Conduct family therapy sessions in which a structural intervention (e.g., parents will not allow the children to get involved in their discussions or disagreements, while assuring the children that the parents can work things out themselves) is developed, assigned, and then implemented by the family. Monitor the implementation and adjust intervention as required.

29. Develop a strategic intervention (parents will be responsible for holding a weekly family meeting and the client will be responsible for raising one personal issue in that forum for them to work out together) and have the family implement it. Monitor the implementation and adjust intervention as needed.

30. Evaluate the client or refer him/her for evaluation for substance abuse, Attention-Deficit/Hyperactivity Disorder (ADHD), affective disorder, or psychotic processes.

21. Comply with all recommendations of the psychiatric or other evaluations. (31)

22. Move to a neutral living environment that meets both own and parents' approval. (9, 32)

31. Monitor the client's and the family's compliance with the evaluation recommendations.

9. Arrange for the client to be placed in respite care or in another secure setting, if necessary, while the family works in family therapy to resolve conflicts that have led to abuse or neglect of the client.

32. Help the parents and the client draw up a contract for the client to live in a neutral setting for an agreed-upon length of time. The contract will include basic guidelines for daily structure and for frequency of contact with the parents and the acceptable avenues by which the contact can take place.

—. _____

_____

—. _____

_____

—. _____

_____

—. _____

_____

—. _____

_____

—. _____

_____

DIAGNOSTIC SUGGESTIONS

Axis I:	314.01	Attention-Deficit/Hyperactivity Disorder, Predominantly Hyperactive-Impulsive Type
	312.82	Conduct Disorder, Adolescent-Onset Type
	313.81	Oppositional Defiant Disorder
	300.01	Panic Disorder Without Agoraphobia
	300.4	Dysthymic Disorder
	309.24	Adjustment Disorder With Anxiety
	309.4	Adjustment Disorder With Mixed Disturbance of Emotions and Conduct
	312.30	Impulse-Control Disorder NOS
	V61.20	Parent-Child Relational Problem
	995.54	Physical Abuse of Child (Victim)

995.53	Sexual Abuse of Child (Victim)
995.52	Neglect of Child (Victim)
_____	_____
_____	_____

Axis II:

799.9	Diagnosis Deferred
V71.09	No Diagnosis
_____	_____
_____	_____

SCHOOL VIOLENCE

BEHAVIORAL DEFINITIONS

1. Threats of violence have been made against students, teachers, and/or administrators.
2. Feels alienated from most peers within the school.
3. Subjected to bullying or intimidation from peers.
4. Subjected to ridicule, teasing, or rejection from peers.
5. Loss of temper has led to violent or aggressive behavior.
6. Engages in drug or alcohol abuse.
7. Has access to or a fascination with weapons.
8. Has a history of hurting animals.
9. History of conflict with authority figures.
10. Exhibits poor academic performance.
11. Feels disrespected by peers and adults.
12. Lacks close attachment to family members.

—. _____
   _____
—. _____
   _____
—. _____
   _____

LONG-TERM GOALS

1. Express hurt and anger in nonviolent ways.
2. Develop trusting relationships with peers.
3. Terminate substance abuse as a means of coping with pain and alienation.

4. Improve degree of connection and involvement with parents, siblings, and extended family.
5. Increase involvement in academic and social activities within the school environment.

—. _____
_____
_____
—. _____
_____
_____
—. _____
_____

SHORT-TERM OBJECTIVES

1. Identify attitudes and feelings regarding school experience as well as general emotional status. (1, 2, 3)

THERAPEUTIC INTERVENTIONS

1. Explore the client's attitude and feelings regarding his/her school experience (e.g., academic performance, peer relationships, staff relationships).

2. Administer or arrange for psychological testing to assess the client's emotional adjustment, especially depth of depression (e.g., MMPI-A, MACI, Beck Depression Inventory); evaluate results and give feedback to the client and his/her parents.

3. Assess the current risk of the client's becoming violent (e.g., depth of anger, degree of alienation from peers and family, substance abuse, fascination with and/or access to weapons, articulation of a violence plan, threats made directly or indirectly); notify the proper authorities, if necessary, and take steps to remove the client's access to weapons.

2. Describe social network and degree of support or rejection felt from others. (4, 5)

4. Develop a sociogram with the client that places friends and other peers in concentric circles, with the client at the center and closest friends on the closest circle; ask him/her to disclose his/her impression of each person.

5. Explore the client's painful experiences of social rejection by peers; use active listening and unconditional positive regard to encourage sharing of feelings.

3. Identify issues that precipitate peer conflict. (6)

6. Assist the client in identifying issues that precipitate his/her conflict with peers.

4. Implement problem-solving skills to resolve peer conflict. (7, 8, 9)

7. Teach the client problem-solving skills (e.g., identify the problem, brainstorm solutions, select an option, implement a cause of action, evaluate the outcome) that can be applied to peer conflict issues.

8. Teach the client means of coping with and improving conflicted peer relationships (e.g., social skills training; outside intervention with bullies; conflict resolution training; reaching out to build new friendships; identifying empathetic resource peers or adults in school to whom the client can turn when hurt, lonely, or angry).

9. Use role-playing, modeling, and behavioral rehearsal to assist the client in learning the application of social problem-solving skills.

5. Increase participation in structured social activities within the school environment. (10, 11)

10. Brainstorm with the client possible extracurricular activities he/she might enjoy being involved in; obtain a commitment to pursue one or two of these choices in order to build a positive attitude toward school and peers.

6. Identify feelings toward family members. (12, 13)

7. Caregivers and client identify common anger-provoking situations that contribute to loss of control and emergence of violent behavior. (14, 15, 16)

8. Identify family issues that contribute to violent behavior. (17)

11. Process the client's experience with increased social involvement; reinforce success and redirect failures.

12. Explore the client's relationships with and feelings toward his/her family members; be especially alert to feelings of alienation, isolation, emotional detachment, resentment, distrust, and anger.

13. In a family therapy session, facilitate an exchange of thoughts and feelings that can lead to increased mutual understanding and a reduction in negative feelings.

14. Assist the client in recognizing early signs (e.g., tiredness, muscular tension, hot face, hostile remarks) that he/she is starting to become frustrated or agitated so that he/she can take steps to remain calm and cope with frustration.

15. Assist the caregivers and school officials in identifying specific situations or events that routinely lead to explosive outbursts or aggressive behaviors. Teach the caregivers and school officials effective coping strategies to help defuse the client's anger and to deter his/her aggressive behavior.

16. Assign the client to read material regarding learning to manage anger more effectively (e.g., *Everything You Need to Know About Anger* by Licata); process the reading with him/her.

17. Conduct family therapy sessions to explore the dynamics (e.g., parental modeling of aggressive behavior; sexual, verbal, or physical abuse of family members;

substance abuse in the home; neglect) that may contribute to the emergence of the client's violent behavior.

9. Uninvolved or detached parent(s) increase time spent with the client in recreational, school, or work activities. (18, 19)

18. Instruct the caregivers to set aside between 5 and 10 minutes each day to listen to the client's concerns and to provide him/her with the opportunity to express his/her anger in an adaptive manner.

19. Give a directive to uninvolved or disengaged parent(s) to spend more time with the client in leisure, school, or work activities.

10. Increase active involvement in family activities. (20)

20. Assist the family in identifying several activities they could engage in together, assigning the family to engage in at least one structured activity together every week; process the experience.

11. Caregivers increase the frequency of praise and positive reinforcement of the client for demonstrating good control of anger. (21)

21. Design a reward system to help the parents reinforce the client's expression of his/her anger in a controlled manner (or employ the "Anger Control" exercise in the *Adolescent Psychotherapy Homework Planner,* 2nd ed. by Jongsma, Peterson, and McInnis).

12. Implement anger management techniques to reduce violent outbursts. (22, 23)

22. Teach the client anger management techniques (e.g., take a time-out, journal feelings, talk to a trusted adult, engage in physical exercise); process his/her implementation of these techniques, reinforcing success and redirecting failure (see Anger Management chapter in this *Planner*).

23. Refer the client to an anger management group. Direct him/her to self-disclose at least one time in each group therapy session about his/her responses to anger-provoking situations.

13. Write a letter of forgiveness to a perpetrator of hurt. (24)

24. Instruct the client to write a letter of forgiveness to a target of anger in the latter stages of treatment as a step toward letting go of anger; process the letter in a follow-up session, and discuss what to do with the letter.

14. Identify and replace the irrational beliefs or maladaptive thoughts that contribute to the emergence of destructive or assaultive/aggressive behavior. (25)

25. Assist the client in identifying his/her irrational thoughts that contribute to the emergence of violent behavior (e.g., believing that aggression is an acceptable way to deal with teasing or name-calling, justifying acts of violence or aggression as a means to meet his/her needs or to avoid restrictions). Replace these irrational thoughts with more adaptive ways of thinking to help control anger.

15. Complete a substance abuse evaluation, and comply with the recommendations that are offered by the evaluation findings. (26)

26. Arrange for substance abuse evaluation to assess whether substance abuse problems are contributing to the client's violent behavior; refer him/her for treatment if indicated (see Chemical Dependence chapter in this *Planner*).

16. Identify and list strengths, interests, or positive attributes. (27, 28)

27. Give the client a homework assignment of identifying between 5 and 10 unique strengths, interests, or positive attributes. Review this list with the client in the following therapy session, and encourage him/her to utilize his/her strengths, interests, or positive attributes to build a positive self-image.

28. Assist the client in taking an inventory of his/her strengths, interests, or accomplishments, then ask him/her to bring objects or symbols to the next therapy session that represent those strengths

17. Identify and implement effective strategies to improve self-esteem. (29, 30)

or interests; encourage him/her to use strengths or interests to build self-esteem (or assign the exercise "Symbols of Self-Worth" from the *Adolescent Psychotherapy Homework Planner,* 2nd ed. by Jongsma, Peterson, and McInnis).

29. Assign the client to view the video entitled *10 Ways to Boost Low Self-Esteem* (available from The Guidance Channel) to learn effective strategies to elevate self-esteem and increase confidence in himself/herself.

30. Instruct the client to complete the exercise entitled "Self-Esteem—What Is It? How Do I Get It?" from *Ten Days to Self-Esteem* (Burns) to help increase his/her self-esteem.

18. Increase the frequency of positive self-descriptive statements. (31, 32)

31. Encourage the client to use positive self-talk (e.g., "I am capable," "I can do this," "I am kind," "I can dance well") as a means of increasing his/her confidence and developing a positive self-image.

32. Instruct the client to make three positive statements about himself/herself daily and record them in a journal; review and reinforce these journal entries in follow-up therapy sessions.

19. Caregivers increase the frequency of praise and positive reinforcement for the client's prosocial or responsible behaviors. (33, 34)

33. Encourage the parents/caregivers and teachers to provide frequent praise and positive reinforcement for the client's prosocial and responsible behavior to help him/her develop a positive self-image.

34. Instruct the parents/caregivers to observe and record between three and five positive responsible

behaviors by the client before the next therapy session. Review these behaviors in the next session, and encourage the client to continue engaging in these behaviors to boost his/her self-esteem.

20. Caregivers cease making overly hostile, critical remarks, and increase conveying positive messages to the client. (35, 36)

35. Confront and challenge the parents/caregivers to cease making overly hostile or critical remarks about the client or his/her behavior that only reinforce his/her feelings of low self-esteem. Encourage the caregivers to verbalize the positive, specific behaviors or changes that they would like to see the client make.

36. Teach the client and his/her parents/caregivers effective communication skills (e.g., practicing active listening, using "I messages," avoiding blaming statements, identifying specific positive changes that other family members can make) to improve the lines of communication, facilitate closer family ties, and resolve conflict more constructively.

21. Verbalize increased feelings of genuine empathy for others. (37, 38, 39)

37. Attempt to sensitize the client to his/her lack of empathy for others by reviewing and listing the negative consequences of his/her aggression on others (e.g., loss of trust, increased fear, distancing, physical pain).

38. Use role reversal techniques to get the client to verbalize the impact of his/her aggression on others.

39. Assign the client to address an empty chair in giving an apology for pain that he/she has caused the victim.

—. _____   —. _____
   _____   _____
—. _____   —. _____
   _____   _____
—. _____   —. _____
   _____   _____

DIAGNOSTIC SUGGESTIONS

Axis I: 312.34   Intermittent Explosive Disorder
               312.30   Impulse-Control Disorder NOS
               312.8   Conduct Disorder
               312.9   Disruptive Behavior Disorder NOS
               314.01   Attention-Deficit/Hyperactivity Disorder,
                         Predominantly Hyperactive-Impulsive Type
               314.9   Attention-Deficit/Hyperactivity Disorder NOS
               V71.02   Adolescent Antisocial Behavior
               V61.20   Parent-Child Relational Problem
               300.4   Dysthymic Disorder
               296.xx   Major Depressive Disorder
               296.89   Bipolar II Disorder
               296.xx   Bipolar I Disorder

               _____   _____
               _____   _____

Axis II: V799.9   Diagnosis Deferred
               V71.09   No Diagnosis

               _____   _____
               _____   _____

SEXUAL ABUSE PERPETRATOR

BEHAVIORAL DEFINITIONS

1. Arrest and conviction for a sexually related crime, such as exhibitionism, exposure, voyeurism, or criminal sexual conduct (first, second, or third degree).
2. Sexual abuse of a younger, vulnerable victim.
3. Frequent use of language that has an easily noted sexual content.
4. Evident sexualization of most, if not all, relationships.
5. Focus on and preoccupation with anything of a sexual nature.
6. Positive familial history of incest.
7. History of being sexually abused as a child.
8. Interest in pornographic content in books, magazines, videos, and/or on the Internet that is more than mere curiosity.

__. _____
   _____
__. _____
   _____
__. _____
   _____

LONG-TERM GOALS

1. Eliminate all inappropriate sexual behaviors.
2. Establish and honor boundaries that reflect a sense of mutual respect in all interpersonal relationships.
3. Form relationships that are not sexualized.
4. Reach the point of genuine self-forgiveness, and make apologies to the violated individual(s), along with an offer of restitution.

5. Acknowledge and take responsibility for all inappropriate sexual be-havior.
6. Resolve issues of his/her own sexual abuse.

—. _____

_____

—. _____

_____

—. _____

_____

SHORT-TERM OBJECTIVES

THERAPEUTIC INTERVENTIONS

1. Develop a working relationship with the therapist that allows for sharing thoughts and feelings openly. (1, 2)

1. Actively build the level of trust with the client in individual sessions through consistent eye contact, active listening, uncon-ditional positive regard, and warm acceptance to help increase his/her ability to identify and express feelings.

2. Use a celebrity interview format in which the client is asked non-threatening questions (e.g., his/her likes and dislikes, best times, favorite holidays) to initiate self-disclosure.

2. Sign a no-sexual-contact agree-ment. (3, 4)

3. Assist the client and his/her family in developing and imple-menting a behaviorally specific no-sexual-contact agreement; ask the client to sign the agreement.

4. Monitor the client's no-sexual-contact agreement along with the parents, making any necessary adjustments and giving construc-tive praise and redirection as warranted; if the client is unable to keep the contract, facilitate a referral to a more restrictive set-ting.

3. Verbally acknowledge the abuse, and take full responsibility for perpetrating it. (1, 5, 6)

1. Actively build the level of trust with the client in individual sessions through consistent eye contact, active listening, unconditional positive regard, and warm acceptance to help increase his/her ability to identify and express feelings.

5. Process all the incidents of sexual misconduct and/or abuse, focusing on getting the whole story out and having the client accept responsibility for his/her behavior.

6. Assign an exercise on sexual boundaries from the Safer Society Press Series (Freeman-Longo and Bays) to begin the client's process of education and treatment of his/her offense cycle (or assign the "Getting Started" exercise from the *Adolescent Psychotherapy Homework Planner,* 2nd ed. by Jongsma, Peterson, and McInnis).

4. Recognize and honor the personal boundaries of others as shown by the termination of inappropriate sexual contact. (6, 7)

6. Assign an exercise on sexual boundaries from the Safer Society Press Series (Freeman-Longo and Bays) to begin the client's process of education and treatment of his/her offense cycle (or assign the "Getting Started" exercise from the *Adolescent Psychotherapy. Homework Planner,* 2nd ed. by Jongsma, Peterson, and McInnis).

7. Assist the client in becoming aware of personal space and boundaries and how to honor and respect them; role-play situations with him/her to reinforce and model appropriate actions that show respect for personal space.

5. Decrease the frequency of sexual references in daily speech and sexual actions in daily behavior. (8, 9)

6. Provide a complete sexual history. (10)

7. Verbally acknowledge ever being a victim of sexual, physical, or emotional abuse. (11)

8. State a connection between being a sexual abuse victim and a sexual abuse perpetrator. (12)

9. Demonstrate the ability to identify and express feelings. (13, 14)

8. Point out to the client sexual references and content in his/her speech and behavior; process the feelings and thoughts that underlie these references.

9. Ask the client to gather feedback from teachers, parents, and so on regarding sexual references in his/her speech and behavior; process the feedback with the client and identify nonsexualized alternatives.

10. Gather a thorough sexual history of the client from the client and his/her parents.

11. Gently explore whether the client was sexually, physically, or emotionally abused by asking specific questions regarding others' respect for the client's physical boundaries when he/she was a child.

12. Assist the client in identifying the connections between his/her own sexual abuse victimization and the development of his/her attitudes and patterns of sexual abuse perpetration.

13. Assist the client in becoming capable of identifying, labeling, and expressing his/her feelings, using various therapeutic tools to increase and reinforce his/her new skills (e.g., The Talking, Feeling, and Doing Game by Gardner, available from Creative Therapeutics; The Ungame by Zakich, available from the Ungame Company).

14. Give feedback to the client when he/she does not show awareness of his/her own feelings or those of others, and positive verbal reinforcement when he/she shows awareness without direction.

10. Tell the story of being a victim of sexual, physical, or emotional abuse with appropriate affect. (15, 16)

15. Encourage and support the client in telling the story of being a sexual, physical, or emotional abuse victim (see Sexual Abuse Victim or Physical/Emotional Abuse Victim chapters in this *Planner*).

16. Prepare, assist, and support the client in telling his/her parents of his/her own abuse experiences.

11. Attend a sexual abuse perpetrators' group treatment. (17)

17. Refer the client to group treatment for sexual abuse perpetrators.

12. Identify thinking errors, feelings, and beliefs that give justification for sexual abuse and ways to handle each effectively. (18)

18. Assist the client in identifying thoughts and beliefs that he/she used as justification for the abuse; assist him/her in identifying socially acceptable thoughts that are respectful, not exploitive, of others.

13. Increase the connection between thinking errors, feelings, and beliefs and sexual offending. (18, 19)

18. Assist the client in identifying thoughts and beliefs that he/she used as justification for the abuse; assist him/her in identifying socially acceptable thoughts that are respectful, not exploitive, of others.

19. Assist the client in making connections between thinking errors and his/her sexually abusive behaviors.

14. Complete psychological testing and comply with the recommendations. (20)

20. Arrange or conduct psychological testing for the client to rule out presence of psychopathology or other severe emotional issue, and interpret the test results for the client and family, emphasizing the importance of following through on each recommendation.

15. Complete a psychiatric evaluation for medications. (21)

21. Refer the client for a psychiatric evaluation as to the need for psychotropic medication.

16. Take the prescribed medications to control impulses, decrease aggression, or stabilize mood. (22)

17. Develop and utilize anger management techniques. (13, 23, 24)

18. Increase the formation of positive peer relationships. (25, 26, 27)

22. Monitor the client's psychotropic medication prescription compliance, effectiveness, and side effects.

13. Assist the client in becoming capable of identifying, labeling, and expressing his/her feelings, using various therapeutic tools to increase and reinforce his/her new skills (e.g., The Talking, Feeling, and Doing Game by Gardner, available from Creative Therapeutics; The Ungame by Zakich, available from the Ungame Company).

23. Assign the client an exercise in *The Anger Workbook* (Blodeau) to learn to recognize anger and ways to effectively handle these feelings (or assign the "Anger Control" exercise in the *Adolescent Psychotherapy Homework Planner,* 2nd ed. by Jongsma, Peterson, and McInnis).

24. Refer the client to a group focused on teaching anger management techniques.

25. Assist the client in identifying specific ways he/she can become more involved with peers (e.g., join sports, music, art, hobby, or church youth groups; invite peers over to watch a DVD/video); role-play these situations to build the client's skill and confidence level in initiating these actions.

26. Ask the client to attempt one new social or recreational activity each week and/or to engage a peer in conversation (5 minutes) once daily; process the experience and the results.

27. Assign the client to read material to help build his/her awareness of what is appropriate and inappropriate behavior when interacting with the opposite sex (e.g., *Dating for Dummies* by Browne; *The Complete Idiot's Guide to Dating* by Kuriansky).

19. Verbalize reasonable guidelines to follow to avoid unhealthy, abusive relationships. (28)

28. Teach the client the SAFE formula for relationships: Avoid a relationship if there is anything *Secret* about it, if it is *Abusive* to oneself or others, if it is used to avoid *Feelings*, or if it is *Empty* of caring and commitment. Monitor his/her use and give feedback and redirection as required.

20. Parents verbalize awareness of the patterns, beliefs, and behaviors that support the client's sexual behavior. (29, 30)

29. Conduct a family session in which a genogram is developed that depicts patterns of interaction and identifies family members who are sexual abuse survivors or perpetrators, or who have been involved in other sexual deviancy.

30. Hold family sessions in which sexual patterns, beliefs, and behaviors are explored; assist the family members in identifying what sexual patterns, beliefs, or behaviors need to be changed and how they can begin to change them.

21. Parents verbalize changes they are trying to make to improve their parenting patterns. (31, 32, 33)

31. Conduct family sessions in which structural interventions are developed and implemented by the family (e.g., family members begin closing doors for privacy within their home, remove children from roles as supervisors of siblings, terminate sexual references within family conversation).

32. Recommend that the parents attend a didactic group on parenting teenagers.

33. Suggest that the parents read material to expand their understanding of adolescents and to build parenting skills (e.g., *Between Parent and Teenager* by Ginott; *Parents, Teens, and Boundaries* by Bluestein; *Raising Self-Reliant Children in a Self-Indulgent World* by Glenn and Nelsen; *The 7 Habits of Highly Effective Families* by Covey).

22. Parents develop and implement new family rituals. (34)

34. Assist the parents and family members in developing rituals of transition, healing, membership, identity, and new beginnings that give structure, meaning, and connection to their family.

23. Report instances of increased awareness of the feelings of others and self. (14, 35)

14. Give feedback to the client when he/she does not show awareness of his/her own feelings or those of others, and positive verbal reinforcement when he/she shows awareness without direction.

35. Teach the client the importance of expanding his/her awareness of his/her feelings and those of others (or assign the exercise "Your Feelings and Beyond" or "Surface Behavior/Inner Feelings" from the *Adolescent Psychotherapy Homework Planner,* 2nd ed. by Jongsma, Peterson, and McInnis).

24. Report an increase in appropriate sexual fantasies. (36, 37)

36. Ask the client to keep a fantasy journal, recording daily what sexual fantasies are experienced; review the fantasies for patterns that are appropriate or inappropriate and process this feedback with the client.

37. Assist the client in creating appropriate sexual fantasies that involve consenting, age-appropriate individuals; reflect feelings for the other party, and reject fantasies that involve receiving or inflicting pain.

25. Verbalize a desire to make an apology to his/her victim(s). (38, 39, 40)

38. Explore the client's attitude regarding apologizing to his/her victim(s) and forgiving himself/herself (or assign the exercise "Opening the Door to Forgiveness" from the *Adolescent Psychotherapy Homework Planner,* 2nd ed. by Jongsma, Peterson, and McInnis).

39. Ask the client to write a letter of apology to one of his/her victims; assess the genuineness of the remorse and guilt present, and give the client feedback.

40. Role-play the client's apology to the victim of sexual abuse to determine if he/she is ready for this step or what additional work may need to be done for him/her to reach that point; use role reversal to sensitize the client to the victim's feelings and reactions.

26. Make an apology to the sexual abuse survivor and the family. (41)

41. Conduct a family session with the families of both the perpetrator and the survivors in which the perpetrator apologizes to the survivor and his/her family.

27. Identify relapse triggers for perpetrating sexual abuse and list strategies to cope with them. (42)

42. Help the client to identify his/her potential relapse triggers (e.g., environmental situations, fantasies, sexually explicit material), assisting him/her in developing behavioral and cognitive coping strategies to implement for each trigger (e.g., avoidance or removing himself/herself from high-risk

situations, thought-stopping of inappropriate fantasies, avoiding being alone with young children).

28. Develop and implement an aftercare plan that includes the support of the family. (43, 44)

43. Ask the client and his/her family to develop a written aftercare plan (e.g., relapse prevention strategies, periodic checkups with therapist, support group participation, legal obligations); process the plan in a family session and make adjustments as necessary.

44. Hold checkup sessions in which the aftercare plan is reviewed for effectiveness and follow-through; give feedback and make adjustments as necessary.

29. Cooperate with a risk assessment for repeating sexual offenses. (45)

45. Refer the client for a sex-offender-specific risk assessment as part of the process of completing treatment.

30. Comply with any investigations by child protective services or criminal justice officials. (46)

46. Report to the appropriate authorities any sexual abuse that comes to light. Ask the client to share the results of the resulting investigation, and then process the results in a session that focuses on the client taking full responsibility for his/her inappropriate sexual behavior(s).

__. _____

_____

__. _____

_____

__. _____

_____

__. _____

_____

__. _____

_____

__. _____

_____

DIAGNOSTIC SUGGESTIONS

Axis I:	312.81	Conduct Disorder, Childhood-Onset Type
	312.82	Conduct Disorder, Adolescent-Onset Type
	302.2	Pedophilia
	302.4	Exhibitionism
	302.82	Voyeurism
	V61.8	Sibling Relational Problem
	995.53	Sexual Abuse of Child (Victim)
	V71.02	Child or Adolescent Antisocial Behavior

_____   _____

_____   _____

| Axis II: | 799.9 | Diagnosis Deferred |
| | V71.09 | No Diagnosis |

_____   _____

_____   _____

SEXUAL ABUSE VICTIM

BEHAVIORAL DEFINITIONS

1. Self-report of being sexually abused.
2. Physical signs of sexual abuse (e.g., red or swollen genitalia, blood in the underwear, constant rashes, a tear in the vagina or rectum, venereal disease, hickeys on the body).
3. Vague memories of inappropriate childhood sexual contact that can be corroborated by significant others.
4. Strong interest in or curiosity about advanced knowledge of sexuality.
5. Pervasive pattern of promiscuity or the sexualization of relationships.
6. Recurrent and intrusive distressing recollections or nightmares of the abuse.
7. Acting or feeling as if the sexual abuse were reoccurring (including delusions, hallucinations, or dissociative flashback experiences).
8. Unexplainable feelings of anger, rage, or fear when coming into contact with the perpetrator or after exposure to sexual topics.
9. Pronounced disturbance of mood and affect (e.g., frequent and prolonged periods of depression, irritability, anxiety, and fearfulness).
10. Marked distrust of others as manifested by social withdrawal and problems with establishing and maintaining close relationships.
11. Feelings of guilt, shame, and low self-esteem.
12. Excessive use of alcohol or drugs as a maladaptive coping mechanism to avoid dealing with painful emotions connected to sexual abuse.
13. Sexualized or seductive behavior with younger or same-aged children, adolescents, or adults (e.g., sexualized kissing, provocative exhibition of genitalia, fondling, mutual masturbation, anal or vaginal penetration).

__. _____

_____

__. _____

_____

—. _____

_____

LONG-TERM GOALS

1. Obtain protection from all further sexual victimization.
2. Work successfully through the issue of sexual abuse with consequent under-standing and control of feelings and behavior.
3. Resolve the issues surrounding the sexual abuse, resulting in an ability to establish and maintain close interpersonal relationships.
4. Establish appropriate boundaries and generational lines in the family to greatly minimize the risk of sexual abuse ever occurring in the future.
5. Achieve healing within the family system as evidenced by the verbal expression of forgiveness and a willingness to let go and move on.
6. Eliminate denial in self and the family, placing responsibility for the abuse on the perpetrator and allowing the survivor to feel supported.
7. Eliminate all inappropriate promiscuous or sexual behaviors.
8. Build self-esteem and a sense of empowerment as manifested by an increased number of positive self-descriptive statements and greater participation in extracurricular activities.

—. _____

_____

_____

—. _____

_____

—. _____

_____

SHORT-TERM OBJECTIVES

1. Tell the entire story of the abuse. (1, 2)

THERAPEUTIC INTERVENTIONS

1. Actively build the level of trust with the client through consistent eye contact, active listening, unconditional positive regard, and warm acceptance to help increase his/her ability to identify and express feelings connected to the abuse.

2. Explore, encourage, and support
the client in verbally expressing
the facts and clarifying his/her
feelings associated with the abuse
(or assign the exercise "My Story"
in the *Adolescent Psychotherapy
Homework Planner,* 2nd ed. by
Jongsma, Peterson, and McInnis).

2. Identify the nature, frequency,
and duration of the abuse.
(2, 3, 4, 5)

2. Explore, encourage, and support
the client in verbally expressing
the facts and clarifying his/her
feelings associated with the abuse
(or assign the exercise "My Story"
in the *Adolescent Psychotherapy
Homework Planner,* 2nd ed. by
Jongsma, Peterson, and McInnis).

3. Report the client's sexual abuse to
the appropriate child protection
agency, criminal justice officials,
or medical professionals.

4. Consult with a physician, criminal
justice officials, or child protection case managers to assess
the veracity of the sexual abuse
charges.

5. Consult with the physician,
criminal justice officials, or child
protection case managers to
develop appropriate treatment
interventions for the client.

3. Decrease secrecy in the family by informing key members
about the abuse. (6, 7)

6. Facilitate conjoint sessions to
reveal the client's sexual abuse to
key family members or caregivers.

7. Actively confront and challenge
denial of the client's sexual abuse
within the family system.

4. Implement steps to protect
the client from further sexual
abuse. (8, 9, 10, 11)

8. Assess whether the perpetrator
should be removed from the home.

9. Implement the necessary steps
to protect the client and other
children in the home from future
sexual abuse.

10. Assess whether the client is safe to remain in the home or should be removed.

11. Empower the client by reinforcing steps necessary to protect himself/herself.

5. Parents establish and adhere to appropriate intimacy boundaries within the family. (12)

12. Counsel the client's family members about appropriate intimacy and privacy boundaries.

6. Identify family dynamics or stressors that contributed to the emergence of sexual abuse. (13, 14, 15)

13. Assess the family dynamics and identify the stress factors or precipitating events that contributed to the emergence of the client's abuse.

14. Assign the client to draw a diagram of the house where the abuse occurred, indicating where everyone slept, and share the diagram with the therapist.

15. Construct a multigenerational family genogram that identifies sexual abuse within the extended family to help the client realize that he/she is not the only one abused and to help the perpetrator recognize the cycle of boundary violation.

7. Identify and express feelings connected to the abuse. (16, 17, 18, 19, 20)

16. Instruct the client to write a letter to the perpetrator that describes his/her feelings about the abuse; process the letter.

17. Utilize the empty-chair technique to assist the client in expressing and working through his/her myriad of feelings toward the perpetrator and other family members.

18. Direct the client to keep a journal in which he/she records experiences or situations that evoke strong emotions pertaining to sexual abuse, and share the journal in therapy sessions.

19. Employ art therapy (e.g., drawing, painting, sculpting) to help the client identify and express his/her feelings toward the perpetrator.

20. Use guided fantasy and imagery techniques to help the client express suppressed thoughts, feelings, and unmet needs associated with sexual abuse.

8. Decrease expressed feelings of shame and guilt and affirm self as not being responsible for the abuse. (21)

21. Explore and resolve the client's feelings of guilt and shame connected to the sexual abuse (or assign the "You Are Not Alone" exercise in the *Adolescent Psychotherapy Homework Planner,* 2nd ed. by Jongsma, Peterson, and McInnis).

9. Verbalize the way sexual abuse has impacted life. (22)

22. Instruct the client to create a drawing or sculpture that reflects how sexual abuse impacted his/her life and feelings about himself/herself.

10. Nonabusive parent and other key family members increase support and acceptance of client. (23, 24, 25)

23. Elicit and reinforce support and nurturance for the client from other key family members.

24. Assign the parents and family members reading material to increase their knowledge of sexually addictive behavior and learn ways to help the client recover from sexual abuse (e.g., *Out of the Shadows* by Carnes; *Allies in Healing* by Davis).

25. Give directive to disengaged, nonabusive parent to spend more time with the client in leisure, school, or household activities.

11. Perpetrator takes responsibility for the abuse. (26, 27)

26. Hold a therapy session in which the client and/or the therapist confronts the perpetrator with the abuse.

27. Hold a session in which the perpetrator takes full responsibility for the sexual abuse and apologizes to the client and/or other family members.

12. Perpetrator agrees to seek treatment. (28)

28. Require the perpetrator to participate in a sexual offenders' group.

13. Verbalize a desire to begin the process of forgiveness of the perpetrator and others connected with the abuse. (29, 30)

29. Assign the client to write a forgiveness letter and/or complete a forgiveness exercise in which he/she verbalizes forgiveness to the perpetrator and/or significant family members (or assign the "Letter of Forgiveness" exercise in the *Adolescent Psychotherapy Homework Planner,* 2nd ed. by Jongsma, Peterson, and McInnis). Process the letter.

30. Assign the client a letting-go exercise in which a symbol of the abuse is disposed of or destroyed; process this experience.

14. Verbally identify self as a survivor of sexual abuse. (31, 32)

31. Ask the client to identify the positive and negative consequences of being a victim versus being a survivor; compare and process the lists.

32. Introduce the idea in later stages of therapy that the client can survive sexual abuse by asking, "What will you be doing in the future that shows you are happy and have moved on with your life?" Process his/her responses and reinforce any positive steps that he/she can take to work through issues related to victimization.

15. Attend and actively participate in group therapy with other sexual abuse survivors. (33)

33. Refer the client to a survivor group with other adolescents to assist him/her in realizing that he/she is not alone in having experienced sexual abuse.

16. Increase the level of trust of others as shown by increased socialization and a greater number of friendships. (34, 35, 36, 37)

34. Encourage the client to participate in positive peer groups and extracurricular activities.

35. Teach the client the share-check method of building trust, in which the degree of shared information is related to a proven level of trustworthiness.

36. Identify appropriate and inappropriate forms of touching and affection; encourage the client to accept and initiate appropriate forms of touching with trusted individuals.

37. Develop a list of resource people outside of the family to whom the client can turn for support, guidance, and affirmation.

17. Decrease the frequency of sexualized or seductive behaviors in interactions with others. (38, 39)

38. Assist the client in making a connection between underlying painful emotions (e.g., fear, hurt, sadness, anxiety) and sexualized or seductive behaviors; help the client identify more adaptive ways to meet his/her needs other than through seductive or sexually promiscuous behaviors.

39. Provide sex education and discuss the risks involved with sexually promiscuous or seductive behaviors.

18. Complete a substance abuse evaluation and comply with the recommendations offered by the evaluation findings. (40)

40. Arrange for a substance abuse evaluation and/or treatment for the client (see Chemical Dependence chapter in this *Planner*).

19. Complete psychological testing. (41, 42)

41. Arrange for psychological testing of the client to rule out the presence of severe psychological disorders.

42. Assess the client's self-esteem by having him/her draw self-portraits during the beginning, middle, and end stages of therapy.

20. Parents comply with rec-ommendations regarding psychiatric or substance abuse treatment. (43)

43. Assess the parents for the pos-sibility of having a psychiatric disorder and/or substance abuse problem. Refer the parents for psychiatric or substance abuse evaluation and/or treatment if it is found that the parents have psychiatric disorders or substance abuse problems.

—. _____   —. _____
    _____   _____
—. _____   —. _____
    _____   _____
—. _____   —. _____
    _____   _____

DIAGNOSTIC SUGGESTIONS

Axis I:	309.81	Posttraumatic Stress Disorder
	308.3	Acute Stress Disorder
	296.xx	Major Depressive Disorder
	309.21	Separation Anxiety Disorder
	995.53	Sexual Abuse of Child (Victim)
	307.47	Nightmare Disorder
	300.15	Dissociative Disorder NOS
	_____	_____
	_____	_____
Axis II:	799.9	Diagnosis Deferred
	V71.09	No Diagnosis
	_____	_____
	_____	_____

SEXUAL ACTING OUT

BEHAVIORAL DEFINITIONS

1. Engagement in sexual intercourse with several different partners with little or no emotional attachment.
2. Engagement in sexual intercourse without birth control and without being at a stage of development to take responsibility for a baby.
3. Sexually active with one partner but with no sense of long-term commitment to each other.
4. No utilization of safe-sex practices.
5. Routine public engagement in sexually provocative dress, language, and behavior.
6. Talking freely of own sexual activity without regard for consequences to reputation or loss of respect from others.
7. Use of drugs and/or alcohol to alter mood and judgment prior to and during sexual activity.
8. Low self-esteem evidenced by self-disparaging remarks and predictions of future failure.
9. Depression evidenced by irritability, social isolation, low energy, and sad affect.
10. Hypomania evidenced by impulsivity, high energy, lack of follow-through, and pressured speech.
11. Angry, oppositional pattern of behavior that is in conflict with social mores, parental rules, and authority figures.
12. Conflict and instability within the family of origin.

__. _____
   _____
__. _____
   _____
__. _____
   _____

LONG-TERM GOALS

1. Terminate sexual activity that does not reflect commitment, emotional intimacy, and a caring, mature relationship.
2. Implement birth control and safe-sex practices.
3. Develop insight into the maladaptive sexual activity as self-defeating and emanating from emotional needs and conflicts not related to sex.
4. Resolve underlying emotional conflicts that energize the maladaptive sexual activity.
5. Terminate substance abuse and understand its interaction with sexual promiscuity.
6. Resolve family-of-origin conflicts.

—. _____

_____

—. _____

_____

—. _____

_____

SHORT-TERM OBJECTIVES

1. Acknowledge history and current practice of sexual activity. (1, 2, 3)

THERAPEUTIC INTERVENTIONS

1. Actively build the level of trust with the client in individual sessions through consistent eye contact, active listening, unconditional positive regard, and warm acceptance to help increase his/her ability to identify and express intimate facts and feelings.

2. Gather a detailed sexual history that includes number of partners, frequency of activity, birth control and/or safe-sex practices used, source of sexual information in childhood, first sexual experience, and degree of emotional attachment to partner.

3. Explore the client's thoughts and feelings that surround the facts of the sexual history and current practice.

2. Identify any and all known motivations for sexual activity. (4, 5)

4. Ask the client to list all possible reasons he/she has chosen to engage in sexual activity at this early stage of life and why specific partners were selected.

5. Process the pros and cons of each reason given for the client's sexual activity.

3. Disclose any history of sexual abuse that has occurred in childhood or adolescence and its effect on current sexual activity. (6, 7)

6. Explore for any history of the client having been sexually abused (see Sexual Abuse Victim chapter in this *Planner*).

7. Assist the client in making a connection between being treated as a sexual object in childhood by a perpetrator and treating himself/herself and others as impersonal sexual objects currently.

4. Verbalize insight into the sources and impact of low self-esteem. (8, 9, 10, 11)

8. Explore the client's feelings of low self-esteem as to his/her awareness, depth of feeling, and means of expression (see Low Self-Esteem chapter in this *Planner*).

9. Assist the client in identifying sources of his/her feelings of low self-esteem (e.g., perceived parental criticism or rejection; physical, sexual, or emotional abuse; academic or social failures).

10. Help the client become aware of his/her fear of rejection and its connection with past rejection or abandonment experiences.

11. Assist the client in making a connection between his/her feelings of low self-esteem, fear of rejection, and current sexual activity.

5. Identify positive ways to build self-esteem. (12, 13)

12. Confront the self-defeating nature of trying to build self-esteem or gain acceptance through sexual activity, and assist the client in developing a constructive plan to build self-esteem.

13. Assign the client a homework exercise in which he/she is asked to draw pictures of the desired changes to himself/herself (or assign "Three Ways to Change Yourself" from the *Adolescent Psychotherapy Homework Planner,* 2nd ed. by Jongsma, Peterson, and McInnis).

6. Describe family interaction patterns that may lead to feelings of rejection. (14, 15, 16)

14. Explore the dynamics of rejection versus affirmation present in the client's family of origin.

15. Hold family therapy sessions that focus on the family members' feelings toward each other and their style of interacting.

16. Interpret the client's sexual activity as a maladaptive means of seeking affirmation and attention that has been missed in the family.

7. Verbalize a value for sexual activity beyond physical pleasure and/or trying to "get someone to like you." (17, 18)

17. Teach the value of reserving sexual intimacy for a relationship that has commitment, longevity, and maturity.

18. Teach that sexual activity is most rewarding when it is a mutual expression of giving oneself as an act of love versus being sexual to try to get someone to love you or only to meet your own needs for pleasure or conquest.

8. Verbalize feelings of depression. (19, 20, 21)

19. Assess the client for signs or symptoms of depression (see Depression chapter in this *Planner*).

20. Administer or arrange for psychological testing to assess for emotional or personality factors that may contribute to the client's sexual behavior.

21. Interpret the client's sexual activity as a means of seeking relief from depression that only ends up deepening his/her depression.

9. Verbalize an understanding of the serious risks involved in not using birth control or safe sex practices and affirm implementation of same. (22, 23)

22. Teach the client the value of using birth control and safe sex practices.

23. Explore any underlying wishes (e.g., pregnancy, death) that have influenced the client's maladaptive behavior in not using birth control or safe sex practices.

10. Admit that the use of drugs and/or alcohol before or during sexual activity is done to escape from feelings of shame, guilt, or fear. (24, 25)

24. Explore for the client's use of mood-altering drugs or alcohol before or during sexual activity.

25. Assist the client in identifying the role of drugs or alcohol as a means of numbing his/her conscience and escaping feelings of shame, fear, and guilt associated with sexual acting out.

11. Terminate the use of mood-altering drugs and alcohol. (26)

26. Ask the client for a commitment to terminate the use of drugs and alcohol (see Chemical Dependence chapter in this *Planner*).

12. Describe a pattern of impulsive behaviors that lead to negative consequences. (27, 28)

27. Assess the client for a pattern of impulsivity that may characterize many aspects of his/her behavior and that may be related to Attention-Deficit/Hyperactivity Disorder (ADHD) or mania (see Attention-Deficit/Hyperactivity Disorder [ADHD] and Mania chapters in this *Planner*).

28. Assess the client for the need for psychotropic medications to alleviate the factors underlying his/her maladaptive sexual activity (e.g., depression, mania, ADHD).

13. Cooperate with an assessment for psychotropic medication. (28, 29)

28. Assess the client for the need for psychotropic medications to alleviate the factors underlying his/her maladaptive sexual activity (e.g., depression, mania, ADHD).

29. Refer the client to a physician to be evaluated for a prescription for psychotropic medication.

14. Take medications as prescribed and report as to effectiveness and side effects. (29, 30)

29. Refer the client to a physician to be evaluated for a prescription for psychotropic medication.

30. Monitor the client's compliance with medication and assess for effectiveness and side effects.

__. _____   __. _____
    _____   _____
__. _____   __. _____
    _____   _____
__. _____   __. _____
    _____   _____

DIAGNOSTIC SUGGESTIONS

Axis I: 296.xx   Major Depressive Disorder
                 300.4   Dysthymic Disorder
                 296.89   Bipolar II Disorder
                 296.4x   Bipolar I Disorder, Most Recent Episode Manic
                 303.90   Alcohol Dependence
                 305.00   Alcohol Abuse
                 304.30   Cannabis Dependence
                 305.20   Cannabis Abuse

314.01   Attention-Deficit/Hyperactivity Disorder,
              Predominantly Hyperactive-Impulsive Type

_____   _____

_____   _____

Axis II: 799.9   Diagnosis Deferred
                V71.09   No Diagnosis

_____   _____

_____   _____

SEXUAL IDENTITY CONFUSION*

BEHAVIORAL DEFINITIONS

1. Uncertainty about sexual orientation.
2. Sexual fantasies and desires about same-sex partners that cause distress.
3. Feelings of guilt, shame, and/or worthlessness.
4. Depressed mood; diminished interest in activities.
5. Concealment of sexual identity from parents.
6. Recent homosexual experimentation that has created questions about sexual orientation.
7. Parents verbalize distress over concern that the client may be homosexual.
8. Recent disclosure of homosexual identity to parents.
9. Parents express feelings of failure because the client is gay/lesbian.

__. _____

_____

__. _____

_____

__. _____

_____

LONG-TERM GOALS

1. Clarify own sexual identity and engage in a wide range of relationships that are supportive of same.

---

*Most of the content of this chapter (with only slight revisions) originates from J. M. Evosevich and M. Avriette, *The Gay and Lesbian Treatment Planner* (New York: John Wiley & Sons, 1999). Copyright © 1999 by J. M. Evosevich and Michael Avriette. Reprinted with permission.

2. Reduce overall frequency and intensity of the anxiety associated with sexual identity so that daily functioning is not impaired.
3. Disclose sexual orientation to parents.
4. Return to previous level of emotional, psychological, and social functioning.
5. Parents accept the client's homosexuality.
6. Resolve all symptoms of depression (e.g., depressed mood, guilt, shame, worthlessness).

—. _____

_____

—. _____

_____

—. _____

_____

SHORT-TERM OBJECTIVES

1. Describe fear, anxiety, and distress related to confusion over sexual identity. (1, 2)

2. Contract not to harm self. (3)

3. Openly discuss history of sexual desires, fantasies, and experiences. (4)

4. Verbalize reasons for questioning own sexual identity. (5, 6)

THERAPEUTIC INTERVENTIONS

1. Actively build trust with the client and encourage the expression of fear, anxiety, and distress over his/her sexual identity confusion.

2. Conduct a suicide assessment and refer the client to the appropriate supervised level of care if a danger to self exists.

3. Encourage the client to verbalize and then sign a no-harm contract.

4. Assess the client's current sexual functioning by asking about his/her history of sexual experiences, fantasies, and desires.

5. Ask the client why he/she has questions about his/her sexuality, with specific questions about when he/she began to question his/her sexuality and why.

6. Educate the client about the commonality of same-sex experiences in youth and emphasize that

these do not necessarily indicate a homosexual identity.

5. Rate sexual attraction to males and females on a scale of 1 to 10. (7)

6. Write a future biography detailing life as a heterosexual and as a homosexual to assist self in identifying primary orientation. (8)

7. Resolve sexual identity confusion by identifying self as homosexual or heterosexual. (9, 10)

8. Identify and verbalize feelings related to identifying self as gay or lesbian. (11, 12)

9. Verbalize an understanding of how religious beliefs have contributed to hiding or denying sexual orientation. (13, 14)

7. Have the client rate his/her sexual attraction to males and females on a scale of 1 to 10 (with 10 being extremely attracted and 1 being not at all attracted).

8. Assign the client the homework of writing a future biography describing his/her life 20 years in the future, both as a heterosexual and as a homosexual; read and process this biography (e.g., ask the client which life was more satisfying, which life had more regrets).

9. Allow the client to evaluate all the evidence from his/her experience in a nonjudgmental atmosphere so as to resolve his/her confusion and identify himself/herself as homosexual or heterosexual.

10. Ask the client to list all the factors that led to a decision regarding his/her sexual identity; process the list.

11. Explore the client's feelings regarding seeing himself/herself as homosexual.

12. Explore the client's negative emotions (e.g., shame, guilt, anxiety, loneliness) related to hiding or denying his/her homosexuality.

13. Explore the client's religious convictions and how these may conflict with identifying himself/herself as homosexual and cause feelings of shame or guilt.

14. Refer the client to a member of the clergy who will listen compassionately to the client's religious struggle over his/her homosexual identity.

10. Verbalize an understanding of safer sex practices. (15)

11. List myths about homosexuals and replace them with more realistic, positive beliefs. (16)

15. Teach the client the details of safer sex guidelines.

16. Assist the client in identifying myths about homosexuals (e.g., bad parenting causes homosexuality, homosexuals are not ever happy) and assist him/her in replacing them with more realistic, positive beliefs (e.g., there is no evidence that parenting causes homosexuality; gay men and lesbians can be as happy as heterosexuals).

12. List the advantages and disadvantages of disclosing one's sexual orientation to significant people in one's life. (17)

17. Assign the client to list advantages and disadvantages of disclosing his/her sexual orientation to family members and other significant people in his/her life. Process the list.

13. Describe social interaction with peers and identify any isolation and/or homophobia experienced because of having a homosexual identity. (18, 19)

18. Explore the client's relationships with peers and assist him/her in describing any homophobic experiences and/or isolation as well as the feelings associated with these experiences.

19. Encourage the client to identify other lesbian and gay adolescents to interact with by reviewing people he/she has met in support groups, at school, or on a job, and encourage him/her to initiate social activities.

14. Attend a support group for gay and lesbian adolescents. (20)

20. Refer the client to a lesbian and gay adolescent support group (e.g., Gay and Lesbian Community Service Center, Youth Services).

15. Write a plan detailing when, where, and to whom sexual orientation is to be disclosed. (21, 22)

21. Assign the client homework to write a detailed plan to disclose his/her sexual orientation, including where, when, and to whom it will be disclosed, and possible questions and reactions the recipient might have.

16. Reveal sexual orientation to family members according to the written plan. (23, 24)

17. Parents attend conjoint sessions that focus on resolving their feelings about the client's disclosure of his/her homosexual orientation. (25, 26)

18. Parents verbalize an increased understanding of homosexuality. (27, 28)

19. Parents attend a support group for families of homosexuals. (29)

20. Parents identify any religious beliefs that contribute to rejecting the client's homosexuality. (30)

22. Have the client role-play the disclosure of his/her sexual orientation to significant others.

23. Encourage the client to disclose his/her sexual orientation to family members according to the previously written plan.

24. Probe the client about the reactions of significant others to his/her disclosure of homosexuality; provide encouragement and positive feedback.

25. Arrange conjoint sessions that allow for a free exchange of thoughts and feelings within the family; encourage the client's parents to attend and participate.

26. Explore the emotional reactions of the parents to the client's disclosure of his/her homosexuality.

27. Educate the parents about homosexuality and answer questions they may have in an honest, direct manner (e.g., assure the parents that homosexuality is not caused by faulty parenting, nor is it considered a mental illness).

28. Assign the parents books that offer positive, realistic information about homosexuality and homosexual adolescents (e.g., *Is It a Choice?* by Marcus; *Beyond Acceptance* by Griffin, Wirth, and Wirth).

29. Refer the parents to a support group for families of homosexuals (e.g., Parents and Friends of Lesbians and Gays) and encourage their attendance.

30. Probe the parents about the impact of their religious beliefs on accepting their child's homosexuality.

21. Parents verbalize an understanding that many religious leaders are accepting of homosexuals. (31, 32)

31. Refer the parents to gay/lesbian-positive clergy to discuss their concerns.

32. Assign the parents to read Chapter 4 in *Beyond Acceptance* (Griffin, Wirth, and Wirth) and "The Bible and Homosexuality: The Last Prejudice" in *The Good Book* (Gomes). Process their reactions to the material read.

—. _____

   _____

—. _____

   _____

—. _____

   _____

—. _____

   _____

—. _____

   _____

—. _____

   _____

DIAGNOSTIC SUGGESTIONS

Axis I:	309.0	Adjustment Disorder With Depressed Mood
	309.28	Adjustment Disorder With Mixed Anxiety and Depressed Mood
	300.00	Anxiety Disorder NOS
	309.24	Adjustment Disorder With Anxiety
	300.4	Dysthymic Disorder
	302.85	Gender Identity Disorder in Adolescents or Adults
	300.02	Generalized Anxiety Disorder
	313.82	Identity Problem
	296.2x	Major Depressive Disorder, Single Episode
	296.3x	Major Depressive Disorder, Recurrent
	V62.89	Phase of Life Problem
	V61.20	Parent-Child Relational Problem
	_____	_____
	_____	_____
Axis II:	799.9	Diagnosis Deferred
	V71.09	No Diagnosis
	_____	_____
	_____	_____

SOCIAL PHOBIA/SHYNESS

BEHAVIORAL DEFINITIONS

1. Excessive shrinking from or avoidance of contact with unfamiliar people.
2. Social isolation and/or excessive involvement in isolated activities (e.g., reading, listening to music in room alone, playing video games alone).
3. Hypersensitivity to the criticism or disapproval of others.
4. No close friends or confidants outside of first-degree relatives.
5. Avoidance of situations that require a degree of interpersonal contact.
6. Reluctant involvement in social situations out of fear of saying or doing something foolish or of becoming emotional in front of others.
7. Debilitating performance anxiety and/or avoidance of required social performance demands.
8. Increased heart rate, sweating, dry mouth, muscle tension, and shakiness in social situations.

—. _____
   _____

—. _____
   _____

—. _____
   _____

LONG-TERM GOALS

1. Interact socially without undue fear or anxiety.
2. Participate in social performance requirements without undue fear or anxiety.
3. Develop the essential social skills that will enhance the quality of relationship life.

4. Develop the ability to form relationships that will enhance a recovery support system.
5. Reach a personal balance between solitary time and interpersonal interaction with others.

—. _____
_____

—. _____
_____

—. _____
_____

SHORT-TERM OBJECTIVES

1. Describe the history and nature of social fears and avoidance. (1, 2, 3)

2. Complete psychological tests designed to assess the nature and severity of social anxiety and avoidance. (4)

THERAPEUTIC INTERVENTIONS

1. Actively build the level of trust with the client through consistent eye contact, active listening, unconditional positive regard, and warm acceptance.

2. Assess the client's frequency, intensity, duration, and history of panic symptoms, fear, and avoidance (e.g., *The Anxiety Disorders Interview Schedule for Children—Parent Version* or *Child Version* by Silverman and Albano).

3. Assess the nature of any stimulus, thoughts, or situations that precipitate the client's social fear and/or avoidance.

4. Administer a measure of social anxiety to further assess the depth and breadth of social fears and avoidance (e.g., *The Social Interaction Anxiety Scale and/or Social Phobia Scale* by Mattick and Clarke).

▽ 3. Cooperate with an evaluation by a physician for psychotropic medication. (5, 6)

5. Arrange for an evaluation for a prescription of psychotropic medications. ▽

6. Monitor the client for prescription compliance, side effects, and overall effectiveness of the medication; consult with the prescribing physician at regular intervals. ▽

▽ 4. Participate in a small group therapy for social anxiety, or individual therapy if the group is unavailable. (7)

7. Enroll clients in a small (closed enrollment) group for social anxiety (see Baer and Garland, 2005) or individual therapy if a group cannot be formed. ▽

▽ 5. Verbalize an accurate understanding of the vicious cycle of social anxiety and avoidance. (8, 9)

8. Discuss how social anxiety derives from cognitive biases that overestimate negative evaluation by others, undervalue the self, distress, and often lead to unnecessary avoidance. ▽

9. Assign the client to read psychoeducational chapters of books or treatment manuals on social anxiety that explain the cycle of social anxiety and avoidance and the rationale for treatment (e.g., *Overcoming Shyness and Social Phobia* by Rapee; *Overcoming Social Anxiety and Shyness* by Butler). ▽

▽ 6. Verbalize an understanding of the rationale for treatment of social anxiety. (10, 11)

10. Discuss how cognitive restructuring and exposure serve as an arena to desensitize learned fear, build social skills and confidence, and reality test biased thoughts. ▽

11. Assign the client to read about cognitive restructuring and exposure-based therapy in chapters of books or treatment manuals on social anxiety (e.g.,

---

▽ indicates that the Objective/Intervention is consistent with those found in evidence-based treatments.

▽ 7. Learn and implement calming and coping strategies to manage anxiety symptoms and focus attention usefully during moments of social anxiety. (12, 13)

▽ 8. Identify, challenge, and replace fearful self-talk with reality-based, positive self-talk. (14, 15, 16)

Managing Social Anxiety by Hope, Heimberg, Juster, and Turk; *Dying of Embarrassment* by Markaway, Carmin, Pollard, and Flynn). ▽

12. Teach the client relaxation and attentional focusing skills (e.g., staying focused externally and on behavioral goals, muscular relaxation, evenly paced diaphragmatic breathing, ride the wave of anxiety) to manage social anxiety symptoms. ▽

13. Assign the client to read about calming and coping strategies in books or treatment manuals on social anxiety (e.g., *Overcoming Shyness and Social Phobia* by Rapee). ▽

14. Explore the client's schema and self-talk that mediate his/her social fear response, challenge the biases; assist him/her in generating appraisals that correct for the biases and build confidence. ▽

15. Assign the client to read about cognitive restructuring in books or treatment manuals on social anxiety (e.g., *The Shyness and Social Anxiety Workbook* by Antony and Swinson). ▽

16. Assign the client a homework exercise in which he/she identifies fearful self-talk and creates reality-based alternatives (or assign "Bad Thoughts Lead to Depressed Feelings" in the *Adolescent Psychotherapy Homework Planner,* 2nd ed. by Jongsma, Peterson, and McInnis); review and reinforce success, providing corrective feedback for failure (see

▽ 9. Participate in gradual repeated exposure to feared social situations within individual or group therapy sessions and review with group members and therapist. (17, 18, 19)

▽10. Participate in gradual repeated exposure to feared social situations outside of individual or group therapy sessions. (20)

The Shyness and Social Anxiety Workbook by Antony and Swinson; *Overcoming Shyness and Social Phobia* by Rapee). ▽

17. Direct and assist the client in construction of a hierarchy of anxiety-producing situations associated with the phobic response. ▽

18. Select initial in vivo or role-played exposures that have a high likelihood of being a successful experience for the client; do cognitive restructuring within and after the exposure, use behavioral strategies (e.g., modeling, rehearsal, social reinforcement) to facilitate the exposure, review with the client and group members, if done in group (*Treatment of Social Anxiety Disorder* by Albano). ▽

19. Assign the client to read about exposure in books or treatment manuals on social anxiety (e.g., *The Shyness and Social Anxiety Workbook* by Antony and Swinson; *Overcoming Shyness and Social Phobia* by Rapee). ▽

20. Assign the client a homework exercise in which he/she does an exposure exercise (or assign "Gradually Facing a Phobic Fear" in the *Adolescent Psychotherapy Homework Planner,* 2nd ed. by Jongsma, Peterson, and McInnis) and records responses (see *The Shyness and Social Anxiety Workbook* by Antony and Swinson; *Treatment of Social Anxiety Disorder* by Albano); review and reinforce success, providing corrective feedback toward improvement. ▽

▼11. Learn and implement social skills to reduce anxiety and build confidence in social interactions. (21, 22)

21. Use instruction, modeling, and role-playing to build the client's general social and/or communication skills (see Turner, Beidel, and Cooley); assign the client to implement these skills in daily life and review the success or failure (or assign "Greeting Peers" or "Reach Out and Call" in the *Adolescent Psychotherapy Homework Planner,* 2nd ed. by Jongsma, Peterson, and McInnis). ▼

22. Assign the client to read about general social and/or communication skills in books or treatment manuals on building social skills (e.g., *Your Perfect Right* by Alberti and Emmons; *Conversationally Speaking* by Garner). ▼

▼12. Learn and implement relapse prevention strategies for managing possible future anxiety symptoms. (23, 24, 25, 26)

23. Discuss with the client the distinction between a lapse and relapse, associating a lapse with an initial and reversible return of symptoms, fear, or urges to avoid and relapse with the decision to return to fearful and avoidant patterns. ▼

24. Identify and rehearse with the client the management of future situations or circumstances in which lapses could occur. ▼

25. Instruct the client to routinely use strategies learned in therapy (e.g., using cognitive restructuring, social skills, and exposure) while building social interactions and relationships. ▼

26. Develop a "coping card" on which coping strategies and other important information (e.g., "Pace your breathing," "Focus on the task at hand," "You can manage it," "It will go away") are written for the client's later use. ▼

13. Family members learn skills that strengthen and support the client's positive behavior change. (27, 28, 29)

27. Hold family sessions in which the family is taught the treatment goals, how to give support as the client faces his/her fears, and how to prevent reinforcing the client's fear and avoidance; offer encouragement, support, and redirection as required.

28. Teach the family problem-solving and conflict resolution skills for managing problems within themselves and between them and the client.

29. Encourage the family to model constructive skills they have learned and the therapeutic skills the client is learning (e.g., calming, cognitive restructuring, nonavoidance of unrealistic fears).

14. Explore past experiences that may be the source of low self-esteem and social anxiety currently. (30, 31)

30. Probe childhood experiences of criticism, abandonment, or abuse that would foster low self-esteem and shame; process these.

31. Assign the client to read the books, *Healing the Shame That Binds You* (Bradshaw) and *Facing Shame* (Fossum and Mason), and process key ideas.

15. Verbally describe the defense mechanisms used to avoid close relationships. (32)

32. Assist the client in identifying defense mechanisms that keep others at a distance and prevent him/her from developing trusting relationships; identify ways to minimize defensiveness.

16. Explore beliefs and communication patterns that cause social anxiety and isolation. (33, 34)

33. Utilize a transactional analysis (TA) approach to uncover and identify the client's beliefs and fears; use the TA approach to alter beliefs and actions.

34. Assign the client to read a book on improving social relationships

using Transactional Analysis (e.g., *Achieving Emotional Literacy* by Steiner)

17. Return for a follow-up session to track progress, reinforce gains, and problem-solve barriers. (35)

35. Schedule a follow-up or "booster session" for the client for 1 to 3 months after therapy ends.

__. _____

__. _____

__. _____

__. _____

__. _____

__. _____

DIAGNOSTIC SUGGESTIONS

Axis I:
300.23 Social Anxiety Disorder (Social Phobia)
300.4   Dysthymic Disorder
296.xx Major Depressive Disorder
300.7   Body Dysmorphic Disorder

_____ _____

_____ _____

Axis II:
799.9   Diagnosis Deferred
V71.09 No Diagnosis

_____ _____

_____ _____

SPECIFIC PHOBIA

BEHAVIORAL DEFINITIONS

1. Describes a persistent and unreasonable fear of a specific object or situation that promotes avoidance behaviors because an encounter with the phobic stimulus provokes an immediate anxiety response.
2. Avoids the phobic stimulus/feared environment or endures it with distress, resulting in interference of normal routines.
3. Acknowledges a persistence of fear despite recognition that the fear is unreasonable.
4. Sleep disturbed by dreams of the feared stimulus.
5. Dramatic fear reaction out of proportion to the phobic stimulus.
6. Parental reinforcement of the phobia by catering to the client's fear.

—. _____
   _____
   _____
—. _____
   _____
   _____
—. _____
   _____

LONG-TERM GOALS

1. Reduce fear of the specific stimulus object or situation that previously provoked phobic anxiety.
2. Reduce phobic avoidance of the specific object or situation, leading to comfort and independence in moving around in public environment.
3. Eliminate interference in normal routines and remove distress from feared object or situation.
4. Live phobia-free while responding appropriately to life's fears.
5. Resolve the conflict underlying the phobia.

—. _____

   _____

—. _____

   _____

—. _____

   _____

SHORT-TERM OBJECTIVES

1. Describe the history and nature of the phobia(s), complete with impact on functioning and attempt to overcome it. (1, 2)

2. Complete psychological tests designed to assess features of the phobia. (3)

▽ 3. Cooperate with an evaluation by a physician for psychotropic medication. (4, 5)

THERAPEUTIC INTERVENTIONS

1. Actively build a level of trust with the client that will promote the open showing of thoughts and feelings, especially fearful ones.

2. Assess the client's fear and avoidance, including the focus of fear, types of avoidance (e.g., distraction, escape, dependence on others), development, and disability (e.g., *The Anxiety Disorders Interview Schedule for Children— Parent Version or Child Version* by Silverman and Albano).

3. Administer a client-report measure (e.g., from *Measures for Specific Phobia* by Antony) to further assess the depth and breadth of phobic responses.

4. Arrange for an evaluation for a prescription of psychotropic medications if the client requests it or if the client is likely to be noncompliant with gradual exposure. ▽

5. Monitor the client for prescription compliance, side effects, and overall effectiveness of the

---

▽ indicates that the Objective/Intervention is consistent with those found in evidence-based treatments.

medication; consult with the prescribing physician at regular intervals. ▽

▽ 4. Verbalize an accurate understanding of information about phobias and their treatment. (6, 7, 8)

6. Discuss how phobias are very common, a natural but irrational expression of our fight or flight response, are not a sign of weakness, but cause unnecessary distress and disability. ▽

7. Discuss how phobic fear is maintained by a "phobic cycle" of unwarranted fear and avoidance that precludes positive, corrective experiences with the feared object or situation, and how treatment breaks the cycle by encouraging these experiences (see *Mastery of Your Specific Phobia—Therapist Guide* by Craske, Antony, and Barlow; *Specific Phobias* by Bruce and Sanderson). ▽

8. Assign the client to read psychoeducational chapters of books or treatment manuals on specific phobias (e.g., *Mastery of Your Specific Phobia—Client Manual* by Antony, Craske, and Barlow; *The Anxiety and Phobia Workbook* by Bourne). ▽

▽ 5. Verbalize an understanding of how thoughts, physical feelings, and behavioral actions contribute to anxiety and its treatment. (8, 9, 10)

8. Assign the client to read psychoeducational chapters of books or treatment manuals on specific phobias (e.g., *Mastery of Your Specific Phobia—Client Manual* by Antony, Craske, and Barlow; *The Anxiety and Phobia Workbook* by Bourne). ▽

9. Discuss how phobias involve perceiving unrealistic threats, bodily expressions of fear, and avoidance of what is threatening that interact to maintain the problem (see *Mastery of Your*

Specific Phobia—Therapist Guide by Craske, Antony, and Barlow; *Specific Phobias* by Bruce and Sanderson). ▽

10. Discuss how exposure serves as an arena to desensitize learned fear, build confidence, and feel safer by building a new history of success experiences (see *Mastery of Your Specific Phobia—Therapist Guide* by Craske, Antony, and Barlow; *Specific Phobias* by Bruce and Sanderson). ▽

▽ 6. Learn and implement calming skills to reduce and manage anxiety symptoms that may emerge during encounters with phobic objects or situations. (11, 12, 13, 14)

11. Teach the client anxiety management skills (e.g., staying focused on behavioral goals, muscular relaxation, evenly paced diaphragmatic breathing, positive self-talk) to address anxiety symptoms that may emerge during encounters with phobic objects or situations. ▽

12. Assign the client to read psychoeducational chapters of books or treatment manuals describing calming strategies (e.g., *Mastery of Your Specific Phobia—Client Manual* by Antony, Craske, and Barlow). ▽

13. Assign the client a homework exercise in which he/she practices daily calming skills; review and reinforce success, providing corrective feedback for failure. ▽

14. Use biofeedback techniques to facilitate the client's success at learning calming skills. ▽

▽ 7. Learn and implement applied tension skills to prevent fainting in response to blood, injection, or injury. (15, 16)

15. Teach the client applied tension in which he/she tenses neck and upper torso muscles to curtail blood flow out of the brain to help prevent fainting during encounters

with phobic objects or situations involving blood, injection, or injury (see "Applied tension, exposure in vivo, and tension-only in the treatment of blood phobia" in *Behaviour Research and Therapy* by Ost, Fellenius, and Sterner). ▽

16. Assign the client a homework exercise in which he/she practices daily applied tension skills; review and reinforce success, providing corrective feedback for failure. ▽

▽ 8. Identify, challenge, and replace fearful self-talk with positive, realistic, and empowering self-talk. (17, 18, 19, 20)

17. Explore the client's schema and self-talk that mediate his/her fear response; challenge the biases; assist him/her in replacing the distorted messages with reality-based, positive self-talk. ▽

18. Assign the client to read about cognitive restructuring in books or treatment manuals on Panic Disorder and Agoraphobia (e.g., *Mastery of Your Specific Phobia—Client Manual* by Antony, Craske, and Barlow; *The Anxiety and Phobia Workbook* by Bourne). ▽

19. Assign the client a homework exercise in which he/she identifies fearful self-talk and creates reality-based alternatives (or assign "Bad Thoughts Lead to Depressed Feelings" in the *Adolescent Psychotherapy Homework Planner,* 2nd ed. by Jongsma, Peterson, and McInnis); review and reinforce success, providing corrective feedback for failure. ▽

20. Use behavioral techniques (e.g., modeling, corrective feedback, imaginal rehearsal, social reinforcement) to train the client

▽ 9. Participate in gradual repeated exposure to feared or avoided phobic objects or situations. (21, 22, 23, 24, 25)

in positive self-talk that pre-pares him/her to endure anxiety symptoms without serious conse-quences. ▽

21. Direct and assist the client in construction of a hierarchy of anxiety-producing situations as-sociated with the phobic response. ▽

22. Select initial exposures that have a high likelihood of being a suc-cessful experience for the client; develop a plan for managing the symptoms and rehearse the plan. ▽

23. Assign the client to read about situational exposure in books or treatment manuals on specific phobias (e.g., *Mastery of Your Specific Phobia—Client Manual* by Antony, Craske, and Barlow). ▽

24. Conduct exposures with the client using graduated tasks, modeling, and reinforcement of the client's success until he/she can do the exposures unassisted (see *Phobic and Anxiety Disorders in Children and Adolescents* by Ollendick and March). ▽

25. Assign the client a homework exercise in which he/she does situational exposures and records responses (or assign "Gradually Facing a Phobic Fear" in the *Ado-lescent Psychotherapy Homework Planner,* 2nd ed. by Jongsma, Pe-terson, and McInnis; see *Mastery of Your Specific Phobia—Client Manual* by Antony, Craske, and Barlow); review and reinforce success or provide corrective feed-back toward improvement. ▽

▼10. Implement relapse prevention strategies for managing possible future anxiety symptoms. (26, 27, 28, 29)

26. Discuss with the client the distinction between a lapse and relapse, associating a lapse with a temporary and reversible return of symptoms, fear, or urges to avoid and relapse with the decision to return to fearful and avoidant patterns. ▼

27. Identify and rehearse with the client the management of future situations or circumstances in which lapses could occur. ▼

28. Instruct the client to routinely use strategies learned in therapy (e.g., cognitive restructuring, exposure), building them into his/her life as much as possible. ▼

29. Develop a "coping card" on which coping strategies and other important information (e.g., "You're safe," "Pace your breathing," "Focus on the task at hand," "You can manage it," "Stay in the situation," "Let the anxiety pass") are written for the client's later use. ▼

11. Collect pleasant pictures or stories regarding the phobic stimulus and share them in therapy sessions. (30, 31)

30. Use pleasant pictures, readings, or storytelling about the feared object or situation as a means of desensitizing the client to the fear-producing stimulus.

31. Use humor, jokes, riddles, and stories to enable the client to see his/her situation/fears as not as serious as believed and to help instill hope without disrespecting or minimizing his/her fears.

12. Family members demonstrate support for the client as he/she tolerates more exposure to the phobic stimulus. (32, 33, 34)

32. Hold family sessions in which the family is instructed to give support as the client faces the phobic stimulus and to withhold support if the client panics and fails to

face the fear (see *Turning Points* by Pittman); offer encouragement, support, and redirection as required.

33. Assist the family in overcoming the tendency to reinforce the client's phobia; as the phobia decreases, teach the family constructive ways to reward the client's progress.

34. Assess and confront family members when they model phobic fear responses for the client in the presence of the feared object or situation.

13. Identify the symbolic significance of the phobic stimulus as a basis for fear. (35)

35. Probe, discuss, and interpret the possible symbolic meaning of the client's phobic stimulus object or situation.

14. Verbalize the separate realities of the irrationally feared object or situation and the emotionally painful experience from the past that is evoked by the phobic stimulus. (36)

36. Clarify and differentiate between the client's current irrational fear and past emotionally painful experiences.

15. Verbalize the feelings associated with a past emotionally painful situation that is connected to the phobia. (37, 38)

37. Encourage the client to share feelings from the past through active listening, unconditional positive regard, and questioning.

38. Reinforce the client's insight into the past emotional pain and its connection to present anxiety.

__. _____

_____

__. _____

_____

__. _____

_____

__. _____

_____

__. _____

_____

__. _____

_____

DIAGNOSTIC SUGGESTIONS

Axis I:	300.00	Anxiety Disorder NOS
	300.29	Specific Phobia
	_____	_____
	_____	_____
Axis II:	799.9	Diagnosis Deferred
	V71.09	No Diagnosis
	_____	_____
	_____	_____

SUICIDAL IDEATION

BEHAVIORAL DEFINITIONS

1. Recurrent thoughts of or a preoccupation with death.
2. Recurrent or ongoing suicidal ideation without any plans.
3. Ongoing suicidal ideation with a specific plan.
4. Recent suicide attempt.
5. History of suicide attempts that required professional or family/friend intervention on some level (e.g., inpatient, safe house, outpatient, supervision).
6. Positive family history of depression and/or suicide.
7. Expression of a bleak, hopeless attitude regarding life.
8. Recent painful life events (e.g., parental divorce, death of a friend or family member, broken close relationship).
9. Social withdrawal, lethargy, and apathy.
10. Rebellious and self-destructive behavior patterns (e.g., dangerous drug or alcohol abuse, reckless driving, assaultive anger) that indicate a disregard for personal safety and a desperate attempt to escape from emotional distress.

___. _____
   _____
___. _____
   _____
___. _____
   _____

LONG-TERM GOALS

1. Alleviate the suicidal impulses or ideation and return to the highest previous level of daily functioning.

2. Stabilize the suicidal crisis.
3. Place in an appropriate level of care to address the suicidal crisis.
4. Reestablish a sense of hope for future life.
5. Terminate the death wish and renew a zestful interest in social activities and relationships.
6. Cease the perilous lifestyle and resolve the emotional conflicts that underlie the suicidal pattern.

—. _____
_____
—. _____
_____
—. _____
_____

SHORT-TERM OBJECTIVES

THERAPEUTIC INTERVENTIONS

1. State the strength of the suicidal feelings, the frequency of the thoughts, and the detail of the plans. (1, 2)

1. Assess the client's suicidal ideation, taking into account the extent of the ideation, the presence of primary and backup plans, past attempts, and family history.

2. Assess and monitor the client's suicide potential on an ongoing basis.

2. Parents, family members, and significant others agree to provide supervision and monitor suicide potential. (3)

3. Notify the client's family and significant others of any severe suicidal ideation. Ask them to form a 24-hour suicide watch until the crisis subsides.

3. Cooperate with psychological testing to assess for the severity of depression and hopelessness. (4)

4. Arrange for psychological assessment of the client (e.g., Minnesota Multiphasic Personality Inventory, Beck Depression Inventory, Reynolds Adolescent Depression Scale) and evaluate the results as to the depth of depression.

4. Cooperate with an evaluation by a physician for antidepressant medication. (5, 6)

5. Cooperate with hospitalization if the suicidal urge becomes uncontrollable. (7)

6. Verbalize a promise (as part of a suicide prevention contract) to contact the therapist or some other emergency helpline if a serious urge toward self-harm arises. (8, 9, 10, 11)

7. Parents increase the safety of the home by removing firearms or other lethal weapons from the client's easy access. (12)

8. Increase communication with the parents, resulting in feeling attended to and understood. (13)

5. Assess the client's need for antidepressant medication and arrange for a prescription, if necessary.

6. Monitor the client for medication compliance, effectiveness, and side effects.

7. Arrange for hospitalization when the client is judged to be harmful to himself/herself.

8. Elicit a promise from the client that he/she will initiate contact with the therapist or a helpline if the suicidal urge becomes strong and before any self-injurious behavior.

9. Provide the client with an emergency helpline telephone number that is available 24-hours a day.

10. Make a written contract with the client, identifying what he/she will and will not do when experiencing suicidal thoughts or impulses (or complete the "No Self-Harm Contract" exercise from the *Adolescent Psychotherapy Homework Planner,* 2nd ed. by Jongsma, Peterson, and McInnis).

11. Offer to be available to the client through telephone contact if a life-threatening urge develops.

12. Encourage the parents to remove firearms or other lethal weapons from the client's easy access.

13. Meet with the parents to assess their understanding of the causes for the client's distress and to explain the client's perspective and need for empathy.

9. Identify feelings of sadness, anger, and hopelessness related to a conflicted relationship with the parents. (14, 15)

10. Verbalize an understanding of the motives for self-destructive behavior patterns. (16, 17, 18)

11. Verbally report and demonstrate an increased sense of hope for self. (19, 20, 21, 22)

14. Probe the client's feelings of despair related to his/her family relationships.

15. Hold family therapy sessions to promote communication of the client's feelings of sadness, hurt, and anger.

16. Explore the sources of emotional pain underlying the client's suicidal ideation and the depth of his/her hopelessness.

17. Interpret the client's sadness, wish for death, or dangerous rebellion as an expression of hopelessness and helplessness (a cry for help).

18. Encourage the client to express his/her feelings related to the suicidal behavior in order to clarify them and increase insight into the causes and motives for the behavior.

19. Teach the client the benefit of sharing emotional pain instead of internalizing it and brooding over it (or assign the client to read the short story "Renewed Hope" from the *Adolescent Psychotherapy Homework Planner,* 2nd ed. by Jongsma, Peterson, and McInnis).

20. Assist the client in finding positive, hopeful things in his/her life at the present time.

21. Reinforce all of the client's statements that reflect hope and resolution of the suicidal urge.

22. Ask the client to bring to session symbols of achievement and personal meaning and reinforce their importance (or assign the exercise "Symbols of Self-Worth" from the

Adolescent Psychotherapy Homework Planner, 2nd ed. by Jongsma, Peterson, and McInnis).

12. Implement more positive cognitive processing patterns that maintain a realistic and hopeful perspective. (23, 24, 25)

23. Assist the client in developing coping strategies for suicidal ideation (e.g., more physical exercise, less internal focus, increased social involvement, more expression of feelings).

24. Assist the client in developing an awareness of the cognitive messages that reinforce hopelessness and helplessness.

25. Identify and confront catastrophizing, fortune-telling, and mind-reading tendencies in the client's cognitive processing, teaching more realistic self-talk of hope in the face of pain.

13. Identify how previous attempts to solve interpersonal problems have failed, resulting in helplessness. (26)

26. Review with the client previous problem-solving attempts and discuss new alternatives that are available (e.g., assertiveness, brainstorming with a friend, sharing with a mentor, compromise, acceptance).

14. Develop and implement a penitence ritual of expressing grief for victims and absolving self of responsibility for surviving an incident fatal to others. (27)

27. Develop a penitence ritual for the client who is a survivor of an incident fatal to others and implement it with him/her.

15. Strengthen the social support network with friends by initiating social contact and participating in social activities with peers. (28, 29, 30)

28. Encourage the client to reach out to friends and participate in enriching social activities by assigning involvement in at least one social activity with his/her peers per week. Monitor and process the experience.

29. Use behavioral rehearsal, modeling, and role-playing to build the client's social skills with his/her peers.

30. Encourage the client to broaden his/her social network by initiating one new social contact per week versus desperately clinging to one or two friends.

16. Reestablish a consistent eating and sleeping pattern. (31)

31. Encourage normal eating and sleeping patterns and monitor the client's compliance.

—. _____   —. _____
    _____   _____

—. _____   —. _____
    _____   _____

—. _____   —. _____
    _____   _____

DIAGNOSTIC SUGGESTIONS

Axis I: 296.2x   Major Depressive Disorder, Single Episode
                296.3x   Major Depressive Disorder, Recurrent
                300.4   Dysthymic Disorder
                296.xx   Bipolar I Disorder
                296.89   Bipolar II Disorder, Most Recent Episode Depressed
                311   Depressive Disorder NOS
                309.81   Posttraumatic Stress Disorder

                _____   _____

                _____   _____

Axis II: 799.9   Diagnosis Deferred
                V71.09   No Diagnosis

                _____   _____

                _____   _____

Appendix A

BIBLIOTHERAPY SUGGESTIONS

GENERAL

Many references are made throughout the chapters to a therapeutic homework resource that was developed by the authors as a corollary to the *Adolescent Psychotherapy Treatment Planner* (Jongsma, Peterson, and McInnis). This frequently cited homework resource book is:

Jongsma, A., Peterson, L. M., and McInnis, W. (2006). *Adolescent Therapy Homework Planner, 2nd ed.* New York: Wiley.

ACADEMIC UNDERACHIEVEMENT

Harwell, J. (1989). *Complete Learning Disabilities Handbook.* Paramus, NJ: Center for Applied Research.

Martin, M., and Greenwood-Waltman, C., ed. (1995). *Solve Your Child's School-Related Problems.* New York: HarperCollins.

Silverman, S. (1998). *13 Steps to Better Grades.* Plainview, NY: Childswork/Childsplay.

Zentil, S., and Goldstein, S. (1999). *Seven Steps to Homework Success.* Plantation, FL: Specialty Press.

ADOPTION

Burlingham-Brown, B. (1994). *Why Didn't She Keep Me?* South Bend, IN: Langford.

Covey, S. (1997). *The 7 Habits of Highly Effective Families: Building a Beautiful Family Culture in a Turbulent World.* New York: Golden Books.

Eldridge, S. (1999). *20 Things Adopted Kids Wish Their Adoptive Parents Knew.* New York: Dell.

Jewett, C. (1979). *Adopting the Older Child.* Boston: Harvard Press.

Jewett, C. (1994). *Helping Children Cope with Separation and Loss.* Harvard, MA: Harvard Common Press.

Korb-Khalsa, K., Azok, S., and Leutenberg, E. (1992). *SEALS & PLUS.* Beachwood, OH: Wellness Reproductions.

Krementz, J. (1996). *How It Feels To Be Adopted.* New York: Alfred Knopf.

Lifton, B. J. (1994). *Journey of the Adopted Self.* New York: Basic Books.

Medina, L. (1984). *Making Sense of Adoption.* New York: Harper & Row.

Schooler, J. (1993). *The Whole Life Adoption Book.* Colorado Springs, CO: Pinon Press.

Schooler, J. (1995). *Searching for a Past.* Colorado Springs, CO: Pinon Press.

Stinson, K. (1998). *I Feel Different.* Los Angeles: Manson Western Co.

Tyson, J. (1997). *Common Threads of Teenage Grief.* Lake Dallas, TX: Helm Seminars.

ANGER MANAGEMENT

Bertolino, B. (1999). *Therapy with Troubled Teenagers.* New York: Wiley.

Bluestein, J. (1993). *Parents, Teens and Boundaries: How to Draw the Line.* Deerfield Beach, FL: Health Communications.

Canter, L., and Canter, P. (1988). *Assertive Discipline for Parents.* New York: HarperCollins.

Clark, L. (1998). *S.O.S.—Help for Emotions.* Bowling Green, KY: Parents' Press.

Deffenbacher, J. L., and McKay, M. (2000). *Overcoming Situational and General Anger: Client Manual (Best Practices for Therapy).* Oakland, CA: New Harbinger.

Forehand, R., and Long, N. (1996). *Parenting the Strong-Willed Child.* Chicago: Contemporary Books.

Garner, A. (1997). *Conversationally Speaking: Tested New Ways to Increase Your Personal and Social Effectiveness.* Los Angeles: Lowell House.

Katherine, A. (1991). *Boundaries: Where You End and I Begin.* New York: Simon & Schuster.

Murphy, T. (2001). *The Angry Child.* New York: Three Rivers Press.

Patterson, G. R. (1976). *Living with Children: New Methods for Parents and Teachers.* Champaign, IL: Research Press.

Patterson, G. R. (1982). *Coercive Family Process.* Eugene, OR: Castalia.

Potter-Efron, R. (1994). *Angry All the Time.* Oakland, CA: New Harbinger.

Robin, A., and Foster, S. (1989). *Negotiating Parent/Adolescent Conflict.* New York: Guilford.

Stewart, J. (2002). *The Anger Workout Book for Teens.* Franklin, CA: Jalmer Press.

Wolf, A. (1992). *Get Out of My Life, But First Could You Drive Me and Cheryl to the Mall?: A Parent's Guide to the New Teenager.* New York: Noonday Press.

ANXIETY

Benson, J. (1975). *The Relaxation Response.* New York: William Morrow.

Bourne, E. (1995). *Anxiety and Phobia Workbook.* Berkeley, CA: Fine Communications.

Burns, D. (1989). *The Feeling Good Handbook.* New York: William Morrow.
Burns, D. (1993). *Ten Days to Self-Esteem.* New York: William Morrow.
Clark, L. (1998). *S.O.S.—Help for Emotions.* Bowling Green, KY: Parents' Press.
Crist, J. J. (2004). *What to Do When You're Scared & Worried: A Guide for Kids.* Minneapolis, MN: Free Spirit.
Elkind, D. (1981). *The Hurried Child: Growing Up Too Fast Too Soon.* New York: Addison-Wesley.
Elkind, D. (1984). *All Grown Up and No Place to Go: Teenagers in Crisis.* New York: Addison-Wesley.
Faber, A., and Mazlish, E. (1987). *How to Talk So Kids Will Listen and Listen So Kids Will Talk.* New York: Avon.
Ginnot, H. (1965). *Between Parent and Child.* New York: Macmillan.
Ginnot, H. (1969). *Between Parent and Teenager.* New York: Macmillan.
Manassis, K. (1996). *Keys to Parenting Your Anxious Child.* Hauppauge, NY: Barron's.
Marks, I. M. (2001). *Living with Fear, 2nd ed.* London: McGraw-Hill.
McCauley, C. S., and Schachter, R. (1988). *When Your Child Is Afraid.* New York: Simon & Schuster.
Rapee, R., Spense, S., Cobham, V., and Wignal, A. (2000*). Helping Your Anxious Child: A Step-By-Step Guide for Parents.* San Francisco: New Harbinger.
Wagner, A. P. (2000). *Up and Down the Worry Hill.* Rochester, NY: Lighthouse Press.
Wagner, A. P. (2002). *Worried No More: Help and Hope for Anxious Children.* Rochester, NY: Lighthouse Press.
Zinbarg, R. E., Craske, M. G., Barlow, D. H., and O'Leary, T. (1993). *Mastery of Your Anxiety and Worry—Client Guide.* San Antonio, TX: Psychological Corporation.

ATTENTION-DEFICIT/HYPERACTIVITY DISORDER (ADHD)

Alexander-Roberts, C. (2001). *ADHD and Teens.* Dallas, TX: Taylor Publishing.
Alexander-Roberts, C., and Elliot, P. (2002). *ADHD and Teens: A Parent's Guide to Making It Through the Tough Years.* Cutten, CA: Taylor Publishing.
Barkley, R. A. (2000). *Taking Charge of ADHD: The Complete Authoritative Guide for Parents.* New York: Guilford.
Barkley, R. A., and Murphy, K. R. (2005). *Attention-Deficit Hyperactivity Disorder: A Clinical Workbook, 3rd ed.* New York: Guilford.
Crist, J. (1997). *ADHD—A Teenager's Guide.* Plainview, NY: Childswork/Childsplay.
Dendy-Zeigler, C. (1995). *Teenagers with ADD: A Parent's Guide.* Bethesda, MD: Woodbine House.
Hallowell, E., and Ratey, J. (1994). *Driven to Distraction.* New York: Pantheon.
Ingersoll, B. (1988). *Your Hyperactive Child.* New York: Doubleday.
Parker, H. (1990). *Put Yourself in Their Shoes: Understanding Teenagers with Attention Deficit Hyperactivity Disorder.* Plantation, FL: Specialty Press.
Parker, H. (1992). *The ADD Hyperactivity Handbook for Schools.* Plantation, FL: Impact Publications.
Quinn, P. (1995). *Adolescents and ADD: Gaining the Advantage.* Washington, DC: Magination Press.

Robin, A., and Foster, S. (2002). *Negotiating Parent/Adolescent Conflict.* New York: Guilford.

Snyder, J. (2001). *AD/HD and Driving: A Guide for Parents of Teens with AD/HD.* Whitefish, MT: Whitefish Consultants.

Zeigler Dendy, C. A. (1995). *Teenagers with ADD: A Parents' Guide.* Bethesda, MD: Woodbine House.

AUTISM/PERVASIVE DEVELOPMENTAL DISORDER

Brill, M. (1994). *Keys to Parenting the Child with Autism.* Hauppauge, NY: Barrons.

Kennedy, D. (2002). *The AD/HD-Autism Connection.* Colorado Springs, CO: WaterBooks Press.

Moyes, R. (2003). *I Need Help with School: A Guide for Parents of Children with Autism and Asperger's Syndrome.* Marquette, MI: Future Horizons.

Siegel, B. (1996). *The World of the Autistic Child.* New York: Oxford.

Simons, J., and Olsihi, S. (1987). *The Hidden Child.* Bethesda, MD: Woodbine House.

Waltz, M. (2002). *Autistic Spectrum Disorders: Understanding the Diagnosis and Getting Help.* Harrington Park, NJ: O'Reily.

BLENDED FAMILY

Brown, M. (1947). *Stone Soup.* New York: Simon & Schuster.

Burns, D. (1993). *Ten Days to Self-Esteem.* New York: William Morrow.

Burt, M. (1989). *Stepfamilies Stepping Ahead.* Lincoln, NE: Stepfamily Association.

Covey, S. (1997). *The 7 Habits of Highly Effective Families.* New York: Golden Books.

Fassler, D., Lash, M., and Ives, S. (1988). *Changing Families.* Burlington, VT: Waterfront Books.

Markman, H., Stanley, S., and Blumberg, S. (1994). *Fighting for Your Marriage.* San Francisco: Jossey-Bass.

Seuss, Dr. (1961). *The Sneetches and Other Stories.* New York: Random House.

Visher, E., and Visher, J. (1982). *How To Win As a Stepfamily.* New York: Brunner/Mazel.

CHEMICAL DEPENDENCE

Ackerman, R. (1978). *Children of Alcoholics: A Guide for Educators, Therapists and Parents.* Holmes Beach, FL: Learning Publications.

Alcoholics Anonymous. (1976). *Alcoholics Anonymous: The Big Book.* New York: AA World Service.

Bell, T. (1990). *Preventing Adolescent Relapse.* Independence, MO: Herald House.

Black, C. (1982). *It Will Never Happen to Me.* Denver, CO: MAC Printing and Publishing.

Bradshaw, J. (1988). *Bradshaw on the Family.* Pompano Beach, FL: Health Communications.

Ellis, D. (1986). *Growing Up Stoned.* Pompano Beach, FL: Health Communications.
Fanning, P., and O'Neil, J. (1996). *The Addiction Workbook.* San Francisco: New Harbinger.
Narcotics Anonymous. (1982). *Narcotics Anonymous.* Van Nuys, CA: NA World Services Office, Inc.
Ohm, D. (1983). *POT.* Belleville, IL: G. Whiteaker.
Woititz, J. G. (1983). *Adult Children of Alcoholics.* Pompano Beach, FL: Health Communications.

CONDUCT DISORDER/DELINQUENCY

Bernstein, N. (2001). *How to Keep Your Teenager Out of Trouble and What To Do if You Can't.* New York: Workman Publications.
Bertolino, B. (1999). *Therapy with Troubled Teenagers.* New York: Wiley.
Canter, L., and Canter, P. (1988). *Assertive Discipline for Parents.* New York: HarperCollins.
Deffenbacher, J. L., and McKay, M. (2000). *Overcoming Situational and General Anger: Client Manual (Best Practices for Therapy).* Oakland, CA: New Harbinger.
Forehand, R., and Long, N. (1996). *Parenting the Strong-Willed Child.* Chicago: Contemporary Books.
Garner, A. (1997). *Conversationally Speaking: Tested New Ways to Increase Your Personal and Social Effectiveness.* Los Angeles: Lowell House.
Katherine, A. (1991). *Boundaries: Where You End and I Begin.* New York: Simon & Schuster.
Patterson, G. R. (1976). *Living with Children: New Methods for Parents and Teachers.* Champaign, IL: Research Press.
Patterson, G. R. (1982). *Coercive Family Process.* Eugene, OR: Castalia.
Robin, A., and Foster, S. (1989). *Negotiating Parent/Adolescent Conflict.* New York: Guilford.
Shapiro, L. E. (1996). *Teens' Solution Workbook.* Plainview, NY: Childswork/Childsplay.
Shore, H. (1991). *The Angry Monster.* King of Prussia, PA: Center for Applied Psychology.
York, P., York, D., and Wachtel, T. (1997). *Toughlove.* New York: Bantam Books.

DEPRESSION

Burns, D. D. (1999). *Feeling Good: The New Mood Therapy.* New York: HarperCollins.
Ingersoll, B., and Goldstein, S. (1995). *Lonely, Sad and Angry: A Parent's Guide to Depression in Children and Adolescents.* New York: Doubleday.
Kerns, L. (1993). *Helping Your Depressed Child.* Rocklin, CA: Prima.
Luciani, J. (2001). *Self-Coaching: How to Heal Anxiety and Depression.* New York: Wiley.

Manassis, K., and Levac, A. M. (2004). *Helping Your Teenager Beat Depression: A Problem-Solving Approach for Families.* Bethesda, MD: Woodbine House.

Marra, T. (2004). *Depressed and Anxious: The Dialectical Behavioral Therapy Workbook.* Oakland, CA: New Harbinger.

Sanford, D. (1993). *It Won't Last Forever.* Sisters, OR: Questar.

Shapiro, L. (2001). *Teen Solutions Workbook.* King of Prussia, PA: Childswork/Childsplay.

DIVORCE REACTION

Clark, L. (1998). *S.O.S.—Help for Emotions.* Bowling Green, KY: Parents' Press.

Grollman, E. (1975). *Talking About Divorce.* Boston: Beacon Press.

Krementz, J. (1988). *How It Feels When Parents Divorce.* New York: Alfred A. Knopf.

Swan-Jackson, A., Shapiro, J., Klebanoff, S., and Rosenfield, L. (1998). *When Your Parents Split: How to Keep Yourself Together.* Los Angeles: Price Stern Sloan.

EATING DISORDER

Berg, F. (1997). *Afraid to Eat.* Hettinger, ND: Healthy Weight Publishing Network.

Fairburn, C. G. (1995). *Overcoming Binge Eating.* New York: Guilford.

Hettner, M., and Eitert, G. (2004). *The Anorexic Workbook.* Oakland, CA: New Harbinger.

McCabe, R., McFarlane, T., and Olmsted, M. (2004). *Overcoming Bulimia Workbook.* Oakland, CA: New Harbinger.

Metropolitan Height and Weight Tables. (1983). New York: Metropolitan Life Insurance Company, Health and Safety Division.

Rodin, J. (1992). *Body Traps.* New York: William Morrow.

Siegel, M., Brisman, J., and Weinshel, M. (1988). *Surviving an Eating Disorder: Strategies for Families and Friends.* New York: Harper & Row.

Wilson, G. T., Fairburn, C. G., and Agras, W. S. (1997). "Cognitive-Behavioral Therapy for Bulimia Nervosa" in D. M. Garner and P. Garfinkel, eds. *Handbook of Treatment for Eating Disorders.* New York: Guilford.

GRIEF/LOSS UNRESOLVED

Fitzgerald, H. (2000). *The Grieving Teen.* New York: Fireside.

Grollman, E. (1967). *Explaining Death to Children.* Boston: Beacon Press.

Hambrook, D., and Eisenberg, E. (1997) *A Mother Loss Workbook.* New York: HarperCollins.

Jewett, C. (1982). *Helping Children Cope with Separation and Loss.* Cambridge, MA: Harvard University Press.

LeShan, E. (1976). *Learning to Say Good-Bye: When A Parent Dies.* New York: Macmillan.

Mellonie, B., and Ingpen, R. (1983). *Lifetimes.* New York: Bantam Books.

O'Toole, D. (1989). *Growing Through Grief.* Burnsville, NC: Mountain Rainbow Publications.

Tyson, J. (1997). *Common Threads of Teenage Grief.* Lake Dallas, TX: Helm Seminars.

LOW SELF-ESTEEM

Burns, D. (1993). *Ten Days to Self-Esteem.* New York: William Morrow.

Covey, S. (1998). *The 7 Habits of Highly Effective Teens.* New York: Fireside.

Dobson, J. (1974). *Hide or Seek: How to Build Self-Esteem in Your Child.* Old Tappan, NJ: F. Revell Co.

Glenn, H., and Nelsen, J. (1989). *Raising Self-Reliant Children in a Self-Indulgent World.* Rocklin, CA: Prima.

Hanson, L. (1996). *Feed Your Head: Some Excellent Stuff on Being Yourself.* Center Court, MN: Hazelden.

Harris, C., Bean, R., and Clark, A. (1978). *How to Raise Teenager's Self-Esteem.* Los Angeles: Price Stern Sloan.

Loomans, D., and Loomans, J. (1994). *Full Esteem Ahead.* Fort Collins, CO: Kramer, Inc.

Pipher, M. (1994). *Reviving Ophelia.* Newburgh, NY: Courage to Change.

Powell, J. (1969). *Why Am I Afraid to Tell You Who I Am?* Allen, TX: Argus Communications.

Sanford, D. (1986). *Don't Look at Me.* Portland, OR: Multnomah Press.

Schiraldi, G. (2001). *The Self-Esteem Workbook.* Oakland, CA: New Harbinger.

Scott, S. (1997). *How to Say No and Keep Your Friends.* Highland Ranch, CO: HRC Press.

Shapiro, L. (2001). *Teen Solutions Workbook.* King of Prussia, PA: Childswork/Childsplay.

MANIA/HYPOMANIA

DePaulo, R., and Ablow, K. (1989). *How to Cope with Depression.* New York: McGraw-Hill.

Dumont, L. (1991). *Surviving Adolescence: Helping Your Child Through the Struggle.* New York: Villard.

Papolos, D., and Papolos, J. (2002). *The Bipolar Child.* West Palm Beach, FL: Broadway.

Waltz, M. (2000). *Bipolar Disorders: A Guide to Helping Children and Adolescents.* Sebastopol, CA: Patient-Centered Guides.

Wilens, T. (2004). *Straight Talk About Psychiatric Medications for Kids.* New York: Guilford.

MEDICAL CONDITION

Babcock, E. (1997). *When Life Becomes Precious: A Guide for Loved Ones and Friends of Cancer Patients.* New York: Bantam Books.

Bluebond-Langner, M. (1996). *In the Shadow of Illness.* Princeton, NJ: Princeton University Press.

Dorfman, E. (1998). *The C-Word: Teenagers and Their Families Living with Cancer, 2nd ed.* New York: NewSage Press.

Fromer, M. (1998). *Surviving Childhood Cancer: A Guide for Families.* Oakland, CA: New Harbinger.

Keene, N., Hobbie, W., and Ruccione, K. (2000). *Childhood Cancer Survivors: A Practical Guide to Your Future.* Sebastopol, CA: O'Reilly & Associates.

Kushner, H. (1981). *When Bad Things Happen to Good People.* New York: Schocken Books.

Smedes, L. (1982). *How Can It Be All Right When Everything Is All Wrong?* San Francisco: Harper.

Westberg, G. (1962). *Good Grief.* Philadelphia: Augsburg Fortress Press.

Woznick, L. (2002). *Living with Childhood Cancer: A Practical Guide to Help Parents Cope.* Washington, DC: American Psychological Association.

MENTAL RETARDATION

Trainer, M. (1991). *Differences in Common.* Rockville, MD: Woodbine House.

NEGATIVE PEER INFLUENCES

Bernstein, N. (2001). *How to Keep Your Teenager Out of Trouble and What To Do if You Can't.* New York: Workman Publications.

Mules, K. (2001). *Teen Relationship Workbook.* King of Prussia, PA: Childswork/ Childsplay.

Scott, S. (1997). *How to Say No and Keep Your Friends.* Highland Ranch, CO: HRC Press.

Shapiro, L. (2001). *Teen Solutions Workbook.* King of Prussia, PA: Childswork/ Childsplay.

OBSESSIVE-COMPULSIVE DISORDER (OCD)

Chansky, T. E. (2000). *Freeing Your Child from Obsessive-Compulsive Disorder: Powerful, Practical Solutions to Overcome Your Child's Fears, Worries, and Phobias.* New York: Random House.

Wagner, A. P. (2002). *What to Do When Your Child Has Obsessive-Compulsive Disorder: Strategies and Solutions.* Rochester, NY: Lighthouse Press.

Waltz, M. (2000). *Obsessive-Compulsive Disorder: Help for Children and Adolescents.* Sebastopol, CA: O'Reilly and Associates.

OPPOSITIONAL DEFIANT

Abern, A. (1994). *Everything I Do You Blame on Me.* Plainview, NY: Childswork/
    Childsplay.

Barkley, R., and Benton, C. (1998). *Your Defiant Child: Eight Steps to Better
    Behavior.* New York: Guilford.

Bayard, R. T., and Bayard, J. (1983). *How to Deal with Your Acting-Up Teenager:
    Practical Self-Help for Desperate Parents.* New York: M. Evans.

Deffenbacher, J. L., and McKay, M. (2000). *Overcoming Situational and General
    Anger: Client Manual (Best Practices for Therapy).* Oakland, CA: New
    Harbinger.

Dobson, J. (1978). *The Strong-Willed Child.* Wheaton, IL: Tyndale House.

Forehand, R., and Long, N. (1996). *Parenting the Strong-Willed Child.* Chicago:
    Contemporary Books.

Gardner, R. (1990). *The Girls and Boys Book About Good and Bad Behavior.*
    Cresskill, NJ: Creative Therapeutics.

Garner, A. (1997). *Conversationally Speaking: Tested New Ways to Increase Your
    Personal and Social Effectiveness.* Los Angeles: Lowell House.

Ginott, H. (1969). *Between Parent and Teenager.* New York: Macmillan.

Greenspan, S. (1995). *The Challenging Child.* Reading, MA: Perseus Books.

Kaye, K. (1991). *Family Rules: Raising Responsible Children.* New York: St. Martins.

Patterson, G. R. (1976). *Living with Children: New Methods for Parents and Teachers.*
    Champaign, IL: Research Press.

Patterson, G. R. (1982). *Coercive Family Process.* Eugene, OR: Castalia.

Satir, V. (1972). *Peoplemaking.* Palo Alto, CA: Science and Behavior Books.

Wenning, K. (1996). *Winning Cooperation from Your Child.* New York: Aronson.

York, P., York, D., and Wachtel, T. (1997). *Toughlove.* New York: Bantam Books.

PANIC/AGORAPHOBIA

Antony, M. M., and McCabe, R. E. (2004*). 10 Simple Solutions to Panic: How
    to Overcome Panic Attacks, Calm Physical Symptoms, and Reclaim Your Life.*
    Oakland, CA: New Harbinger.

Marks, I. M. (2001). *Living With Fear, 2nd ed.* London: McGraw-Hill.

Wilson, R. R. (1996). *Don't Panic: Taking Control of Anxiety Attacks, 2nd ed.* New
    York: Harper & Row.

PARENTING

Bluestein, J. (1993). *Parents, Teens and Boundaries: How to Draw the Line.* Deerfield
    Beach, FL: Health Communications.

Dobson, J. (2000). *Preparing for Adolescence: How to Survive the Coming Years of
    Change.* New York: Regal Press.

Forehand, R., and Long, N. (1996). *Parenting the Strong-Willed Child.* Chicago:
    Contemporary Books.

Ginott, H. (1969). *Between Parent and Teenager.* New York. Macmillan.
Gordon, T. (1970). *Parent Effectiveness Training (P.E.T.).* New York: Wyden Books.
Kellner, M. (2003). *Staying in Control (Anger Management Skills for Parents of Young Adolescents).* Ottawa, Ontario: Research Press Publishers.
Patterson, G. R. (1976). *Living with Children: New Methods for Parents and Teachers.* Champaign, IL: Research Press.
Patterson, G. R. (1982). *Coercive Family Process.* Eugene, OR: Castalia.
Phelan, T. (1998). *Surviving Your Adolescents: Parenting Under Stress Manual.* Glen Ellyn, IL: Parentmagic, Inc.
Renshaw-Joslin, K. (1994). *Positive Parenting from A to Z.* New York: Fawcett Books.
Taffel, R. (2001). *The Second Family: How Adolescent Power is Challenging the American* Family. New York: St. Martin's Press.
Tracy, F. (1994). *Grounded for Life: Stop Blowing Your Fuse and Start Communicating.* Seattle, WA: Parenting Press.
Wolf, A. (1992). *Get Out of My Life but First Could You Drive Me and Cheryl to the Mall?: A Parent's Guide to the New Teenager.* New York: Noonday Press.

PEER/SIBLING CONFLICT

Baruch, D. (1949). *New Ways in Discipline.* New York: Macmillan.
Bieniek, D. (1996). *How to End the Sibling Wars.* King of Prussia, PA: Childswork/Childsplay.
Dellasega, C., and Nixon, C. (2003). *Girl Wars.* New York: Fireside.
Faber, A., and Mazlish, E. (1982). *How to Talk So Kids Will Listen and Listen So Kids Will Talk.* New York: Avon.
Faber, A., and Mazlish, E. (1987). *Siblings Without Rivalry.* New York: Norton.
Ginott, H. (1965). *Between Parent and Child.* New York: Macmillan.
Ginott, H. (1969). *Between Parent and Teenager.* New York: Macmillan.
Mules, K. (2001). *Teen Relationship Workbook.* King of Prussia, PA: Childswork/Childsplay.
Nevick, R. (1996). *Helping Your Child Make Friends.* King of Prussia, PA: Childswork/Childsplay.
Shapiro, L. (2001). *Teen Solutions Workbook.* King of Prussia, PA: Childswork/Childsplay.

PHYSICAL/EMOTIONAL ABUSE VICTIM

Copeland, M. E., and Harris, M. (2000). *Healing the Trauma of Abuse: A Woman's Workbook.* Oakland, CA: New Harbinger.
Miller, A. (1984). *For Your Own Good.* New York: Farrar Straus Group.
Monahon, C. (1983). *Children and Trauma: A Parent's Guide to Helping Children Heal.* New York: Lexington Press.

POSTTRAUMATIC STRESS DISORDER

Allen, J. (1995). *Coping with Trauma: A Guide to Self-Understanding.* American Psychiatric Press.
Brooks, B., and Siegel, P. M. (1996). *The Scared Child: Helping Kids Overcome Traumatic Events.* New York: Wiley.
Carter, W. L. (2002). *It Happened to Me.* Oakland, CA: New Harbinger.
Eifert, G. H., Forsyth, J. P., and McKay, M. (2006). *ACT on Life Not on Anger.* Oakland, CA: New Harbinger.
Flannery Jr., R. (1995). *Posttraumatic Stress Disorder: The Victim's Guide to Healing and Recovery.* New York: Crossroad Publishing.
Foa, E. B., Davidson, J., and Frances, A. (1999). The Expert Consensus Guideline Series: Treatment of Posttraumatic Stress Disorder. *Journal of Clinical Psychiatry, 60*(Suppl 16). Also available online at: http://www.psychguides .com/ptsdhe.pdf
Kennerly, H. (2000). *Overcoming Childhood Trauma: A Self-Help Guide Using Cognitive Behavioral Techniques.* New York: New York University Press.
Matsakis, A. (1996). *I Can't Get Over It: A Handbook for Trauma Survivors, 2nd ed.* Oakland, CA: New Harbinger.
Williams, M. B., and Poijula, S. (2002). *The PTSD Workbook.* Oakland, CA: New Harbinger.

PSYCHOTICISM

Dumont, L. (1991). *Surviving Adolescence: Helping Your Child Through the Struggle.* New York: Villard.
Torry, M. D., and Fuller, E. (1988). *Surviving Schizophrenia: A Family Manual.* New York: Harper & Row.
Wilens, T. (2004). *Straight Talk About Psychiatric Medications for Kids.* New York: Guilford.

RUNAWAY

Carter, W. L. (2002). *It Happened to Me.* Oakland, CA: New Harbinger.
Elkind, D. (1984). *All Grown Up and No Place to Go: Teenagers in Crisis.* New York: Addison-Wesley.
Glenn, H., and Nelsen, J. (1989). *Raising Self-Reliant Children in a Self-Indulgent World.* Rocklin, CA: Prima.
Gordon, T. (1970). *Parent Effectiveness Training (P.E.T.).* New York: Wyden Books.
Millman, H., and Schaefer, C. (1977). *Therapies for Children: A Handbook of Effective Treatment for Problem Behaviors.* San Francisco: Jossey-Bass.
Wegscheider, S. (1981). *Another Chance: Hope and Health for the Alcoholic Family.* Palo Alto, CA: Science and Behavioral Books.

SCHOOL VIOLENCE

Burns, D. (1993). *Ten Days to Self-Esteem.* New York: William Morrow.
Fried, S., and Fried, P. (1998). *Bullies & Victims: Helping Your Child Survive the Schoolyard Battlefield.* New York: M. Evans & Co.
Huml, F. (1998). *Ready-to-Use Violence Prevention Skills Lessons and Activities for Secondary Students.* New York: Jossey-Bass.
Licata, R. (1994). *Everything You Need to Know About Anger.* New York: Rosen Publishing Group.
Shearin-Karres, E. (2000). *Violence-Proof Your Kids Now.* Berkeley, CA: Conari Press.

SEXUAL ABUSE PERPETRATOR

Blodeau, L. (1997). *The Anger Workbook.* New York: Fine Communications.
Bluestein, J. (1993). *Parents, Teens and Boundaries: How to Draw the Line.* Deerfield Beach, FL: Health Communications.
Browne, J. (1997). *Dating for Dummies.* Foster City, CA: IDG Books.
Carnes, D. (1983). *Out of the Shadows: Understanding Sexual Addictions.* Minneapolis, MN: Comp Care Publishers.
Covey, S. (1997). *The 7 Habits of Highly Effective Families: Building a Beautiful Family Culture in a Turbulent World.* New York: Golden Books.
Ginott, H. (1969). *Between Parent and Teenager.* New York: Macmillan.
Glenn, H., and Nelsen, J. (1989). *Raising Self-Reliant Children in a Self-Indulgent World.* Rocklin, CA: Prima.
Katherine, A. (1991). *Boundaries: Where You End and I Begin.* New York: Simon & Schuster.
Kuriansky, J. (1999). *The Complete Idiot's Guide to Dating.* New York: Alpha Books.
Scieszka, J. (1989). *The True Story of the Three Little Pigs by A. Wolf.* New York: Viking.

SEXUAL ABUSE VICTIM

Carnes, P. (1992). *Out of the Shadows: Understanding Sexual Addictions.* Minneapolis, MN: Comp Care Publications.
Carter, W. L. (2002). *It Happened to Me.* Oakland, CA: New Harbinger.
Copeland, M. E., and Harris, M. (2000). *Healing the Trauma of Abuse: A Woman's Workbook.* Oakland, CA: New Harbinger.
Davis, L. (1991). *Allies in Healing.* New York: HarperCollins.
Katherine, A. (1991). *Boundaries: Where You End and I Begin.* New York: Simon & Schuster.

SEXUAL ACTING OUT

Pipher, M. (1994). *Reviving Ophelia.* Newburgh, NY: Courage to Change.
Scott, S. (1997). *How to Say No and Keep Your Friends.* Highland Ranch, CO: HRC Press.

SEXUAL IDENTITY CONFUSION

Bradley, S., and Zucker, K. (1995). *Gender Identity Disorder and Psychosexual Problems in Children and Adolescents.* New York: Guilford.
Gomes, P. (1998). *The Good Book: Reading the Bible with Mind and Heart.* New York: Avon.
Griffin, C., Wirth, A., and Wirth, M. (1996). *Beyond Acceptance: Parents of Lesbian and Gays Talk About Their Experiences.* New York: St. Martin's Press.
Grima, T., ed. (1995). *Not the Only One: Lesbian and Gay Fiction for Teens.* Boston: Alyson.
Heron, A., ed. (1995). *Two Teenagers in 20: Writings by Gay and Lesbian Youth.* Boston: Alyson.
Jennings, K., ed. (1994). *Becoming Visible: A Reader in Gay and Lesbian History for High School and College Students.* Los Angeles: Alyson.
Marcus, E. (1999). *Is It a Choice? Answers to 300 of the Most Frequently Asked Questions About Gays and Lesbians.* San Francisco: Harper.
Silber, S. (1981). *The Male.* New York: C. Scribner's Sons.

SOCIAL PHOBIA/SHYNESS

Antony, M. M., and Swinson, R. P. (2000). *The Shyness and Social Anxiety Workbook: Proven, Step-by-Step Techniques for Overcoming Your Fear.* Oakland, CA: New Harbinger.
Butler, G. (1999). *Overcoming Social Anxiety and Shyness: A Self-Help Guide Using Cognitive Behavioral Techniques.* London: Robinson.
Cohen, C. (2000). *Raising Your Child's Social IQ.* Alfamonte Springs, FL: Advantage Books.
Desberg, P. (1996). *No More Butterflies: Overcoming Shyness, Stage Fright, Interview Anxiety, and Fear of Public Speaking.* Oakland, CA: New Harbinger.
Garner, A. (1997). *Conversationally Speaking: Tested New Ways to Increase Your Personal and Social Effectiveness.* Los Angeles: Lowell House.
Hope, D. A., Heimberg, R. G., Juster, H. R., and Turk, C. L. (2000). *Managing Social Anxiety.* Boulder, CO: Graywind Publications.
Markway, B. G., Carmin, C. N., Pollard, C. A., and Flynn, T. (1992). *Dying of Embarrassment: Help for Social Anxiety and Phobia.* Oakland, CA: New Harbinger.
Martin, M., and Greenwood-Waltman, C., ed. (1995). *Solve Your Child's School-Related Problems.* New York: HarperCollins.
Mattick, R. P., and Clarke, J. C. (1998). Development and validation of measures

of social phobia scrutiny fear and social interaction anxiety. *Behaviour Research and Therapy, 36,* 455–70.

Millman, M., Schaefer, C., and Cohen, J. (1980). *Therapies for School Behavioral Problems.* San Francisco: Jossey-Bass.

Rapee, R. M. (1998). *Overcoming Shyness and Social Phobia: A Step-by-Step Guide.* Northvale, NJ: Jason Aronson.

Schneier, F., and Welkowitz, L. (1996). *The Hidden Face of Shyness: Understanding and Overcoming Social Anxiety.* New York: Avon.

Soifer, S., Zgourides, G. D., Himle, J., and Pickering, N. L. (2001). *Shy Bladder Syndrome: Your Step-by-Step Guide to Overcoming Paruresis.* Oakland, CA: New Harbinger.

Stein, M. B., and Walker, J. R. (2001). *Triumph Over Shyness: Conquering Shyness and Social Anxiety.* New York: McGraw-Hill.

Steiner, C. (1997). *Achieving Emotional Literacy: A Personal Program to Improve Your Emotional Intelligence.* New York: Avon.

Zimbardo, P. (1987). *Shyness: What It Is and What to Do About It.* New York: Addison-Wesley.

SPECIFIC PHOBIA

Antony, M. M., Craske, M. C., and Barlow, D. H. (1995). *Mastery of Your Specific Phobia—Client Manual.* San Antonio, TX: Psychological Corporation.

Bourne, E. (1995). *Anxiety and Phobia Workbook.* Berkeley, CA: Fine Communications.

Burns, D. (1989). *The Feeling Good Handbook.* New York: William Morrow.

Burns, D. (1993). *Ten Days to Self-Esteem.* New York: William Morrow.

Chansky, T. E. (2004). *Freeing Your Child from Anxiety: Powerful, Practical Solutions to Overcome Your Child's Fears, Worries, and Phobias.* New York: Random House.

Garber, S., Garber, M., and Spitzman, R. (1993). *Monsters Under the Bed and Other Childhood Fears.* New York: Villard.

Manassis, K. (1996). *Keys to Parenting Your Anxious Child.* Hauppauge, NY: Barron's.

Marks, I. M. (2001). *Living With Fear, 2nd ed.* London: McGraw-Hill.

Rapee R., Spense, S., Cobham, V., and Wignal, A. (2000). *Helping Your Anxious Child: A Step-by-Step Guide for Parents.* San Francisco: New Harbinger.

Wilson, R. (1986). *Don't Panic: Taking Charge of Anxiety Attacks.* New York: Harper & Row.

SUICIDAL IDEATION

Butler, P. (1991). *Talking to Yourself: Learning the Language of Self-Affirmation.* New York: Perigee.

Dumont, L. (1991). *Surviving Adolescence: Helping Your Child Through the Struggle.* New York: Villard.

Luciani, J. (2001). *Self-Coaching: How to Heal Anxiety and Depression.* New York: Wiley.

Marra, T. (2004). *Depressed and Anxious: The Dialectical Behavioral Therapy Workbook.* Oakland, CA: New Harbinger.

McCoy, K. (1994). *Understanding Your Teenager's Depression.* New York: Perigee.

Appendix B

PROFESSIONAL REFERENCES FOR EVIDENCE-BASED CHAPTERS

GENERAL

Many references are made throughout the chapters to a therapeutic homework resource that was developed by the authors as a corollary to the *Adolescent Psychotherapy Treatment Planner* (Jongsma, Peterson, and McInnis). This frequently cited homework resource book is:

Jongsma, A., Peterson, L. M., and McInnis, W. (2006). *Adolescent Therapy Homework Planner, 2nd ed.* New York: Wiley.

Albano, A. M., and Silverman, W. K. (1996). *Clinician's Guide to the Anxiety Disorders Interview Schedule for DSM-IV, Child Version.* Boulder, CO: Graywind Publications.

Bertolino, B. (1999). *Therapy with Troubled Teenagers.* New York: Wiley.

Brown, S. (1985). *Treating the Alcoholic: A Developmental Model of Recovery.* New York: Wiley.

Bruce, T. J., and Sanderson, W. C. (2005). Evidence-based psychosocial practices: Past, present, and future. In C. Stout and R. Hayes (Eds.), *The Handbook of Evidence-Based Practice in Behavioral Healthcare: Applications and New Directions.* New York: Wiley.

Chambless, D. L., Baker, M. J., Baucom, D., Beutler, L. E., Calhoun, K. S., Crits-Christoph, P., Daiuto, A., DeRubeis, R., Detweiler, J., Haaga, D. A. F., Johnson, S. B., McCurry, S., Mueser, K. T., Pope, K. S., Sanderson, W. C., Shoham, V., Stickle, T., Williams, D. A., Woody, S. R. (1998). Update on empirically validated therapies: II. *The Clinical Psychologist, 51*(1), 3–16.

Chambless, D. L., and Ollendick, T. H. (2001). Empirically supported psychological interventions: Controversies and evidence. *Annual Review of Psychology, 52,* 685–716.

Chambless, D. L., Sanderson, W. C., Shoham, V., Johnson, S. B., Pope, K. S.,

Crits-Christoph, P., Baker, M., Johnson, B., Woody, S. R., Sue, S., Beutler, L., Williams, D. A., and McCurry, S. (1996). An update on empirically validated therapies. *The Clinical Psychologist, 49*(2), 5–18.

Compton, S., March, J., Brent, D., Albano, A., Weersing, R., and Curry, J. (2004). Cognitive-behavioral psychotherapy for anxiety and depressive disorders in children and adolescents: An evidence-based medicine review. *Journal of the American Academy of Child and Adolescent Psychiatry, 43,* 930–59.

Friedman, E. (1990). *Friedman's Fables.* New York: Guilford.

Grigoryev, P. (1997). "The Therapist on the Inside." In H. Kaduson and C. Schaefer (Eds.), *101 Favorite Play Therapy Techniques.* Northvale, NJ: Jason Aronson, Inc.

Hesley, J. W., and Hesley, J. G. (2001). *Rent Two Films and Let's Talk in the Morning: Using Popular Movies in Psychotherapy, Second Edition.* New York: Wiley.

James, B. (1989). *Treating Traumatized Children.* New York: Lexington Books.

Joshua, J. Maidman, and DiMenna, D. (2000). *Read Two Books and Let's Talk Next Week: Using Bibliotherapy in Clinical Practice.* New York: Wiley.

Kaduson, H., and Schaefer, C. (Eds.). (1990). *101 Favorite Play Therapy Techniques.* Northvale, NJ: Jason Aronson, Inc.

Kaslow, N. J., and Thompson, M. P. (1998). Applying the criteria for empirically supported treatments to studies of psychosocial interventions for child and adolescent depression. *Journal of Clinical Child Psychology, 27,* 146–55.

Kendall, P. (1994). Treating anxiety disorders in children: Results of a randomized clinical trial. *Journal of Consulting and Clinical Psychology, 62,* 100–10.

Kendall, P. (2005). *Child and Adolescent Therapy: Cognitive-Behavioral Procedures, 3rd ed.* New York: Guilford.

Kendall, P., Chu, B., Pimentel, S., and Choudhury, M. (2000). Treating anxiety disorders in youth. In P. C. Kendall (Ed.), *Child and Adolescent Therapy: Cognitive-Behavioral Procedures, 2nd ed.* (pp. 235–87). New York: Guilford.

Kendall, P., Flannery-Schroeder, E., Panichelli-Mindel, S., Southam-Gerow, M., Henin, A., and Warman, M. (1997). Therapy for youths with anxiety disorders: A second randomized clinical trial. *Journal of Consulting and Clinical Psychology, 65,* 366–80.

March, J., and Wells, K. (2003). Combining medication and psychotherapy. In A. Martin, L. Scahill, D. S. Charney, and J. F. Leckman (Eds.), *Pediatric Psychopharmacology: Principles and Practice* (pp. 426–46). London: Oxford University Press.

Marlatt, G., and Gordon, J. (1985). *Relapse Prevention: Maintenance Strategies in the Treatment of Addictive Behaviors.* New York: Guilford.

McClellan, J., and Werry, J. S. (2003). Evidence-based treatments in child and adolescent psychiatry: An inventory. *Journal of the American Academy of Child and Adolescent Psychiatry, 42,* 1388–400.

Mendlowitz, S. L., Manassis, K., Bradley, S., Scapillato, D., Miezitis, S., and Shaw, B. F. (1999). Cognitive-behavioral group treatments in childhood anxiety disorders: The role of parental involvement. *Journal of the American Academy of Child and Adolescent Psychiatry, 38,* 1223–29.

Millman, H., Schaefer, C., and Cohen, J. (1980). *Therapies for School Behavioral Problems.* San Francisco: Jossey-Bass.

Nathan, P. E., and Gorman, J. M. (Eds.). (1998). *A Guide to Treatments That Work.* New York: Oxford University Press.

Nathan, P. E., and Gorman, J. M. (Eds.). (2002). *A Guide to Treatments That Work* (Vol. II). New York: Oxford.

Norcross, J. C., Santrock, J. W., Campbell, L. F., Smith, T. P., Sommer, R., and Zuckerman, E. L. (2003). *The Authoritative Guide to Self-Help Resources in Mental Health, Revised Edition.* New York: Guilford.

O'Hanlon, B., and Beadle, S. (1997). *A Guide to Possibility Land.* New York: W. W. Norton.

Ollendick, T. H., and March, J. C. (2004). *Phobic and Anxiety Disorders in Children and Adolescents: A Clinician's Guide to Effective Psychosocial and Pharmacological Interventions.* New York: Oxford.

Pennington, B. (1991). *Diagnosing Learning Disorders.* New York: Guilford.

Pina, A. A., Silverman, W. K., Fuentes, R. M., Kurtines, W. M., and Weems, C. F. (2003). Exposure-based cognitive-behavioral treatment for phobic and anxiety disorders: Treatment effects and maintenance for Hispanic/Latino relative to European-American youths. *Journal of the American Academy of Child and Adolescent Psychiatry, 42,* 1179–87.

Pittman, F. (1987). *Turning Points.* New York: W. W. Norton.

Pruitt, D. B. (1999). *Your Adolescent: What Every Parent Needs to Know: What's Normal, What's Not, and When to Seek Help.* New York: HarperCollins.

Robin, A., and Foster, S. (1989). *Negotiating Parent/Adolescent Conflict.* New York: Guilford.

Satir, V. (1991). *Peoplemaking.* Palo Alto, CA: Science and Behavior Books.

Selekman, M. (1997). *Solution-Focused Therapy with Children.* New York: Guilford.

Silverman, W. K. (1987). *Anxiety Disorders Interview Schedule for Children.* Boulder, CO: Graywind.

Silverman, W. K., and Albano, A. (1996a). *The Anxiety Disorders Interview Schedule for DSM-IV: Child Interview Schedule.* Boulder, CO:Graywind.

Silverman, W. K., and Albano, A. (1996b). *The Anxiety Disorders Interview Schedule for DSM-IV: Parent Interview Schedule.* Boulder, CO:Graywind.

Theiss, S. (1997). Pretending to know how. In H. Kaduson and C. Schaefer (Eds.), *101 Favorite Play Therapy Techniques.* Northvale, NJ: Jason Aronson, Inc.

Treatment for Adolescents with Depression Study. (2003). Treatment for Adolescents with Depression Study (TADS): Rationale, design, and methods. *Journal of the American Academy of Child Adolescent Psychiatry, 42,* 531–42.

Wadeson, H. (1980). *Art Psychotherapy.* New York: Wiley.

Wadeson, H. (1995). *The Dynamics of Art Psychotherapy.* New York: Wiley.

Wallas, L. (1985). *Stories for the Third Ear.* New York: W. W. Norton.

Watson, G.S., and Gross, A. (1997). Mental Retardation and Developmental Disorders. In R.T. Ammerman and M. H. Herson (Eds.), *Handbook of Prevention and Treatment with Children and Adolescents* (pp. 495–520). New York: Wiley.

Watzlawick, P., Weakland, J., and Fisch, R. (1974). *Change.* New York: W. W. Norton.

ANGER MANAGEMENT

Feindler, E. L., Marriott, S.A., and Iwata, M. (1984). Group anger control training for junior high school delinquents. *Cognitive Therapy & Research, 8,* 299–311.

Huey, W. C., and Rank, R. C. (1984). Effects of counselor and peer-led group assertiveness training on black adolescent aggression. *Journal of Counseling Psychology, 31,* 95–98.

Lochman, J. E., Lampron, L. B., Gemmer, T. C., Harris, S. R., and Wyckoff, G. M. (1989). Teacher consultation and cognitive-behavioral interventions with aggressive boys. *Psychology in the Schools, 26,* 179–88.

Meichenbaum, D. (1985). *Stress Inoculation Training.* New York: Pergamon Press.

Meichenbaum, D. (1993). Stress inoculation training: A twenty-year update. In R. L. Woolfolk and P. M. Lehrer (Eds.), *Principles and Practices of Stress Management.* New York: Guilford.

Meichenbaum, D. (2001). *Treatment of Individuals with Anger Control Problems and Aggressive Behaviors: A Clinical Handbook.* Clearwater, FL: Institute Press.

Novaco, R. (1975). *Anger Control: The Development and Evaluation of an Experimental Treatment.* Lexington, MA: Lexington Books.

ANXIETY

Barrett, P. M. (1998). Evaluation of cognitive-behavioral group treatments for childhood anxiety disorders. *Journal of Clinical Child Psychology, 27,* 459–68.

Barrett, P. M., Dadds, M. R., and Rapee, R. M. (1996). Family treatment of childhood anxiety: A controlled trial. *Journal of Consulting Clinical Psychology, 64,* 333–42.

Barrett, P. M., Duffy, A. L., Dadds, M. R., and Rapee, R. M. (2001). Cognitive-behavioral treatment of anxiety disorders in children: Long-term (6-year) follow-up. *Journal of Consulting Clinical Psychology, 69,* 135–41.

Bernstein, D. A., Borkovec, T. D., and Hazlett-Stevens, H. (2000). *New Directions in Progressive Relaxation Training: A Guidebook for Helping Professionals.* Westport, CT: Praeger.

Kendall P. C., Krain, A., and Treadwell, K. R. (1999). Generalized anxiety disorder. In R. T. Ammerman, M. Hersen, and C. G. Last (Eds.), *Handbook of Prescriptive Treatments for Children and Adolescents, 2nd ed.* (pp. 155–71). Boston: Allyn and Bacon.

Meyer, T. J., Miller, M. L., Metzger, R. L., and Borkovec, T. D. (1990). Development and validation of the Penn State Worry Questionnaire. *Behaviour Research and Therapy, 28,* 487–95.

Ollendick, T. H., and March, J. C. (2004). *Phobic and Anxiety Disorders in Children and Adolescents : A Clinician's Guide to Effective Psychosocial and Pharmacological Interventions.* New York: Oxford.

Pina, A. A., Silverman, W. K., Fuentes, R. M., Kurtines, W. M., and Weems, C. F. (2003). Exposure-based cognitive-behavioral treatment for phobic and anxiety disorders: Treatment effects and maintenance for Hispanic/Latino relative to

European-American youths. *Journal of the American Academy of Child and Adolescent Psychiatry, 42,* 1179–87.

ATTENTION-DEFICIT/HYPERACTIVITY DISORDER (ADHD)

American Academy of Child & Adolescent Psychiatry. (1997). Practice parameters for the assessment and treatment of children, adolescents, and adults with attention deficit/hyperactivity disorder. *Journal of the American Academy of Child and Adolescent Psychiatry, 36,* 85S–121S.

Barkley, R. A. (2005). *Attention-Deficit Hyperactivity Disorder: A Handbook for Diagnosis and Treatment, 3rd ed.* New York: Guilford.

Barkley, R. A. (1998). *ADHD: A Handbook For Diagnosis and Treatment, 2nd ed.* New York: Guilford.

Pelham, W. E. Jr., Wheeler, T., and Chronis, A. (1998). Empirically supported psychosocial treatments for attention deficit hyperactivity disorder. *Journal of Clinical Child Psychology, 27,* 190–205.

Robin, A. L. (2000). *ADHD in Adolescents: Diagnosis & Treatment.* New York: Guilford.

Smith, B. H., Waschbusch, D., Willoughby, M., and Evans, S. (2000). The efficacy, safety, and practicality of treatments for adolescents with attention-deficit/hyperactivity disorder. *Clinical Child & Family Psychology Review, 3,* 243–67.

Webster-Stratton, C. (1994). Advancing videotape parent training: A comparison study. *Journal of Consulting and Clinical Psychology, 62,* 583–93.

CHEMICAL DEPENDENCE

Azrin, N. H., Acierno, R., Kogan, E., Donahue, B., Besalel, V., and McMahon, P. (1996). Follow-up results of supportive versus behavioral therapy for illicit drug abuse. *Behavioral Research & Therapy, 34,* 41–46.

Azrin, N. H., Donohue, B., Besalel, V., Kogan, E., and Acierno, R. (1994). Youth drug abuse treatment: A controlled outcome study. *Journal of Child & Adolescent Substance Abuse, 3,* 1–16.

Azrin, N. H., McMahon, P., Donahue, B., Besalel, V., Lapinski, K., Kogan, E., Acierno, R., and Galloway, E. (1994). Behavioral therapy for drug abuse: A controlled treatment outcome study. *Behavioral Research & Therapy, 32,* 857–66.

Carroll, K., Rounsaville, B., and Keller, D. (1991). Relapse prevention strategies for the treatment of cocaine abuse. *American Journal of Drug and Alcohol Abuse, 17,* 249–65.

Carroll, K., Rounsaville, B., Nich, C., Gordon, L., Wirtz, P., and Gawin, F. (1994). One-year follow-up of psychotherapy and pharmacotherapy for cocaine dependence: Delayed emergence of psychotherapy effects. *Archives of General Psychiatry, 51,* 989–97.

Crits-Cristoph, P., Siqueland, L., Blaine, J., Frank, A., Luborsky, L., Onken, L., Muenz, L., Thase, M., Weiss, R., Gastfriend, D., Woody, G., Barber, J., Butler,

S., Daley, D., Bishop, S., Najavits, L., Lis, J., Mercer, D., Griffin, M., Moras, K., and Beck, A. (1999). Psychosocial treatments for cocaine dependence: Results of the NIDA Cocaine Collaborative Study. *Archives of General Psychiatry, 56,* 493–502.

Higgins, S. T., Budney, A., Bickel, H., Badger, G., Foerg, F., and Ogden, D. (1995). Outpatient behavioral treatment for cocaine dependence: One-year outcome. *Experimental & Clinical Psychopharmacology, 3,* 205–12.

Higgins, S. T., Budney, A., Bickel, W., Foerg, F., Donham, R., and Badger, G. (1994). Incentives improve outcome in outpatient behavioral treatment of cocaine dependence. *Archives of General Psychiatry, 51,* 568–76.

Schmidt, S. E., Liddle, H., and Dakof, G. (1996). Effects of multidimensional family therapy: Relationship of changes in parenting practices to symptom reduction in adolescent substance abuse. *Journal of Family Psychology, 10,* 1–16.

Silverman, K., Higgins, S., Brooner, R., Montoya, I., Cone, E., Schuster, C., and Preston, K. (1996). Sustained cocaine abstinence in methadone maintenance patients through voucher-based reinforcement therapy. *Archives of General Psychiatry, 53,* 409–15.

Silverman, K., Wong, C., Higgins, S., Brooner, R., Montoya, I., Contoreggi, C., Umbricht-Schneiter, A., Schuster, C., and Preston, K. (1996). Increasing opiate abstinence through voucher-based reinforcement therapy. *Drug and Alcohol Dependence, 41,* 157–65.

Woody, G. E., McLellan, A., Luborsky, L., and O'Brien, C. (1987). Twelve month follow-up of psychotherapy for opiate dependence. *American Journal of Psychiatry, 144,* 590–96.

CONDUCT DISORDER/DELINQUENCY

Alexander, J. F., and Parsons, B. (1973). Short-term behavioral intervention with delinquent families: Impact on family process and recidivism. *Journal of Abnormal Psychology, 81,* 219–25.

Bernstein, D. A., Borkovec, T., and Hazlett-Stevens, H. (2000). *New Directions in Progressive Relaxation Training: A Guidebook for Helping Professionals.* Westport, CT: Praeger.

Borduin, C. M., Mann, B., Cone, L., Henggeler, S., Fucci, B., Blaske, D., and Williams, R. (1995). Multisystemic treatment of serious juvenile offenders: Long-term prevention of criminality and violence. *Journal of Consulting and Clinical Psychology, 63,* 569–78.

Brestan, E. V., and Eyberg, S. (1998). Effective psychosocial treatments of conduct-disorders children and adolescents: 29 years, 82 studies, and 5,272 kids. *Journal of Clinical Child Psychology, 27,* 180–89.

Curtis, N. M., Ronan, K., and Borduin, C. (2004). Multisystemic treatment: A meta-analysis of outcome studies. *Journal of Family Psychology, 18,* 411–19.

Feindler, E. L., Marriott, S., and Iwata, M. (1984). Group anger control training for junior high school delinquents. *Cognitive Therapy & Research, 8,* 299–311.

Henggeler, S. W., Melton, G., and Smith, L. (1992). Family preservation using multisystemic therapy: An effective alternative to incarcerating serious juvenile offenders. *Journal of Consulting & Clinical Psychology, 60,* 953–61.

Henggeler, S. W., Rodick, J., Bourdin, C., Hanson, C., Watson, S., and Urey, J. (1986). Multisystemic treatment of juvenile offenders: Effects on adolescent behavior and family interaction. *Developmental Psychology, 22,* 132–41.

Henggeler, S. W., Schoenwald, S., Borduin, C., Rowland, M., and Cunningham, P. (1998). *Multisystemic Treatment of Antisocial Behavior in Children and Adolescents.* New York: Guilford.

Huey, W. C., and Rank, R. (1984). Effects of counselor and peer-led group assertiveness training on black adolescent aggression. *Journal of Counseling Psychology, 31,* 95–98.

Kazdin, A. E., Esveldt-Dawson, K., French, N. H., and Unis, A. S. (1987a). Problem-solving skills training and relationship therapy in the treatment of antisocial child behavior. *Journal of Consulting & Clinical Psychology, 55,* 76–85.

Kazdin, A. E., Esveldt-Dawson, K., French, N. H., and Unis, A. S. (1987b). Effects of parent management training and problem-solving skills training combined in the treatment of antisocial child behavior. *Journal of the American Academy of Child and Adolescent Psychiatry, 26,* 416–24.

Kazdin, A. E., Siegel, T. C., and Bass, D. (1992). Cognitive problem-solving skills training and parent management training in the treatment of antisocial behavior in children. *Journal of Consulting & Clinical Psychology, 60,* 733–47.

Lochman, J. E., Lampron, L. B., Gemmer, T. C., Harris, S. R., and Wyckoff, G. M. (1989). Teacher consultation and cognitive-behavioral interventions with aggressive boys. *Psychology in the Schools, 26,* 179–88.

Meichenbaum, D. (1985). *Stress Inoculation Training.* New York: Pergamon Press.

Meichenbaum, D. (1993). Stress inoculation training: A twenty-year update. In R. L. Woolfolk and P. M. Lehrer (Eds.), *Principles and Practices of Stress Management.* New York: Guilford.

Meichenbaum, D. (2001). *Treatment of Individuals with Anger Control Problems and Aggressive Behaviors: A Clinical Handbook.* Clearwater, FL: Institute Press.

Novaco, R. (1975). *Anger Control: The Development and Evaluation of an Experimental Treatment.* Lexington, MA: Lexington Books.

Webster-Stratton, C. (1994). Advancing videotape parent training: A comparison study. *Journal of Consulting and Clinical Psychology, 62,* 583–93.

DEPRESSION

Beck, A. T., Rush, A. J., Shaw, B. F., and Emery, G. (1979). *Cognitive Therapy of Depression.* New York: Guilford.

Birmaher, B., Ryan, N. D., Williamson, D. E., Brent, D. A., Kaufman, J., Dahl, R. E., Perel, J., and Nelson, B. (1996). Childhood and adolescent depression: A review of the past 10 years: Part I. *Journal of the American Academy of Child and Adolescent Psychiatry, 35,* 1427–39.

Clarke, G., Lewinsohn, P., and Hops, H. (1990). *Instructor's Manual for the Adolescent Coping with Depression Course, 4th ed.* Eugene, OR: Castalia Press.

Clarke, G. N., Hornbrook, M., and Lynch, F., et al. (2002). Group cognitive-behavioral treatment for depressed adolescent offspring of depressed parents in a health maintenance organization. *Journal of the American Academy of Child and Adolescent Psychiatry, 41,* 305–13.

Clarke, G. N., Lewinsohn, P. M., and Hops, H. (1990). *Adolescent Coping with Depression Course.* Eugene, OR: Castalia Publishing.

Clarke, G. N., Lewinsohn, P., and Hops, H. (1990). *Instructor's Manual for the Adolescent Coping with Depression Course, 4th ed.* Eugene, OR: Castalia Press

Clarke, G. N., Rohde, P., Lewinsohn, P. M., Hops, H., and Seeley, J. R. (1999). Cognitive-behavioral treatment of adolescent depression: Efficacy of acute group treatment and booster sessions. *Journal of the American Academy of Child and Adolescent Psychiatry, 38,* 272–79.

Kovacs, M. (1980). Rating scales to assess depression in school-aged children. *Acta Paediatrica, 46,* 305–15.

Lewinsohn, P., Clarke, G., Rhode, P., Hops, H., and Seeley, J. (1996). A course in coping: A cognitive-behavioral approach to the treatment of adolescent depression. In E. D. Hibbs and P. S. Jensen (Eds.), *Psychosocial Treatments for Child and Adolescent Disorders: Empirically Based Strategies for Clinical Practice* (pp. 109–35). Washington DC: American Psychological Association.

Lewinsohn, P. M., Clarke, G. N., Hops, H., and Andrews, J. (1990). Cognitive-behavioral treatment for depressed adolescents. *Behavior Therapy, 21,* 385–401.

March, J., Silva, S., and Petrycki, S., et al. (2004). Fluoxetine, cognitive-behavioral therapy, and their combination for adolescents with depression: Treatment for Adolescents With Depression Study (TADS) randomized controlled trial. *Journal of the American Medical Association, 292,* 807–20.

Mufson, L., Weissman, M. M., Moreau, D., and Garfinkel, R. (1999). Efficacy of interpersonal psychotherapy for depressed adolescents. *Archives of General Psychiatry, 56,* 573–79.

Mufson, L., Dorta, K. P., Wickramaratne, P., Nomura, Y., Olfson, M., and Weissman, M. M. (2004). A randomized effectiveness trial of interpersonal psychotherapy for depressed adolescents. *Archives of General Psychiatry, 61,* 577–84.

Reinecke, M. A., Ryan, N. E., and DuBois, D. L. (1998). Cognitive-behavioral therapy of depression and depressive symptoms during adolescence: A review and meta-analysis. *Journal of the American Academy of Child and Adolescent Psychiatry, 37,* 26–34.

Rossello J., and Bernal, G. (1999). The efficacy of cognitive-behavioral and interpersonal treatments for depression in Puerto Rican adolescents. *Journal of Consulting and Clinical Psychology, 67,* 734–45.

Sommers-Flanagan, J., and Sommers-Flanagan, R. (1996). Efficacy of anti-depressant medication with depressed youth: What psychologists should know. *Professional Psychology: Research and Practice, 27,* 145–53.

Stark, K. D., Rouse, L., and Livingston, R. (1991). Treatment of Depression During Childhood and Adolescence: Cognitive Behavioral Procedures for the Individual and Family. In P. Kendall (Ed.), *Child and Adolescent Therapy* (pp. 165–206). New York: Guilford.

Vostanis P., Feehan, C., Grattan, E., and Bickerton, W. L. (1996a). A randomised controlled out-patient trial of cognitive-behavioural treatment for children and adolescents with depression: 9-month follow-up. *Journal of Affective Disorders, 40,* 105–16.

Wilkes, T. C. R., Belsher, G., Rush, A. J., and Frank, E. (1994). *Cognitive Therapy for Depressed Adolescents.* New York: Guilford.

Wood, A., Harrington, R., and Moore, A. (1996). Controlled trial of a brief cognitive-behavioural intervention in adolescent patients with depressive disorders. *Journal of Child Psychology and Psychiatry, 37,* 737–46.

Zimmerman, M., Coryell, W., Corenthal, C., and Wilson, S. (1986). A self-report scale to diagnose major depressive disorder. *Archives of General Psychiatry, 43,* 1076–81.

EATING DISORDER

Agras, W. S., Walsh, B. T., Fairburn, C. G., Wilson, G. T., and Kreamer, H. C. (2000). A multicenter comparison of cognitive-behavioural therapy and interpersonal psychotherapy for bulimia nervosa. *Archives of General Psychiatry, 57,* 459–66.

Fairburn, C. G., and Carter, J. C. (1997). Self-help and guided self-help for binge-eating problems. In D. M. Garner and P. E. Garfinkel (Eds.), *Handbook of Treatment for Eating Disorders* (pp. 494–99). New York: Guilford.

Fairburn, C. G., Jones, R., Peveler, R. C., Carr, S. J., Solomon, R. A., O'Conner, M. E., Burton, J., and Hope, D. A. (1991). Three psychological treatments for bulimia nervosa: A comparative trial. *Archives of General Psychiatry, 48,* 463–69.

Fairburn, C. G., Marcus, M. D., and Wilson, G. T. (1993). Cognitive-behavioral therapy for binge eating and bulimia nervosa. In C. G. Fairburn and G. T. Wilson (Eds.), *Binge Eating: Nature, Assessment, and Treatment.* New York: Guilford.

Garner, D. M. (1991). *Eating Disorders Inventory-2.* Odessa, FL: Psychological Assessment Resources.

MEDICAL CONDITION

Rodgers, M., Fayter, G., Richardson, G., Ritchie, R., Lewin, and Sowden, A. J. (2005). *The Effects of Psychosocial Interventions in Cancer and Heart Disease: A Review of Systematic.* York, England: Centre for Reviews and Dissemination, University of York.

OBSESSIVE-COMPULSIVE DISORDER (OCD)

Albano, A. M., Knox, L. S., and Barlow, D. H. (1995). Obsessive-compulsive disorder. In A. Eisen, C. Kearney, and C. Schafer (Eds.), *Clinical Handbook of Anxiety Disorders in Children and Adolescents* (pp. 282–316). Northvale, NJ: Jason Aronson.

de Haan, E., Hoogduin, K., Buitelaar, J., and Keijsers, G. (1998). Behavior therapy versus clomipramine for the treatment of obsessive-compulsive disorder in children and adolescents. *Journal of the American Academy of Child and Adolescent Psychiatry, 37,* 1022–29.

Franklin, M. E., Rynn, M., March, J. S., and Foa, E. B. (2002). Obsessive-compulsive disorder. In M. Hersen (Ed.), *Clinical Behavior Therapy: Adults and Children* (pp. 276–303). New York: Wiley.

Fitzgibbons, L., and Pedrick, C. (2003). *Helping Your Child with OCD*. Oakland, CA: New Harbinger.

March J., and Mulle, K. (1998). *OCD in Children and Adolescents: A Cognitive-Behavioral Treatment Manual*. New York: Guilford.

Pediatric OCD Treatment Study (POTS) Team. (2004). Cognitive-behavior therapy, sertraline and their combination for children and adolescents with obsessive-compulsive disorder: The Pediatric OCD Treatment Study (POTS) randomized controlled trial. *JAMA, 292,* 1969–76.

Scahill, L., Riddle, M., McSwiggin-Hardin, M., Ort, S., King, R., Goodman, W., Cicchetti, D., and Leckman, J. (1997). Children's Yale-Brown Obsessive-Compulsive Scale: Reliability and validity. *Journal of the American Academy of Child and Adolescent Psychiatry, 36,* 844–52.

OPPOSITIONAL DEFIANT

Bernstein, D. A., Borkovec, T. D., and Hazlett-Stevens, H. (2000). *New Directions in Progressive Relaxation Training: A Guidebook for Helping Professionals*. Westport, CT: Praeger.

Block, J. (1978). Effects of a rational-emotive mental health program on poorly achieving disruptive high school students. *Journal of Counseling Psychology, 25,* 61–65.

Feindler, E. L., Marriott, S. A., and Iwata, M. (1984). Group anger control training for junior high school delinquents. *Cognitive Therapy & Research, 8,* 299–311.

Huey, W. C., and Rank, R. C. (1984). Effects of counselor and peer-led group assertiveness training on black adolescent aggression. *Journal of Counseling Psychology, 31,* 95–98.

Kazdin, A. E., Esveldt-Dawson, K., French, N., and Unis, A. (1987a). Problem-solving skills training and relationship therapy in the treatment of antisocial child behavior. *Journal of Consulting & Clinical Psychology, 55,* 76–85.

Kazdin, A. E., Esveldt-Dawson, K., French, N., and Unis, A. (1987b). Effects of parent management training and problem-solving skills training combined in the treatment of antisocial child behavior. *Journal of the American Academy of Child and Adolescent Psychiatry, 26,* 416–24.

Kazdin, A. E., Siegel, T. C., and Bass, D. (1992). Cognitive problem-solving skills training and parent management training in the treatment of antisocial behavior in children. *Journal of Consulting & Clinical Psychology, 60,* 733–47.

Lochman, J. E., Lampron, L. B., Gemmer, T. C., Harris, S. R., and Wyckoff, G. M. (1989). Teacher consultation and cognitive-behavioral interventions with aggressive boys. *Psychology in the Schools, 26,* 179–88.

Meichenbaum, D. (1985). *Stress Inoculation Training*. New York: Pergamon Press.

Meichenbaum, D. (1993). Stress inoculation training: A twenty-year update. In R. L. Woolfolk and P. M. Lehrer (Eds.), *Principles and Practices of Stress Management*. New York: Guilford.

Meichenbaum, D. (2001). *Treatment of Individuals with Anger Control Problems and Aggressive Behaviors: A Clinical Handbook*. Clearwater, FL: Institute Press.

Novaco, R. (1975). *Anger Control: The Development and Evaluation of an Experimental Treatment*. Lexington, MA: Lexington Books.

Webster-Stratton, C. (1994). Advancing videotape parent training: A comparison study. *Journal of Consulting and Clinical Psychology, 62,* 583–93.

PANIC/AGORAPHOBIA

Barlow, D. H., and Craske, M. G. (2000). *Mastery of Your Anxiety and Panic (MAP-3)*. San Antonio, TX: Graywind/Psychological Corporation.

Chambless, D. L., Caputo, G. C., Jasin, S. E., Gracel, E. J., and Williams, C. (1985). The mobility inventory for agoraphobia. *Behaviour Research and Therapy, 23,* 35–44.

Compton, S., March, J., Brent, D., Albano, A., Weersing, R., and Curry, J. (2004). Cognitive-behavioral psychotherapy for anxiety and depressive disorders in children and adolescents: An evidence-based medicine review. *Journal of the American Academy of Child and Adolescent Psychiatry, 43,* 930–59.

Craske, M. G., Barlow, D. H., and Meadows, E. (2000). *Mastery of Your Anxiety and Panic: Therapist's Guide for Anxiety, Panic, and Agoraphobia (MAP-3)*. San Antonio, TX: Graywind/Psychological Corporation.

Craske, M. G., and Barlow, D. H. (2000). *Mastery of Your Anxiety and Panic (MAP-3): Agoraphobia Supplement*. San Antonio, TX: Graywind/Psychological Corporation.

Landon, T. M., and Barlow, D. H. (2004). Cognitive-behavioral treatment for panic disorder: Current status. *Journal of Psychiatric Practice, 10,* 211–26.

Reiss, S., Peterson, R. A., Gursky, D. M., and McNally, R. J. (1986). Anxiety sensitivity, anxiety frequency, and the prediction of fearfulness. *Behaviour Research and Therapy, 24,* 1–8.

PARENTING

Bernal, M. E., Klinnert, M. D., and Schultz, L. A.. (1980). Outcome evaluation of behavioral parent training and client-centered parent counseling for children with conduct problems. *Journal of Applied Behavior Analysis, 13,* 677–91.

Brestan, E. V., and Eyberg, S. M. (1998). Effective psychosocial treatments of conduct-disorders children and adolescents: 29 years, 82 studies, and 5,272 kids. *Journal of Clinical Child Psychology, 27,* 180–89.

Webster-Stratton, C. (1994). Advancing videotape parent training: A comparison study. *Journal of Consulting and Clinical Psychology, 62,* 583–93.

POSTTRAUMATIC STRESS DISORDER (PTSD)

AACAP. (1998). Summary of the practice parameters for the assessment and treatment of children and adolescents with posttraumatic stress disorder.

American Academy of Child and Adolescent Psychiatry. *Journal of the American Academy of Child and Adolescent Psychiatry, 37,* 997–1001.

Amaya-Jackson, L., Reynolds, V., Murray, M., McCarthy, G., Nelson, A., and Cherney, M., et al. (2003). Cognitive behavioral treatment for pediatric post-traumatic stress disorder: Protocol and application in school and community settings. *Cognitive and Behavioral Practice, 10,* 204–13.

Cohen, J., Berliner, L., and March, J. (2000). Treatment of PTSD in Children and Adolescents: Guidelines. In E. Foa, J. Davidson, and T. Keane (Eds.), *Effective Treatments for PTSD* (pp. 330–32). New York: Guilford.

Cohen, J., Mannarino, A., and Deblinger, E. (2006). *Treating Trauma and Traumatic Grief in Children & Adolescents.* New York: Guilford.

Cohen, J., March, J., and Berliner, L. (2000). Treatment of PTSD in Children and Adolescents. In E. Foa, J. Davidson, and T. Keane (Eds.), *Effective Treatments for PTSD* (pp. 106–38). New York: Guilford.

Davidson, J., and March, J. (1996). Traumatic stress disorders. In A. Tasman, J. Kay, and J. Lieberman (Eds.), *Psychiatry, Vol. 2* (pp. 1085–98). Philadelphia: Saunders.

Deblinger, E., and Heflin, A. (1996). *Treatment for Sexually Abused Children and Their Non-offending Parents: A Cognitive-behavioral Approach.* Thousand Oaks, CA: Sage.

Donnelly, C., Amaya-Jackson, L., and March, J. (1999) Psychopharmacology of pediatric posttraumatic stress disorder. *Journal of Child Adolescent Psychopharmacology, 9,* 203–20.

Foa, E. B., Keane T. M., and Friedman, M. J. (2004). *Effective Treatments for PTSD: Practice Guidelines from the International Society for Traumatic Stress Studies.* New York: Guilford.

Foa, E. B., and Meadows, E. A. (1997), Psychosocial treatments for posttraumatic stress disorder: A critical review. *Annual Review of Psychology, 48,* 449–80.

Foy, D. W. (Ed.). (1992). *Treating PTSD: Cognitive Behavioral Strategies.* New York: Guilford.

Francis, G., and Beidel, D. (1995). Cognitive Behavioral Psychotherapy. In J. March (Ed.), *Anxiety Disorders in Children and Adolescents* (pp. 321–40). New York: Guilford.

March, J., Amaya-Jackson, L., Murray M., and Schulte, A. (1998). Cognitive-behavioral psychotherapy for children and adolescents with post-traumatic stress disorder following a single incident stressor. *Journal of the American Academy of Child and Adolescent Psychiatry, 37,* 585–93.

Meichenbaum, D. A. (1995). *Clinical Handbook/Practical Therapist Manual for Assessing and Treating Adults with Post-Traumatic Stress Disorder (PTSD).* Clearwater, FL: Institute Press.

Nader, K., Blake, D., Kriegler, J., and Pynoos, R. (1994). *Clinician Administered PTSD Scale for Children (CAPS-C), Current and Lifetime Diagnosis Version, and Instruction Manual.* UCLA Neuropsychiatric Institute and National Center for PTSD.

Najavits, L. M. (2002). *Seeking Safety: A Treatment Manual for PTSD and Substance Abuse.* New York: Guilford.

Resick, P. A., and Calhoun, K. S. (2001). Posttraumatic Stress Disorder. In D. H.

Barlow (Ed.), *Clinical Handbook of Psychological Disorders: A Step-by-step Treatment Manual, 3rd ed.* (pp. 60–113). New York: Guilford.

Rothbaum, B. O., and Foa, E. B. (2004). *Reclaiming Your Life After Rape: Cognitive-Behavioral Therapy for Posttraumatic Stress Disorder—Client Workbook.* New York: Oxford University Press.

Saunders, B. E., and Hanson, R. F. (eds). (2002). *Child Physical and Sexual Abuse: Guidelines for Treatment.* Charleston, SC: Authors.

Silverman, W. K., and Albano, A. M. (1996). *The Anxiety Disorders Interview Schedule for DSM-IV: Child Interview Schedule.* Boulder, CO: Graywind.

Solomon, S. D., Gerrity, E. T., and Muff, A. M. (1992). Efficacy of treatments for posttraumatic stress disorder. An empirical review. *Journal of the American Medical Association, 268,* 633–38.

SOCIAL PHOBIA/SHYNESS

Albano, A. M. (2003). Treatment of Social Anxiety in Adolescents. In M. Reinecke, F. Datillo, and A. Freeman (Eds.), *Casebook of Cognitive Behavioral Therapy with Children and Adolescents, 2nd ed.* (pp. 128–61). New York: Guilford.

Baer, S., and Garland, E. (2005). Pilot Study of Community-Based Cognitive Behavioral Group Therapy for Adolescents with Social Phobia. *Journal of the American Academy of Child and Adolescent Psychiatry, 44,* 258–64.

Beidel, D. C., and Turner, S. M. (1998). *Shy Children, Phobic Adults: Nature and Treatment of Social Phobia.* Washington, DC: American Psychological Association.

Beidel, D. C., Turner, S. M., and Morris, T. L. (2000). Behavioral treatment of childhood social phobia. *Journal of Consulting Clinical Psychology, 68,* 1072–80.

Bernstein, D. A., Borkovec, T. D., and Hazlett-Stevens, H. (2000). *New Directions in Progressive Relaxation Training: A Guidebook for Helping Professionals.* Westport, CT: Praeger.

Spence, S., Donovan, C., and Brechman-Toussaint, M. (2000). The treatment of childhood social phobia: The effectiveness of a social skills training-based, cognitive-behavioural intervention, with and without parental involvement. *Journal of Child Psychology and Psychiatry, 41,* 713–26.

Turk, C., Heimberg, R., and Hope, D. (2001). Social anxiety disorder. In D. H. Barlow (Ed.), *Clinical Handbook of Psychological Disorders, 3rd ed.* (pp. 114–53). New York: Guilford.

Turner, S. M., Beidel, D. C., and Cooley, M. (1997). *Social Effectiveness Therapy: A Program for Overcoming Social Anxiety and Phobia.* Toronto, Canada: Multi-Health Systems.

SPECIFIC PHOBIA

Antony, M. M. (2001). Measures for specific phobia. In M. M. Antony, S. M. Orsillo, and I. Roemer (Eds.), *Practitioner's Guide to Empirically-Based Measures of Anxiety.* New York: Kluwer Academic/Plenum.

Barrett, P. M. (1998). Evaluation of cognitive-behavioral group treatments for childhood anxiety disorders. *Journal of Clinical Child Psychology, 27,* 459–68.

Barrett, P. M., Dadds, M. R., and Rapee, R. M. (1996). Family treatment of childhood anxiety: A controlled trial. *Journal of Consulting Clinical Psychology, 64,* 333–42.

Barrett, P. M., Duffy, A. L., Dadds, M. R., and Rapee, R. M. (2001). Cognitive-behavioral treatment of anxiety disorders in children: Long-term (6-year) follow-up. *Journal of Consulting Clinical Psychology, 69,* 135–41.

Bernstein, D. A., Borkovec, T. D., and Hazlett-Stevens, H. (2000). *New Directions in Progressive Relaxation Training: A Guidebook for Helping Professionals.* Westport, CT: Praeger.

Kendall, P. C. (1994). Treating anxiety disorders in children: Results of a randomized clinical trial. *Journal of Consulting and Clinical Psychology, 62,* 100–10.

Kendall, P. C., Chu, B. C., Pimentel, S. S., and Choudhury, M. (2000). Treating anxiety disorders in youth. In P. C. Kendall (Ed.), *Child and Adolescent Therapy: Cognitive-Behavioral Procedures, 2nd ed.* (pp. 235–87). New York: Guilford.

Kendall, P. C., Flannery-Schroeder, E., Panichelli-Mindel, S., Southam-Gerow, M., Henin, A., and Warman, M. (1997). Therapy for youths with anxiety disorders: A second randomized clinical trial. *Journal of Consulting and Clinical Psychology, 65,* 366–80.

Ollendick, T. H., and March, J. C. (2003). *Phobic and Anxiety Disorders in Children and Adolescents: A Clinician's Guide to Effective Psychosocial and Pharmacological Interventions.* New York: Oxford.

Pina, A. A., Silverman, W., Fuentes, R., Kurtines, W., and Weems, C. (2003). Exposure-based cognitive-behavioral treatment for phobic and anxiety disorders: Treatment effects and maintenance for Hispanic/Latino relative to European-American youths. *Journal of the American Academy of Child and Adolescent Psychiatry, 42,* 1179–87.

Ost, L., Fellenius, J., and Sterner, U. (1991). Applied tension, exposure in vivo, and tension-only in the treatment of blood phobia. *Behaviour Research and Therapy, 29*(6), 561–74.

Appendix C

INDEX OF THERAPEUTIC GAMES, WORKBOOKS, TOOL KITS, VIDEO TAPES, AND AUDIO TAPES

PRODUCT	*AUTHOR*
The Anger Control Game	B. Berg
The Anger Workbook	L. Blodeau
Anxiety and Phobia Workbook	E. Bourne
Bradshaw on Eating Disorders video	J. Bradshaw
The Goodbye Game	Unknown
The Good Mourning Game	Bisenius and Norris
Heartbeat Audiotapes	Lamb
The Helping, Sharing, Caring Game	R. Gardner
Let's See About Me game	Unknown
A Mother Loss Workbook	D. Hambrook
My Home and Places game	Flood
Odyssey Islands Game	Bridge
Refusal Skills video	Bureau for At Risk Youth
Skillsstreaming: The Adolescent Kit	McGinnis and Goldstein
The Self-Control Game	Shapiro
The Social Conflict Game	B. Berg
The Stress and Anxiety Game	B. Berg
The Talking, Feeling, and Doing Game	R. Gardner
Defiant Disorder in Children video	R. Barkley
Teens' Solutions Workbook	L. E. Shapiro
Ten Minutes to Relax audiotape	L. E. Shapiro
The Ungame	Zakich

The products listed above can be purchased by contacting the following companies:

A.D.D. Warehouse
300 Northwest 70th Avenue, Suite 102
Plantation, FL 33317
Phone: 1-800-233-9273
www.addwarehouse.com

Childswork/Childsplay, LLC
P.O. Box 1604
Secaucus, NJ 07096-1604
Phone: 1-800-962-1141
www.childswork.com

Courage to Change
P.O. Box 1268
Newburgh, NY 12551
Phone: 1-800-440-4003

Creative Therapeutics
P.O. Box 522
Cresskill, NJ 67626-0522
Phone: 1-800-544-6162
www.rgardner.com

Western Psychological Services
Division of Manson Western Corporation
12031 Wilshire Boulevard
Los Angeles, CA 90025-1251
Phone: 1-800-648-8857
www.wpspublish.com

Appendix D

INDEX OF DSM-IV-TR CODES ASSOCIATED WITH PRESENTING PROBLEMS

Academic Problem   **V62.3**
  Academic Underachievement

Acute Stress Disorder   **308.3**
  Physical/Emotional Abuse
    Victim
  Posttraumatic Stress Disorder
    (PTSD)
  Sexual Abuse Victim

Adjustment Disorder   **309.xx**
  Posttraumatic Stress Disorder
    (PTSD)

**Adjustment Disorder With
Anxiety**   **309.24**
  Blended Family
  Divorce Reaction
  Medical Condition
  Runaway
  Sexual Identity Confusion

**Adjustment Disorder With
Depressed Mood**   **309.0**
  Adoption
  Blended Family
  Depression
  Divorce Reaction
  Grief/Loss Unresolved
  Medical Condition
  Sexual Identity Confusion

**Adjustment Disorder With
Disturbance of Conduct**   **309.3**
  Blended Family
  Divorce Reaction
  Medical Condition
  Parenting

**Adjustment Disorder With
Mixed Anxiety and Depressed
Mood**   **309.28**
  Divorce Reaction
  Medical Condition
  Sexual Identity Confusion

**Adjustment Disorder With
Mixed Disturbance of
Emotions and Conduct**   **309.4**
  Adoption
  Divorce Reaction
  Grief/Loss Unresolved
  Medical Condition
  Parenting
  Runaway

**Adolescent Antisocial
Behavior**   **V71.02**
  Negative Peer Influences
  School Violence

Agoraphobia Without History of Panic Disorder   300.22
   Panic/Agoraphobia

Alcohol Abuse   305.00
   Chemical Dependence
   Sexual Acting Out

Alcohol Dependence   303.90
   Adoption
   Chemical Dependence
   Low Self-Esteem
   Obsessive-Compulsive
     Disorder (OCD)
   Sexual Acting Out

Alcohol-Induced Persisting Dementia   291.2
   Chemical Dependence

Alcohol-Induced Persisting Amnestic Disorder   291.1
   Chemical Dependence

Anorexia Nervosa   307.1
   Eating Disorder
   Low Self-Esteem

Antisocial Personality Disorder   301.7
   Parenting

Anxiety Disorder Not Otherwise Specified   300.00
   Anxiety
   Medical Condition
   Obsessive-Compulsive
     Disorder (OCD)
   Sexual Identity Confusion
   Specific Phobia

Asperger's Disorder   299.80
   Autism/Pervasive
     Developmental Disorder
   Mental Retardation

Attention-Deficit/Hyperactivity Disorder, Combined Type   314.01
   Academic Underachievement
   Adoption
   Anxiety

Attention-Deficit/Hyperactivity Disorder (ADHD)
   Parenting

Attention-Deficit/Hyperactivity Disorder Not Otherwise Specified   314.9
   Attention-Deficit/Hyperactivity
     Disorder (ADHD)
   Conduct Disorder/Delinquency
   Negative Peer Influences
   Oppositional Defiant
   Peer/Sibling Conflict
   School Violence

Attention-Deficit/Hyperactivity Disorder, Predominantly Hyperactive-Impulsive Type   314.01
   Attention-Deficit/Hyperactivity
     Disorder (ADHD)
   Conduct Disorder/Delinquency
   Low Self-Esteem
   Mania/Hypomania
   Negative Peer Influences
   Oppositional Defiant
   Peer/Sibling Conflict
   Runaway
   School Violence
   Sexual Acting Out

Attention-Deficit/Hyperactivity Disorder, Predominantly Inattentive Type   314.00
   Academic Underachievement
   Attention-Deficit/Hyperactivity
     Disorder (ADHD)

Autistic Disorder   299.00
   Autism/Pervasive
     Developmental Disorder
   Mental Retardation

Bereavement   V62.82
   Depression
   Grief/Loss Unresolved

Bipolar Disorder Not Otherwise Specified   296.80
   Mania/Hypomania

Bipolar I Disorder   296.xx
Anger Management
Attention-Deficit/Hyperactivity
   Disorder (ADHD)
Depression
Mania/Hypomania
Psychoticism
School Violence
Suicidal Ideation

**Bipolar I Disorder, Most
Recent Episode Manic**   296.4x
Sexual Acting Out

Bipolar II Disorder   296.89
Anger Management
Depression
Mania/Hypomania
Psychoticism
School Violence
Sexual Acting Out

**Bipolar II Disorder, Most
Recent Episode Depressed**   296.89
Suicidal Ideation

Body Dysmorphic Disorder   300.7
Social Phobia/Shyness

**Borderline Intellectual
Functioning**   V62.89
Academic Underachievement
Mental Retardation

**Borderline Personality
Disorder**   301.83
Parenting

Brief Psychotic Disorder   298.8
Psychoticism

Bulimia Nervosa   307.51
Eating Disorder

Cannabis Abuse   305.20
Chemical Dependence
Sexual Acting Out

Cannabis Dependence   304.30
Chemical Dependence
Low Self-Esteem
Sexual Acting Out

**Childhood Disintegrative
Disorder**   299.10
Autism/Pervasive
   Developmental Disorder
Mental Retardation

**Child or Adolescent
Antisocial Behavior**   V71.02
Conduct Disorder/Delinquency
Peer/Sibling Conflict
Sexual Abuse Perpetrator

Cocaine Abuse   305.60
Chemical Dependence

Cocaine Dependence   304.20
Chemical Dependence

Conduct Disorder   312.8
Anger Management
School Violence

**Conduct Disorder,
Adolescent-Onset Type**   312.82
Adoption
Attention-Deficit/Hyperactivity
   Disorder (ADHD)
Conduct Disorder/Delinquency
Negative Peer Influences
Oppositional Defiant
Parenting
Peer/Sibling Conflict
Runaway
Sexual Abuse Perpetrator

**Conduct Disorder,
Childhood-Onset Type**   312.81
Adoption
Attention-Deficit/Hyperactivity
   Disorder (ADHD)
Conduct Disorder/Delinquency
Oppositional Defiant
Peer/Sibling Conflict
Physical/Emotional Abuse
   Victim
Sexual Abuse Perpetrator

Cyclothymic Disorder   301.13
Depression
Mania/Hypomania

Delusional Disorder   297.1
  Psychoticism

**Dependent Personality
Disorder**   301.6
  Parenting

Depersonalization Disorder   300.6
  Physical/Emotional Abuse
    Victim

**Depressive Disorder Not
Otherwise Specified**   311
  Medical Condition
  Suicidal Ideation

**Disorder of Written
Expression**   315.2
  Academic Underachievement

**Disruptive Behavior Disorder
Not Otherwise Specified**   312.9
  Academic Underachievement
  Attention-Deficit/Hyperactivity
    Disorder (ADHD)
  Conduct Disorder/Delinquency
  Negative Peer Influences
  Oppositional Defiant
  Parenting
  Peer/Sibling Conflict
  School Violence

**Dissociative Disorder Not
Otherwise Specified**   300.15
  Physical/Emotional Abuse
    Victim
  Sexual Abuse Victim

Dysthymic Disorder   300.4
  Academic Underachievement
  Adoption
  Blended Family
  Chemical Dependence
  Depression
  Divorce Reaction
  Grief/Loss Unresolved
  Low Self-Esteem
  Physical/Emotional Abuse
    Victim
  Runaway
  School Violence
  Sexual Acting Out

  Sexual Identity Confusion
  Social Phobia/Shyness
  Suicidal Ideation

**Eating Disorder Not
Otherwise Specified**   307.50
  Eating Disorder

Exhibitionism   302.4
  Sexual Abuse Perpetrator

**Gender Identity Disorder in
Adolescents or Adults**   302.85
  Sexual Identity Confusion

Generalized Anxiety Disorder   300.02
  Anxiety
  Divorce Reaction
  Low Self-Esteem
  Medical Condition
  Obsessive-Compulsive
    Disorder (OCD)
  Physical/Emotional Abuse
    Victim
  Sexual Identity Confusion

Identity Problem   313.82
  Sexual Identity Confusion

**Impulse-Control Disorder Not
Otherwise Specified**   312.30
  Runaway
  School Violence

**Intermittent Explosive
Disorder**   312.34
  Anger Management
  Chemical Dependence
  Conduct Disorder/Delinquency
  School Violence

**Learning Disorder Not
Otherwise Specified**   315.9
  Peer/Sibling Conflict

Major Depressive Disorder   296.xx
  Low Self-Esteem
  Medical Condition
  Obsessive-Compulsive
    Disorder (OCD)
  Physical/Emotional Abuse
    Victim

Sexual Abuse of Child　　　**V61.21**
　Parenting

Sexual Abuse of Child
(if focus of clinical attention
is on the victim)　　　**995.53**
　Low Self-Esteem
　Posttraumatic Stress Disorder
　　(PTSD)
　Runaway
　Sexual Abuse Perpetrator
　Sexual Abuse Victim

Sibling Relational Problem　　**V61.8**
　Sexual Abuse Perpetrator

Social Anxiety Disorder
(Social Phobia)　　　**300.23**
　Low Self-Esteem
　Social Phobia/Shyness

Specific Phobia　　　**300.29**
　Specific Phobia

Stereotypic Movement
Disorder　　　**307.3**
　Autism/Pervasive
　　Developmental Disorder

Undifferentiated Somatoform
Disorder　　　**300.81**
　Divorce Reaction

Voyeurism　　　**302.82**
　Sexual Abuse Perpetrator